Holy book and holy tradition; International
Colloquium held in the Faculty of Theology,
University of Manchester, edited by F.F.
Bruce and E.G. Rupp. [Manchester] Manchest
University Press [c1968]
viii, 244 p. 23 cm.

Bibliographies.

1. Sacred books. 2. Traditon (Theology
I. Bruce, Frederick Fyvie, 1910-   ed.
II. International   Colloquium. Uni
ity of Manchester,   1968.

HOLY BOOK AND HOLY TRADITION

HOLY BOOK
AND
HOLY TRADITION

INTERNATIONAL COLLOQUIUM
HELD IN THE FACULTY OF THEOLOGY
UNIVERSITY OF MANCHESTER

edited by

F. F. BRUCE *and* E. G. RUPP

MANCHESTER UNIVERSITY PRESS

© 1968 MANCHESTER UNIVERSITY PRESS
Published by the University of Manchester
at THE UNIVERSITY PRESS
316–324 Oxford Road, Manchester 13

G.B. SBN 7190 0303 2

Printed in Great Britain by Butler & Tanner Ltd, Frome and London

Preface

In the first week of November 1966, an International Colloquium was held in the Faculty of Theology of the University of Manchester on the topic 'Holy Book and Holy Tradition'. The papers read at this Colloquium are now presented to a wider public in the pages that follow.

The various aspects of the topic dealt with in these papers cover a wide range—from cave drawings of the Upper Palaeolithic period to issues that are being warmly debated in the world today. While some aspects lent themselves readily to the most detached objectivity in their treatment, others were dealt with by scholars actively engaged in the issues which they raise. The treatment of these contemporary aspects, which could not be ignored in a comprehensive survey, shows (we trust) that personal involvement is no deterrent to academic appraisal.

The members of the Manchester Faculty of Theology express their thanks to the Vice-Chancellor of the University, whose initiative made the Colloquium possible, and to their colleagues from other parts of Great Britain and Ireland and from the European continent whose generous giving of their time and learning made the occasion so successful and memorable.

Professor Widengren's paper on 'Holy Book and Holy Tradition in Islam' was not delivered at the Colloquium but was written specially for this volume; for this additional service we are the more grateful to him.

F. F. B. and E. G. R.

Contents

vii

Illustrations

PLATES

FIGURES

The Holy Book, the Holy Tradition and the Holy Ikon

A PHENOMENOLOGICAL SURVEY

S. G. F. BRANDON

I

The situation in which I find myself, in introducing the theme of this colloquium, is a rather ambiguous one. It is a situation that has advantages; but it also has its perils. Among the advantages is the opportunity of telling my colleagues in advance what they should talk about in their papers. It is an unfair advantage. Because, if they are going to talk about the topics that I might mention, I have anticipated them, and so enjoy an air of omniscience. If they do not deal with them, then they might feel obliged to explain why. But there are also dire perils for me. If I try to be omniscient and stress what I consider to be all the essential aspects of the theme—what happens, if none of these is mentioned in the succeeding papers, and I appear in a minority of one: a voice crying alone in the wilderness, or a false prophet!

I shall, therefore, play for safety. I shall try to avoid trespassing on any of the specialist topics that will be dealt with in the other papers. Instead, I shall endeavour to discuss what might be called 'The Phenomenology of the Holy Book and the Holy Tradition'. This will enable me to range widely and lightly over the whole subject, and to draw attention to some aspects which are unlikely to be touched upon in the papers dealing with the specific themes. My approach will be both historical and comparative.

II

It is always advisable, though dull, to start with definitions and implications. The double form of our theme: the Holy Book and

the Holy Tradition, includes two terms obviously needing definition, and also implying some interconnection or relationship
between them. Let us briefly consider these aspects.

The idea of the 'Holy Book' is a familiar one to those brought
up in the Hebraeo-Christian tradition, for the Bible at once
appears as the supreme example of a Holy Book. I use the
words 'supreme example', advisedly, because few of us here
would, I think, regard it as the *only* 'Holy Book'. And doubtless
one other example immediately springs to mind, namely, the
Qur'ān. In a truer sense than the Bible, the *Qur'ān* is a book, and
it is venerated as sacred or holy by Muslims.[1]

Although the Bible and the *Qur'ān* immediately present
themselves to our minds as 'holy books', without further qualification, we know that there are many other writings, both
ancient and modern, that might claim such a designation. Let
me just mention a few titles to remind us how many and how
strange are the possible claimants: the ancient Egyptian *Book
of the Dead*;[2] the Babylonian *Enuma Elish*;[3] the *Gathas* of Zara-
thustra;[4] the Sanskrit *Rig-Veda*;[5] the Chinese *Tao Te Ching*;[6]
the Latin *Sibylline Oracles*;[7] the Buddhist '*Lotus of the True Doctrine*';[8] the Sikh '*Book of Granth*';[9]—and to, give two modern
examples, which we must also treat seriously in this connection:
the so-called *Book of Mormon*[10] and Mrs Mary Baker Eddy's
Science and Health.[11]

Quite clearly the term 'Holy Book', unless we are to define
it in some very narrow sense, covers a great multitude of
writings, of diverse ages and cultures, and of very varying content. I have only mentioned some of the more obvious examples
of sacred writings that merit the designation: 'Holy Book'. But
there is another category that also claims consideration. This is
the so-called *Himmelsbuch* or *Schicksalbuch*—a book or record of
destiny, kept in heaven or by some deity, from which the fate
of individual men and women, or nations, will be determined
at a *post-mortem* judgment.[12] Such a book was an imaginative
concept; but it has played an important rôle in the ideology of
many religions, including Christianity,[13] and so cannot be dis-
regarded by us.

III

The holy character or status of any Holy Book necessarily raises the question of its recognition as such. Now, despite whatever claim may be made about its supernatural origin or production, every known example of a Holy Book has had a human author or authors, and it has been written in the language current in the cultural environment concerned. How, then, we may ask, has any such writing ever come to be regarded as holy? Obviously, not because it has been self-authenticating. It is true, of course, that some Holy Books have recommended themselves as such by their intrinsic qualities; such a claim has often been advanced on behalf of the Bible by Christians or for the *Qur'ān* by Muslims, and many other instances could be cited, where the faithful are so sincerely impressed by the contents of their sacred scriptures as to think that they must, therefore, be of divine origin. However, this will always be a subsequent evaluation, and the status of a Holy Book has first to be established by some recognized spiritual authority within the community concerned. In other words, the Holy Book receives its original authentication from persons already accepted as being peculiarly endowed with a numinous prestige and authority.

We are, accordingly, brought to the second part of our subject, namely, the Holy Tradition. For the authority that endorses the sacred character of the Book must clearly be the recognized embodiment or exponent of the Holy Tradition within the community concerned. Thus, we reach the significant conclusion that the Holy Tradition precedes the Holy Book, and that the Holy Tradition inheres in, and is interpreted by, a person or persons, whose supernatural character or status is already established and accepted. This conclusion means that in studying any specific example of a Holy Book, we find that we must give prior consideration to the Holy Tradition, on which that Book is founded, which in turn means that we are led back to consider some sacred person or order— perhaps of shamans, or prophets, or a priesthood.

IV

It is illuminating in this connection, I think, to look at the earliest pre-literary stage of human culture, namely, that of the

Upper Palaeolithic period (*circa* 40,000–10,000 B.C.). Already, in this remote age there is evidence of the existence of a religio-magical tradition which represented the established praxis, governing the community's relations with the supernatural.[14] This praxis, moreover, found expression in two distinctive forms of activity which clearly involved specialists, who knew the traditions and the techniques concerned, and who evidently were accepted as uniquely qualified by other members of the community.

I will briefly illustrate. In the famous Palaeolithic caves of the Trois Frères, Ariège, and of Lascaux in the Dordogne, there are depictions of what appear to be men disguised as animals or birds. The most notable example is perhaps that in the Trois Frères cave, which prehistorians call the 'Dancing Sorcerer'. It seems to represent a man crowned with the antlers of a stag and clothed in the hairy pelt of an animal. The posture of the figure suggests that it is dancing. Now, there is reason for believing that a hunting ritual was practised in these Palaeo-lithic communities, which included the miming by masked dancers of the movements of animals, in order to gain control over them in a subsequent hunt.[15] In the light of modern ethno-logical parallels, it is probable that these masked dancers were specialists in the magic art, and were Palaeolithic prototypes of the shamans of the Central Asian nomads. Such specialists were undoubtedly exponents of a traditional ritual magic, into which they were specially initiated and which endowed them with a supernatural status and character in their community. The ritual they practised, moreover, was not likely to have been of their own private invention; it would derive from a tradition inherited from their predecessors. Doubtless individual shamans or sorcerers varied this ritual in some details or added to it; but it is unlikely that revolutionary changes would ever have been made; for any drastic departure from tradition would surely have disturbed the community, on whose behalf the ritual was performed, and it would not have been tolerated.

Palaeolithic cave-art not only presupposes an established tradition of ritual magic and experts equipped with the requisite knowledge and skill to practise it. According to prehistorians, this art itself was magical in intent, being designed either to secure success in hunting or to promote the fertility of the

Fig. I. The 'Dancing Sorcerer' (Cave of the Trois Frères, Ariège). Possible Palaeolithic evidence of established tradition of ritual-dance

animals hunted. Although we are not informed on how the very considerable task of drawing or painting these animals, generally in the more inaccessible parts of the caves, was managed, it is obvious that the undertaking had so vital a communal significance that it must have been carefully regulated. How the practice originated we can only speculate; but the many painted caves attest an established tradition of

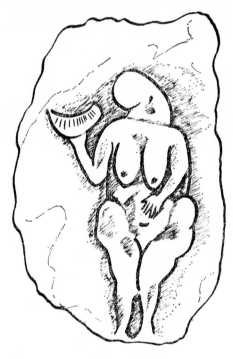

Fig. II. The so-called 'Venus of Laussel' (Dordogne). Possible Palaeolithic evidence of established tradition of religious iconography

Reproduced by courtesy of Hodder & Stoughton, from *Creation Legends of the Ancient Near East*, by S. G. F. Brandon

magical depiction and imply the existence of accredited practitioners of it.[16]

This Palaeolithic cave-art has yet a further significance for us. Tens of thousands of years before the invention of writing, which made possible the concept of the Holy Book, man had already developed a medium fraught with supernatural power, namely, linear or plastic representation. The picture of a bison transfixed by a lance, for example, was believed to be so potent that it would cause such a happening to occur on the occasion of some future hunt.[17] Naturally we know nothing certain of the thought-processes of Palaeolithic man; we can only suppose that he conceived of some nexus existing between the picture and some mysterious power which resulted in the guiding of the hunter's weapon to kill the animal concerned.

There is another product of this art, which has an even greater significance for our theme. On a number of Palaeolithic sites carvings have been found of women which greatly exaggerate the maternal attributes but leave the faces blank. These so-called 'Venus'-figures are generally recognized as not being portraits of individual women, but as being symbolic representations of 'Woman'. One of the most notable specimens, the so-called Venus of Laussel, when found, formed the focal-point of a rock-sanctuary. Many scholars have, accordingly, seen in such a figure a Palaeolithic prototype or anticipation of the Great Goddess of the Neolithic peoples and of the early civilizations of the Near East and of the Indus Valley.[18]

The supposition is a reasonable one, though it obviously cannot be substantiated. However that may be, the recent discoveries at Çatal Hüyük definitely show that the linear depiction of a Great Goddess was already current in the seventh millennium B.C.[19] For us this fact must have a great significance. It means that, long before the conception of a Holy Book, a 'Holy Ikon' existed. In other words, long before men believed that deity could reveal itself in writing, they believed that the form of deity could be revealed in linear or plastic art.

v

This reference to Palaeolithic art brings me on to an issue which is very pertinent to our theme. I am myself becoming increasingly convinced that in the history of religions, owing to our natural preoccupation with texts, we seriously neglect the significance of religious art. The neglect is indeed serious when we recall that human beings are naturally disposed to think pictorially—to have in their mind's eye an image of that with which they are concerned. Unless we can visualize an object about which we are told, we find the task of comprehending it exceedingly difficult. Very few persons can train themselves to think wholly in abstract terms—even mathematical symbols have a linear form, an image.

As we have just noted, man could draw long before he could write. He presented his concept of deity in linear and plastic form long ages before he sought to describe it verbally. The iconography of deity should, therefore, command our attention before we study its presentation in texts. The subject, moreover, should not only precede the study of texts in any specific religion where the relevant material exists, but it should also proceed *pari passu* with it. For example, it is becoming increasingly apparent that Hebrew religion, despite the many denunciations of iconographic representation in the texts, was not aniconic in practice. The synagogue of Dura-Europos, together with much other evidence, attests the existence of a Jewish tradition of pictorial representation of the sacred history.[20] And we may legitimately hazard the guess that when a Hebrew thought of Yahweh, he visualized him in some anthropomorphic form—a form that was conditioned by the cultural tradition in which he was nurtured. And the same conclusion may also be drawn about another aniconic faith, namely, Islam—indeed many manuscripts exist attesting a rich treasury of Islamic sacred art.[21]

A holy iconography must always have been closely linked with a holy tradition, and the two must constantly have reacted on each other. As to which must be accorded priority of origin, we have something like the problem of the chicken and the egg: which came first, since they are interdependent?

To take an obvious example of the point at issue here. I am sure that my colleague, Professor Bleeker, has often pondered, as I have done, on the origin of the ancient Egyptian representation of deity. It appears in the archaeological record, dating from about the third millennium B.C., already well developed and established.[22] It continues from that time as the holy tradition of iconography unchallenged, except for the brief period of Akhenaten's reformation, on for more than three thousand years, indeed until the suppression of paganism enforced by the Christian emperors of the Roman Empire. How the Egyptians came first to visualize their deities in this form is unknown. Doubtless various causes operated; for the Egyptian deities, male and female, are variously represented in human or in animal, or in partly human and animal, forms, and they are endowed with distinctive insignia. It would seem that somewhere back in the predynastic era this iconography must have started. But how was it initiated? Did some unknown genius once draw his idea of a god, and what he drew, did it so impress his fellow-tribesmen that they regarded it as a divine revelation? We do not know, and can only speculate. But it seems a necessary assumption that some time in the remote past of ancient Egyptian culture the figure of a god must have originally been drawn and accepted as the form that all thought a god to have. To have been thus accepted, it must have concretized the image of deity already current in the general mind. Once accepted, it became established as a holy tradition, and, as such it exercised a definitive influence on all subsequent generations. Consequently an Egyptian living about 2000 B.C., and another a thousand years later, would have conceived of any specific deity in the form in which he saw it depicted in statues or on the walls of temples or in illuminated papyri.

The process, which I have briefly outlined here concerning ancient Egyptian religious iconography, would apply, with necessary qualifications, to the iconographic traditions of all other religions. It also raises an interesting problem, which has not yet been properly investigated: why should the iconographic conceptions of deity in the various religions of mankind differ so strikingly? In other words, why should a Hindu god appear so different in form and character from a Chinese god, or from an ancient Egyptian or Mesopotamian, or Greek god, or from the mediaeval Christian depictions of God the Father?

There is an aspect of this subject which I think that we might also pursue profitably in connection with Christianity. As is well known, the Holy Tradition preceded the Holy Book in Christianity. This statement, of course, requires qualification. From the beginning Christians had a Holy Book in the Old Testament, which they inherited from the Jewish origins of their faith. But a specifically Christian Holy Book had to be created, and we are all familiar with the gradual formation of the canon of the New Testament. Now, the New Testament documents provided no information as to the physical appearance of Jesus of Nazareth. The Johannine Apocalypse does, of course, describe the appearance of the Glorified Christ; but the portrait is so clearly a symbolical one that it did not greatly help—it is indeed instructive to note the attempts of later

B

Christian artists to depict the Apocalyptic Christ with a sword proceeding out of his mouth, according to Revelation 1:16.[23]

However that may be, the vivid narrative element in the Christian Gospels must excite all who hear them to visualize Jesus in human form. The earliest depictions of Jesus in the catacombs and on the sculptured sarcophagi, dating from the third and fourth centuries, are, accordingly, very instructive. Without a Holy Tradition or a Holy Book to guide the imagination, the early Christians were compelled to fall back on categories current in contemporary Graeco-Roman society. Accordingly, they were led to imagine Jesus as a young Greek hero, beardless and attired in a classical costume.[24] The fact that ordinary Christian people today, when shown these earliest portraits of Jesus, are puzzled and often shocked by their apparent violation of their own conception, indicates how far the existing Christian view differs from the earliest tradition.

There is, I think, a very great significance for us in this fact. It shows that, probably for the first four centuries, Christians, when they thought of Jesus and addressed themselves to him in worship and prayer, imagined him in a form wholly different from that which has subsequently become the traditional image. The early Christians did this, moreover, although depending on the same holy scriptures as used by Christians of later generations. It would seem, therefore, that we may justly conclude that the image which the devotee has in his mind's eye of the deity he worships and serves may be quite independent of the Holy Book of his faith. It is, of course, unlikely that such an image would be incompatible with the nature of the divinity that finds expression in the Holy Book. But the fact must be recognized that the image or portrait of deity, which is an emotional factor of tremendous power, can be generated independently of the guidance or authority of a Holy Book.

The fact that the original conception of Jesus in Christian art did not finally establish itself, and so become a Holy Tradition, requires explanation, and the fact of its substitution by another conception is also of considerable interest to our theme. What appears to be one of the earliest representations of a bearded Jesus occurs on the wooden doors of the church of Santa Sabina, Rome, and dates from the first half of the fifth century.[25] Whether the description of the bearded Jesus in the spurious

PLATE I

Last Judgment (thirteenth century), on tympanum of central portal of the Cathedral of Bourges. Classic example of mediaeval 'Doom', with *psychostasia* represented as the crucial action of the drama.

(Photo: I. A. Brandon)

PLATE II

The Archangel Michael weighing souls at Last Judgment. The resurrected
dead arise from their graves. Christ, with saints, is depicted above the
psychostasia. From the fifteenth-century polyptych of Van der Weyden in the
Hospice de Beaune (Bourgogne).

Letter of Lentulus was derived from some earlier document, as Robert Eisler suggested, is a good topic for ingenious speculation; but it raises too many complicated problems to permit of the assumption that it was the publication of the prototype of the *Letter of Lentulus* which caused the change-over from the earlier conception.[26] But, however the change came about, once the bearded Christ-figure was established, it quickly became a sacred tradition, from which only certain Renaissance artists dared to depart.[27] In popular Christianity, both Catholic and Protestant, this Christ-portrait has become almost sacrosanct, and its influence upon Christian thought and devotion has been incalculable. The majority of Christians acquire this image of Christ from pictures seen in their childhood, and it abides with them to their life's end. Its influence even with those who are later informed about its origins seems to remain profound. It is, in other words, a most notable instance of a Holy Tradition, of immense emotive and formative power, which has no authorization in the Holy Book of the faith, i.e. the New Testament.

I should like to draw your attention also to another notable instance of the establishment of a tradition, once of considerable importance, in Christian art, for which there was no sanction in Holy Writ.

I have recently been making a special study of the mediaeval 'Doom', i.e. the representation of the Last Judgment as it was portrayed in either sculpture or painting in churches and cathedrals throughout Europe during the Middle Ages. The idea of the Last Judgment has, of course, scriptural warranty; but its depiction in either plastic or linear form included certain features or episodes that had no such sanction. Yet one of these features constituted the most crucial action in the mediaeval rendering of the Judgment of the Dead. These 'Dooms', incidentally, came into fashion in the twelfth century, and they continued to be produced until the Reformation period; their production ended abruptly in countries converted to Protestantism, and it gradually died out in Catholic lands. We may note also that these 'Dooms' were sited in prominent positions in churches and cathedrals, in order to command the attention of the faithful, and so to warn them of the grim experience that awaited them.[28]

The particular feature on which I want to comment is the

depiction of the weighing of souls by the Archangel Michael. Generally this episode is placed in the centre of a three-tiered scene, with Christ seated in the top register, accompanied by the symbols of his Passion, and the Resurrection of the Dead occurring in the bottom register. The Archangel is shown as holding a pair of balances; in one scale-pan a little nude human figure represents a human soul, and in the other there is generally a demon or another little human figure, perhaps symbolizing the individual's evil-self. This weighing of the soul appears in the Doom as the one crucial transaction, by which the eternal fate of each individual is decided.[29]

To the unlettered mediaeval Christian looking at such a depiction of the Last Judgment, which the Church assured him he must surely, some day, face, it would seem that his fate would then depend absolutely on Michael's assessment. It is, accordingly, understandable that the cult of the Archangel figured so prominently in mediaeval Christianity. The significant thing for us, however, is that this weighing of the soul by Michael at the Last Judgment had no sanction in either the Old or the New Testament. The idea, in fact, seems to have entered Christianity from ancient Egypt, where it featured as the crucial episode of the Osirian *post-mortem* judgment in the *Book of the Dead*. The first occurrence of the idea in a Christian writing seems to be in the apocryphal *Testament of Abraham*, a second-century document that, significantly, originated in Christian Egypt. How the idea, from such beginnings, came to establish itself so firmly in Christian tradition, that it forms the crucial transaction of the mediaeval Doom, is obscure.[30] Whatever the process may have been, the fact that it did so establish itself has much significance for our theme. For it means that a tradition was established, having all the prestige of sacred revelation and concerned with a vital aspect of Christian belief, that was quite independent of the Church's Holy Book.

I trust that my commentary on these two aspects of Christian art has not caused me to digress too far from my subject, namely, the phenomenology of the Holy Book and the Holy Tradition. I have hoped that it would be useful to our consideration of the theme to be reminded of the fundamental importance of religious art in this connection: that it is a mode of revelation of the nature of deity which preceded the emergence of the Holy

Book by many millennia. Further, that it is inextricably bound up in the idea of a Holy Tradition—indeed, it seems often to have created such a tradition, as well as becoming an integral part of it.

VI

From the evidence of religious art we should turn to consider that of liturgy. In the ancient religions the two were closely linked. Much of religious iconography took the form of the depiction of cultic acts. The motive was probably the desire to perpetuate the efficacy of some ritual transaction by representing it in durable form on the walls of a temple or tomb.[31] Now, the liturgical service of the gods implies a holy tradition of ritual action that must be punctiliously enacted. Sometimes the ritual will be accompanied by a kind of libretto, recited either by the celebrant or by an assisting officiant. Often this libretto will be read from a written record. The vignette illustrating the ceremony of 'Opening the Mouth' in the *Papyrus of Ani*, one of the finest examples of the Egyptian *Book of the Dead*, provides an early depiction of such a linkage between ritual action and the reading of a holy text.[32] However, there is an abundance of evidence attesting the chronological priority of liturgy to sacred scripture. And I scarcely need to remind the members of this colloquium that the basic thesis of the so-called 'Myth and Ritual' school has been that ritual preceded myth, and that myth originated as an explanation of ancient ritual practice, of which the original purpose was forgotten.

Ritual thus, in the history of religions, also greatly antedates the emergence of the Holy Book. It forms in most religions a holy tradition, which is essential to the being and purpose of the religion concerned. The Holy Book will, indeed, often provide a later *rationale* of the rites. Notable examples of this process are to be found in both the Old and New Testaments. The account of the Passover ritual in Exodus 12 is a later historicized explanation of two ancient rites concerning the sacrifice of the First Born and the use of Unleavened Bread.[33] The accounts of the Last Supper in 1 Corinthians 11:23–30 and in the Gospels involve some very complicated problems; but in the evolution of the Eucharist they have been used to explain the primitive cultic act of the 'breaking of bread', which may have originated from the action of Jesus on other occasions than the Last Supper.[34]

VII

But liturgy implies priesthood, and so we are brought back again to the initial problem of authority: who authenticates or authorizes the Holy Tradition, exemplified in either art or ritual, and the Holy Book?

We have already seen that experts or specialists in the magic art existed in the Palaeolithic communities, and that they must have exercised a determining authority over matters of faith and practice. When we reach the first literate societies we see at once how vital is the rôle of priesthoods in authorizing, developing and maintaining a sacred tradition with which they are identified professionally and economically. Let me cite two examples by way of illustration. The cosmogonies of ancient Egypt, embodied as they were in sacred texts, were the work of rival priesthoods at Heliopolis, Memphis and Hermopolis, and later at Thebes, and they were each designed to present the god of the particular sanctuary concerned as the Creator of the world, and hence to enhance the prestige of that sanctuary from which, of course, the priesthood profited.[35] The *Enuma elish*, the famous *Creation Epic* of Babylon, was similarly the product of the priesthood of the great temple of Marduk there, and it was designed to demonstrate the precedence of Marduk over the more ancient deities of the Mesopotamian pantheon.[36]

VIII

The way in which the status of the sacred literature of the great religions of mankind has originally derived from what we may fairly term 'ecclesiastical authority' may also be briefly noted. The *Rig-Veda* of India, and the other *Vedas* that depend upon it, owe both their existence and their prestige to the Brahmanic priesthood, whose members originally transmitted the knowledge of them orally only to members of their own caste.[37] The formation of the canon of the Old Testament, or, in other words, the decision on what books should be included and what excluded, was ultimately the work of the rabbis in synod at Jamnia at the close of the first century A.D.[38] Similarly ecclesiastical authority finally decreed what writings should have canonical status by inclusion in the corpus of the New Testament.[39] The contents of the *Qur'ān* were likewise decided by others than Muhammad, to whom the revelations were allegedly made by Allah. After Muhammad's death, at the command of the first caliph, Abu Bakr, Zaid, the Prophet's adopted son, in the words of the tradition, 'brought together the *Qur'ān* from the leaves of date-palms, white stones and from the breasts of men, who bore them in their thoughts'.[40] According to Pali tradition, three councils were held after the Buddha's death to determine the Buddhist canon of holy scripture.[41]

Ecclesiastical authority, although it has thus, in all the religions, played the decisive rôle in determining the status of the Holy Book, and in selecting its contents, has generally been careful to disguise its part in the transaction. For the writings, which it has decreed as sacred, it has invariably claimed a divine origin or authorship. For example, the 30th chapter of the Egyptian *Book of the Dead*, which concerns the witness of the heart at the *post-mortem* judgment, is stated, in the accompanying rubric, to have been found under a statue of the god Thoth, and written 'in the writing of the god himself'.[42] According to 2 Kings 22:8, the '*Book of the Law*' was found during building operations in the Jerusalem Temple, in the 18th year of king Josiah, thus implying its supernatural origin. It is claimed that the surahs of the *Qur'ān* were revealed to Muhammad by the angel Gabriel, acting as the messenger of Allah,[43] and most of the Buddhist *sutras* have the form of a discourse of the Buddha to his disciples or various inquirers.

But Holy Books not only owe their status as such, and their contents, to priestly or ecclesiastical authority; upon such authority their proper interpretation also depends. In non-literate societies, and before the invention of printing multiplied the production of books, the faithful knew only of their Holy Books as they were recited or expounded to them by those appointed by authority for this office. Such official interpretation necessarily meant that the Holy Book conformed in its witness to the Holy Tradition; even where there might be some variation in exegesis as in rabbinical Judaism, it was inconceivable that layfolk should have claimed the right to interpret the scriptures for themselves. In Christianity, when the monolithic authority of the Church was shattered at the Reformation, its Holy Book entered into a new phase of its existence, and a new principle of evaluation was introduced, which finally resulted in the claim of the individual to make his own interpretation. The innumerable splinter-groups of Protestantism attest the consequences of a Holy Book's becoming detached from the Holy Tradition and the authority that originally sponsored it.

IX

This brief survey of the phenomenology of the Holy Book and the Holy Tradition has left untouched many other topics such as the religious origins of the art of writing, the magical potency of words, the significance of the calendar, the stars as 'the writing of the heavens' in the Babylonian phrase, and the oracle when controlled by a priesthood such as that at Delphi. However, I trust that I have succeeded in sketching in the main proportions of our subject, and in indicating some other pertinent issues which may not be directly relevant to the more specialized themes to be dealt with in the other papers. I believe that we have a subject of great importance for our colloquium, and I shall look forward to hearing the contributions of my colleagues on the various selected themes, on which they have expert knowledge from specialized study and research.

NOTES

[1] The Bible is 'the Book' in a derived sense. When the Greek plural was translated into Latin, it came to be treated as a feminine singular substantive. The *Qur'ān* is conscious of itself as a single entity, an Arabic *Qur'ān* (Surah 20:112). See pp. 210 ff. below.

[2] Cf. H. Bonnet, *Reallexikon der ägyptischen Religionsgeschichte* (Berlin, 1952), pp. 824–8; T. G. Allen, *The Egyptian Book of the Dead* (University of Chicago Press, 1960), pp. 1–3.

[3] Cf. A. Heidel, *The Babylonian Genesis* (Chicago University Press, 1951), pp. 1–17; P. Garelli and M. Leibovici in *Sources orientales*, I (Paris, 1959),

pp. 117–27; G. Furlani, *Miti babilonese e assiri* (Firenze, 1958), pp. 3–38; S. G. F. Brandon, *Creation Legends of the Ancient Near East* (London, 1963), pp. 91–110.

⁴ Cf. J. Duchesne-Guillemin, *Zoroastre* (Paris, 1948), pp. 163–5; R. C. Zaehner, *The Dawn and Twilight of Zoroastrianism* (London, 1961), pp. 25–6, 28–9; Ed. Lehmann in *Lehrbuch der Religionsgeschichte* (hrg. A. Bertholet u. Ed. Lehmann, 4 Aufl., Tübingen, 1925), II, pp. 208–9.

⁵ Cf. A. A. Macdonell, *A History of Sanskrit Literature* (London, 1928), pp. 40 ff.; J. Gonda, *Die Religionen Indiens*, I (Stuttgart, 1960), pp. 9–10.

⁶ Cf. J. J. L. Duyvendak, *Tao Te Ching* (London, 1954), pp. 1 ff.; M. Granet, *La pensée chinoise* (Paris, 1950), pp. 502–3; A. Waley, *The Way and its Power* (London, 1936), pp. 86–91, 106.

⁷ Cf. F. Altheim, *A History of Roman Religion* (E.T., London, 1938), pp. 241–2; J. Leipoldt in *Reallexikon für Antike und Christentum* (hrg. T. Klauser), II (Stuttgart, 1954), 708.

⁸ Cf. E. J. Thomas, *The History of Buddhist Thought* (London, 1951²), pp. 177 ff.

⁹ Cf. H. A. Rose in *Encyclopaedia of Religion and Ethics* (ed. J. Hastings), VI, pp. 389b–90b.

¹⁰ Cf. I. W. Riley in *Encyclopaedia of Religion and Ethics*, XI, pp. 85a–6b.

¹¹ Cf. C. L. Ramsay in *Encycl. Rel. and Ethics*, III, pp. 576b–9b.

¹² Cf. L. Koep, *Das himmlische Buch in Antike und Christentum* (*Theophaneia* 8, 1952), *passim*; in *Reallexikon für Antike u. Christentum*, II, 726–30.

¹³ E.g. Revelation 20:12–15.

¹⁴ Cf. S. G. F. Brandon, *Man and his Destiny in the Great Religions* (Manchester University Press, 1962), pp. 8–30, where references are given to the relevant literature.

¹⁵ Cf. H. Breuil, *Quatre cent siècles d'art pariétal* (Montignac, 1954), pp. 166, 176–7; Th. Mainage, *Les religions de la Préhistoire: l'âge paléolithique* (Paris, 1921), pp. 296–314; H. Kühn, *Die Felsbilder Europas* (Zürich/Wien, 1952), pp. 15–17; J. Maringer, *Vorgeschichtliche Religion* (Einseideln, 1956), pp. 184–90.

¹⁶ Cf. S. Giedon, *The Eternal Present: the Beginnings of Art* (Oxford, 1962), pp. 275–9, 499–512.

¹⁷ Cf. E. O. James, *Prehistoric Religion* (London, 1957), pp. 174–81.

¹⁸ Cf. Breuil, pp. 279–81, and figs 318–20; Maringer, pp. 193–201; E. O. James, *The Cult of the Mother Goddess* (London, 1959), pp. 13–14, 20–5; Giedon, pp. 437–44, 469–84.

¹⁹ J. Mellaart, *Earliest Civilizations of the Near East* (London, 1965), pp. 89–101.

²⁰ Cf. J. Neusner, 'Judaism at Dura-Europos', in *History of Religions* (University of Chicago), 4 (1964), pp. 81–102; J. Leveen, *The Hebrew Bible in Art* (Schweich Lectures, 1939), *passim*; K. Weitzmann, 'Zur Frage des Einflusses jüdischer Bilderquellen auf die Illustrationen des Altes Testaments', in *Mullus. Festschrift T. Klauser* (Münster, 1964).

²¹ See the scenes from the life of Muhammad reproduced in D. T. Rice, *Islamic Art* (London, 1965), ill. 221 and p. 218; also 'Temptation' scene, ill. 113.

[22] See the splendid sculptured group of the pharaoh Menkaure (Myker-inus), between two goddesses; it dates from about 2600 B.C. Cf. R. Hamman, *Aegyptische Kunst* (Berlin, 1944), Abb. 132. For earlier, but less impressive, examples see C. Aldred, *Egypt to the End of the Old Kingdom* (London, 1965), ill. 32–5, 39, 55, 68, 109.

[23] E.g. Van der Weyden's *Last Judgment* at Beaune or the *Last Judgment* in painted glass in the church of St Vincent, Rouen.

[24] Cf. F. Grossi Gondi, *I monumenti cristiani* (Roma, 1923), pp. 57 (fig. 23), 107 (fig. 32), 109 ff., 116 (fig. 34), 118 (fig. 35); F. van der Meer and C. Mohrmann, *Atlas of the Early Christian World* (E.T., London, 1958), ill. 168–70, 174, 175–6, 197, 198, 398, 467; P. du Bourguet, *Early Christian Painting* (E.T., London, 1965), ill. 12, 14, 15, 20, 23, 25, 45, 46, 71, 84, 138, 142.

[25] Cf. M. Gough, *The Early Christians* (London, 1961), ill. 66 and p. 261. The Shepherd-Teacher painted on the wall of the Hypogaeum of the Aurelii on the Viale Manzoni, Rome, seems to be bearded (cf. *Atlas of the Early Christian World*, ill. 63, where it is dated for the third century). It is clearly a symbolical representation and is to be compared with the bearded 'Good Shepherd' on the sarcophagus of the Three Shepherds (cf. *Atlas of the Early Christian World*, ill. 64, 67): the other two 'Good Shepherds', incident-ally, are beardless, which seems to be the established form of portrayal of this symbolic figure in Early Christian Art. In the Catacomb of Commodilla there is an impressive depiction of a bearded Christ, which Bourguet dates for the mid-fourth century (op. cit., ill. 22, and note). However, since both a well-developed halo and the Apocalyptic A and Ω are shown, it may possibly be somewhat later in date (but see the Christ-Helios found in the pre-Constantine cemetery under the Basilica of St Peter: in Bourguet, op. cit., ill. 130). On the complicated origins of the Christ-figure see T. Klauser, 'Studien zur Entstehungsgeschichte der christlichen Kunst', in *Jahrbuch für Antike u. Christentum*, I (1958), pp. 24–51, III (1960), pp. 112–33.

[26] R. Eisler, *ΙΗΣΟΥΣ ΒΑΣΙΛΕΥΣ ΟΥ ΒΑΣΙΛΕΥΣΑΣ* (Heidelberg, 1930), II, pp. 327–41. According to the *Letter of Lentulus*, Christ had 'a full beard of the colour of his hair, not long, but a little forked at the chin' (cf. M. R. James, *The Apocryphal New Testament* [Oxford, 1926], p. 478).

[27] Cf. D. Talbot Rice, *The Beginnings of Christian Art* (London, 1957), pp. 65–6.

[28] Cf. Brandon, *The Judgment of the Dead* (London, 1967), chap. V.

[29] Cf. L. Kretzenbacher, *Die Seelenwaage* (Klagenfurt, 1958), *passim*; M. P. Perry, 'On the Psychostasis in Christian Art', in *The Burlington Magazine*, XXII (1912–13); J. Fournée, *Le Jugement Dernier* (Paris, 1964), pp. 97–102.

[30] The question is discussed at length by the author in his book *The Judgment of the Dead*, chap. V.

[31] Cf. Brandon, *History, Time and Deity* (Manchester University Press, 1965), chap. II, 'The Ritual Perpetuation of the Past'.

[32] Cf. Brandon in *The Saviour God* (Manchester University Press, 1963), p. 22.

[33] Cf. *History, Time and Deity*, pp. 112–13, 130, where references are given.

[34] Cf. M. Goguel, *L'Église primitive* (Paris, 1947), pp. 343–62.

[35] Cf. Brandon, *Creation Legends of the Ancient Near East*, pp. 14–61.

[36] Op. cit., 91 ff.

[37] Cf. R. C. Zaehner, *Hinduism* (London, 1962), pp. 143–5.

[38] Cf. A. Jepson in *Religion in Geschichte und Gegenwart*³, I, 1123–5.

[39] Cf. W. G. Kümmel in op. cit., I, 1131–8.

[40] Cf. D. S. Margoliouth in *Encycl. Religion and Ethics*, X, pp. 542a–5a.

[41] Cf. B. Jinananda in *2,000 Years of Buddhism*, ed. P. V. Bapat (Delhi, 1959), pp. 35 ff.

[42] Cf. E. A. W. Budge, *The Book of the Dead*² (London, 1953), II, p. 151.

[43] Cf. Margoliouth, in *Encycl. Religion and Ethics*, X, p. 542a.

Religious Tradition and Sacred Books in Ancient Egypt

C. J. BLEEKER

I

In Christian theology the question of the relation between scripture and tradition is a well-known and much debated problem. It is a question which logically arises from the character of Christian faith and from the structure of Christian theology. It is not very hard to disclose the presuppositions of this issue. The Christian assents to the truth, which God has revealed to the patriarchs, to Moses and to the prophets of Israel, and to which Jesus Christ has given the supreme testimony by his preaching, his life and his death. The Christian faith rests on the revelation of the one God, who charged his servants to preach His message to mankind. Being a message the word of God is a living reality, transferred from mouth to mouth. It is a well-known fact that this message, at first handed down orally, soon was put down in writing. Thus two collections of holy books, containing the religious literature of Judaism and of early Christianity, came into existence. Furthermore it should be recalled, that the Christian Church made a choice from this literature, combined the two collections, called the Old and the New Testament, and invested them together with the dignity of a canon, meant to function as touchstone of orthodox belief and as defence against heresy. However, tradition did not fully die out after the scriptures, which contained the word of God, had been codified. On the contrary, continually theologians, who appealed to it, made themselves heard. Everybody knows that the adherents of two outstanding types of theology stress the significance respectively of scripture and of tradition: Protestant theologians underline the value of the Bible as the source of Christian truth; Roman Catholic theologians are convinced that the Christian Church cannot dispense with her tradition. Though these few remarks do not exhaust the subject in question, they suffice to show that the problem of the nature and of the function of scripture and of tradition has its fixed locus in Christian theology, because it originates from the character of Christian faith itself.

II

This conference aims among other things at clarifying the relation of scripture and tradition in the non-Christian religions. There are good reasons for entering upon this research. Most religions possess holy books. In some religions these books function as a canon. On the other hand, tradition plays an important part in many religions. There are even religions, primarily those of illiterate peoples, which are totally based on tradition. Therefore an inquiry into the function and relation of scripture and tradition in the non-Christian religions is quite relevant.

Yet one should be cautious in transferring this issue too hastily into the field of the study of foreign religions. For the subject in question obviously is a typical Christian problem. It is dubious whether we are entitled to impose these notions on other religions. It is clear that in some religions people never reflected on the question. And even if the problem in some cases actually is present it was not thought out or formulated in any way. Actually we touch here on one of the key-questions of the methodology of the study of the history of religions. The historian of religions, who is Christian by birth and who is daily handling the terminology of western scholarship, must continually ask himself whether he rightly uses certain notions in order to clarify the essence and the structure of non-Christian religions.

Special caution is required when one intends to apply the apparatus of western theological conceptions to the study of one of the religions of antiquity. For the subject of this paper is taken from that field of study. It has to deal with the relation of religious tradition to sacred books in ancient Egypt. In order to clarify the question one should sharply envisage the nature and the structure of the ancient Egyptian religion. That means, one must raise the question whether this religion contains the presuppositions that create the problem in question, as it is known in Christian theology. The answer cannot be dubious. It turns out to be negative and that for reasons which will by and by be explained. The conclusion presents itself: though the problem is by no means irrelevant, it must be reworded. This transposition is expressed in the title of this paper. My lecture does not deal with scripture and tradition in ancient Egypt, but with religious tradition and sacred books in the land of the Nile in antiquity. What are the reasons for this formulation?

The main reason arises from the character of the ancient Egyptian religion. The Egyptian was no monotheist, but he adored many gods. He did not derive his knowledge about these gods from the preaching of prophets, who appeared in the course of history in order to disclose the nature and the will of God, as was the case in Israel, but he believed in the existence of those gods, thanks to cosmic occurrences which best can be called hierophanies, if we use a term introduced by M. Eliade. These gods were surrounded by groups of worshippers. However, in ancient Egypt there never existed a spiritual community comparable to the Christian Church.

Thus there was no authoritative body, guarding the purity of the doctrine and the orthodoxy of the faithful. In ancient Egypt the secular and the holy community totally overlapped each other. By being a member of a family, a clan or the state, one participated at the same time in the truth and in the blessing which religion and especially the cultic rites could offer. In this connection special attention should be paid to the importance and the function of the cult. In my opinion it is generally overlooked, that the nature of the ancient Egyptian religion was cultic to a high degree, that means, the religious consciousness expressed itself not so much in a doctrine, in myths, but rather in the cult.

As no church existed in ancient Egypt, it is likewise dubious whether there really were theologians in the literal sense of the word. True theology presupposes a certain ability of thinking in a rational and unbiased way. It is doubtful whether the ancient Egyptians reached that stage of critical reflection. In my opinion one should make a clear distinction between two spheres of thinking in the ancient Near East and in ancient

Egypt, i.e. between antiquity in the strict sense of the word on the one hand and the classical world on the other. This is a thesis which I cannot substantiate at this moment. Let me only point to the fact, that in classical Greece—i.e. since the appearance of the famous philosophers—a new and original art of thinking was born, namely the unprejudiced quest for the truth, inventive and independent thought. Though the ancient Egyptians possessed a bright intellect, technical skill and organizational ability, as appears from their highly organized society and from their beautiful and impressive buildings, it is evident that rational thinking, which deduces its conclusions from reasoning and experiment, was foreign to them. Their science was primitive, a mixture of practical knowledge, technical skill and magic. In none of the fields of science did they reach remarkable achievements. A well-known Egyptologist, E. Drioton, defines the level of the ancient Egyptian culture in the following way: 'Elle a marqué la fin, prolongée si on le veut en apothéose, d'un stade de civilisation de l'humanité, celui de l'âge de la pierre.' His judgment on the so-called scientific books of the Egyptians runs like this: 'Ce ne sont pas des traités proprement dits, car ils ne disposent pas logiquement leur matière ni la traitent par voie de principe et de conséquence.'[1] If this is right—and there is no reason to question the truth of these pronouncements made by a famous Egyptologist—it is *a priori* improbable that there were theologians, who could raise and clarify the question of the relation between scripture and tradition. It is true that many learned and pious priests lived in the valley of the Nile. However, their knowledge was no real scholarship but had a bearing on the rites which were performed in the cult and on the mythical insight on which their religion was founded.

III

The last remark gives occasion to throw light on another feature of the ancient Egyptian religion which should be taken into account. That is the modest part which myth plays in the religious texts. It is a well-known and yet amazing fact, that none of the many Egyptian texts presents a coherent description of the life, death and resurrection of Osiris. It was a Greek author, i.e. Plutarch, who first put the myth in full down in writing. The Egyptian texts only hint at the myth. What is the function of these allusions? They are not intended to tell the myth, but to sanction certain ritual acts. This is a clear proof of the thesis, which I put forward, namely that the heart of the Egyptian religion beats in the cult. What is true of Osiris, can also be said of Re, the sun-god, who acted as Creator. It is very astonishing indeed that in the texts no coherent desscription of creation is to be found.[2] And then we know that the ancient Egyptians constantly looked back to this mythical act for their religious orientation. The best proof of this is the hour of the ascension to the throne by a new king. This ceremony took place in the early morning after the day in which the old king passed away. This was the very hour to be chosen, because the king by his ascension to the throne should repeat the mythical act of the sun-god, who by climbing the primaeval hill became the first king. Even the same verb, *ḫꜥj* was used to indicate both the act of the sun-god and his daily rising and the ascension to the throne by the king.[3] What has been said concerning Osiris and Re, can in an even higher degree be repeated in regard to certain other gods, as Min[4] and Sokaris.[5] They can best be characterized as non-mythical figures, i.e. deities with whom hardly any myth is connected. Yet they are personifications of profound mythical ideas. These observations lead to the conclusion that the ancient Egyptian religion hardly created any doctrines, clad in a mythical garment. When there is no doctrine to be taught or preached, no authoritative holy books can come about. However, the absence of myth does not exclude original mythical conceptions. They are actually present.

To these mythical conceptions two notions belong which possess paramount importance in the framework of this argument, i.e. the idea of the divine word and the idea of the divine script. The Egyptians thoroughly reflected on the nature and the function of the creative word. This is proved by a remarkable divine figure, called Ḥu. A. H. Gardiner has defined Ḥu as 'authoritative, creative utterance'.[6] Ḥu is no blood-warm deity. It is a kind of a numen, called by Gardiner a 'personification'. Ḥu is the divine creative word. Ḥu is generally accompanied by Sia, the wisdom, the insight into the mystery of divine life. A spell from the book of the dead tells that Ḥu and

Sia originated from Re.[7] Furthermore it is told that they assisted the sun-god at the creation.

The function of Ḥu is not restricted to his cosmogonic task. It also extends to the present. The sun-god needs his help in order to conquer the dangers which threaten him in the nether world. Thus Ḥu belongs to the crew of the ship of the sun-god, which passes the realm of death. This creative word also sounds from the mouth of the Pharaoh, who is of divine descent and therefore is called to guard Ma-a-t, the order, which the sun-god has instituted as creator. It is no flattery when the courtiers say to the king: 'Ḥu is in thy mouth, Sia in thy heart, the place of thy tongue is a temple of Ma-a-t, a God sits on thy lips, so that thy orders daily are carried out.'[8] Reflection on the divine word has even fostered a more profound insight. This appears from the famous document of the Memphite theology, to be found on the so-called stone slab of Shabaka. This Pharaoh, who belonged to the XXVth dynasty, of Ethiopian origin, took care that a very ancient myth on the creative word, in which the god Ptah from Memphis played the main part, was inscribed in stone, in order to prevent it from oblivion. This text is rightly supposed to contain a kind of doctrine of the Logos. This appears from the following quotation:

there arose in the heart (of Ptah), there arose on the tongue a thought . . . it happened that heart and tongue got control over all the members (i.e. of the deity), because they taught, that he (Ptah) was as heart in every body, as tongue in every mouth, of all gods, of all men, of all cattle, of all creeping animals and of all that is alive, because he thinks as heart and because he orders all things, as he likes, by his tongue.[9]

Here we find the idea of the divine, creative word, which dwells in all creatures and speaks from them. You might call this a presupposition of the conception of religious tradition.

From the text on the stone slab of Shabaka it appears that the ancient Egyptians conceived of the idea of the divine word, immanent in all living creatures and moreover in the social order and in the cult of the gods. They were also convinced that this word had been put in writing. In their opinion the script had divine meaning.[10] This generation, which writes hastily and excessively, has lost sight of the significance of the art of

c

writing. The ancient Egyptians knew that as the word was the audible thought so the script was the visible thought. What has been written down is alive and exercises influence, even after the death of the writer. In the script dwells a magical, creative power. Therefore some texts in the graves, namely those which adorn the walls of hidden rooms, were not intended to be read, but served to provide the dead with the goods enumerated in them. No wonder that creation could be conceived of as an act of writing. The texts mention the seven wise architects who wrote at the creation. In the pyramid texts the dead king is called 'the scribe of the divine book, who speaks what is and creates what does not yet exist' (Pyr. 1146). It is said about Thoth: 'Thoth daily writes Ma-a-t for thee' (i.e. the sun-god),[11] that means Thoth arranges the course of the sun-god, so to say, by an act of writing. There are two gods, who are specially connected with the art of writing, namely Seshat and Thoth. Seshat is the goddess of the art of writing and of reckoning.[12] Her writing has mythical significance, for she is called 'she who wrote for the first time'. She fixes the number of the years of the reign of the Pharaoh. With her measuring rod she defines the scope of sacred buildings, to be constructed. She keeps the annals. In the last capacity she is called 'she, who is the head of the house of books (or the house of life)'. Thoth is still more directly connected with the actual script and with books.[13] As the wise moon-god he is said to have given mankind the art of writing. Libraries and archives are under his charge. He is particularly the author of the so-called 'words of God', i.e. the prescriptions for the cult, that is to say the rituals and the books of magic, as appears from the following quotation: 'the scribe of the sacred books is Thoth, and it is he who will recite the ritual glorification (for the dead) in the course of every day, unseen, unheard'.[14] In this connection I must refrain from a further description of the significance of the two fascinating deities.

However, it is important to mention, that Thoth is the patron of the scribes. No scribe would forget to make libation to Thoth before he started his work. For writing was considered to be a lofty art. The office of the scribe was considered to be a desirable position. To the self-esteem and professional pride of the scribe testifies the saying: 'Look, there is no occupation without

a supervisor, except that of the scribe; he is supervisor himself.'
Significant is the admonition: 'Become a scribe; he is free from
work; he is not obliged to cut the earth.' The ambition to
become a scribe can have a deeper motive than the desire for
a position which releases a man from manual work. This appears from the exhortation which the wise Duauf gave to his son,
when he—as we read—'travelled to the city in order to place
him on the school of books'. He said to him: 'Might I let you
love the books more than your mother, might I let you see their
beauty. It is greater than any other occupation.'[15]

IV

The ancient Egyptians kept the art of writing and the books in
high esteem. They knew the significance of the creative word,
which endures as a living reality. They must have realized the
significance of oral tradition. There are actually several indications that there existed a tradition, which was partly secular,
partly sacred. As for the more secular tradition there existed a
folk-tale tradition.[16] Like all Eastern peoples, the ancient
Egyptians were great lovers of adventurous stories. They eagerly
listened to the born story-tellers, who in the market-place or
in the shadow of the gate of a temple told their tales. Obviously
these stories were handed down by word of mouth. The subjects of these stories were partly of a secular nature; for instance, the trials and tribulations of a shipwrecked person; the
adventures of a courtier, called Sinuhe, who fled to Syria at
the ascension to the throne of a new king; the tale of the doomed
prince, to whom it has been predicted at his birth that he could
become a victim of three hostile animals. These stories partly
have the character of sagas in which old mythical ideas are
elaborated in a popular way. To the last category some famous
stories can be reckoned, e.g. firstly the well-known story of the
two brothers, Anubis and Bata, two persons who obviously
represent the gods Anubis and Osiris, and secondly the long
text in which the course of the lawsuit between Horus and Seth
is related, a story in which many droll and even scabrous episodes, not to be found in the original myth, occur. One can
deduce the existence of this oral tradition of folk-tale from a
series of stories, mostly dating from the Middle Kingdom, and

written on papyri. They must be the literary fixation of the art of telling stories for many generations.

V

Beside this folk-tale tradition and loosely connected therewith a religious tradition existed which handed down mythical conceptions, magic spells and ritual prescriptions from generation to generation. We have several proofs that such a tradition existed and that it was very ancient. Its great age appears, e.g., from the fact that at the close of spell 130 of the *Book of the Dead* it is told that it dates from the time of Usaphaïs, a king of the first dynasty, whilst spell 64 is supposed to date back to the days of the famous king Mycerinus of the IVth dynasty.[17] At that time these spells had not yet assumed their written form. They were part of the oral tradition. One can become familiar with this tradition by paying attention to the commentaries on some funerary texts. Famous and well-known instances of such commentaries are to be found in spell 17 of the *Book of the Dead*. A few years ago Dr M. S. H. G. Heerma van Voss, a Dutch Egyptologist, traced the oldest version of the first part of this spell and its commentaries, namely in spell 335[a] of the Coffin Texts.[18] He reports that there are thirty-three versions of the spell. This fact in itself speaks for a rich variety of the religious tradition. Let me for clarity's sake make some quotations from spell 17 of the *Book of the Dead*, because this text and its commentaries are really striking.

In verse 6 the dead says: 'I am the great God, who came into being of himself.' The commentary, in which tradition makes itself heard, starts with the stereotyped question: 'What does that mean?' The answer is: 'The great God who came into being of himself, that means the water, that is Nun, the father of the gods.' Then there follows: 'Variant: it means Re, who created his names as lord of the Ennead.' The commentary goes on: 'What does that mean?' The answer is: 'It means Re, who created his body; thus came into being these gods who are in the train of Re.'

In verse 15 the original text runs: 'I am Min at his going forth. He has put his twin plumes on his head.' The commentary asks: 'What does that mean?' The answer is; 'Min means Horus who saved his father Osiris. His going forth means his birth. As for his twin plumes on his head, Isis and Nephtys went, they put themselves on his head as two hawks. Variant: they are the great large uraei that are on the brow of his father Atum. Variant of it: they are the two eyes, which were lacking in his head.'

These quotations not only present interesting instances of the mythical way of thinking of the ancient Egyptians, but they also prove, that there were great varieties in the religious tradition.

In itself the *Book of the Dead* is the illustrious example of the codification of religious tradition. The name which the Egyptologists gave to these spells suggests that it was a real book and as such comparable with the holy books of other religions. The specialist is better informed. The *Book of the Dead* contains a series of funerary spells which the Egyptologist R. Lepsius has arranged after the example of a late (i.e. the Saitic) version of this bundle of spells. Thereby the wrong impression is created that the spells are chapters of a book.

However, the ancient Egyptians did possess sacred texts, more numerous than the number that survived. Clement of Alexandria even contends that they had forty-two holy books.[19] One should not attach too great importance to this figure. Forty-two was a holy figure, which had symbolic value. At any rate this notice discloses that there was an extensive religious literature in ancient Egypt. Thus the question arises: what were the nature and the function of these sacred books?

In order to answer this question one should first get acquainted with the nature of Egyptian literature as such. The question arises: which literary genres did the ancient Egyptian pursue and which types are lacking? Likely to the surprise of many people the answer is that both the epos and the drama are absent.[20] Apparently the Egyptians did not possess the sense of the epic and the dramatic. On the other hand they excelled in the narration of short stories, in the formulation of proverbs full of wisdom and in lyrics. They wrote many beautiful love-songs and sang the praise of their kings and their gods in a flowery way. When this is realized, it is not difficult to understand that the religious texts are devoid of the epic or dramatic vein. They have a novelistic or lyric character and are conspicuous by their short concise formulations. Furthermore, attention should be paid to another interesting feature. Many texts, primarily the younger ones, are accompanied by pictures. So several spells of the *Book of the Dead* are illustrated by vignettes. Some funerary papyri mainly consist of religious representations, to which a few explanations are added. In the description of the journey of the sun-god through the nether world, generally called *Am Duat*, the main thing is the representation of the voyage of the sun-god during the twelve hours of the night. Though there is a text which links up the different scenes, the texts, written around the pictures, have no significance in themselves, but serve as explanations. This means that the illustrations of the texts are not artistic extras, but form an essential part of the texts, and sometimes even the main part. One should therewith keep in mind, that the hieroglyphs were originally a picture-writing. This cannot be purely accidental. Obviously the ancient Egyptians were endowed with imagination. Their artistic taste expressed itself mainly in a plastic way. They therefore expressed religious ideas in pictorial representations. Thus the illustrations form an intrinsic part of the sacred books and hint at their nature and function.

VI

These general remarks should be followed by a description and an assessment of the different categories of holy texts or of sacred books, if you like. The sagas, which are popular paraphrases of mythical ideas, have already been mentioned. It has also been mentioned that the Egyptians collected wisdom-sayings. Several collections are extant. Some examples are the teachings of Ptah-hotep, of Kagemni, of Duauf, of king Amenemhet and the book of wisdom of Amenemope. A special genre is formed by the texts which contain charms, e.g. the book of overthrowing Apap, the snake, which tries to thwart the voyage of the sun-god, and the book with curses against Seth. Next come the hymns, written in a lofty style and full of mythological allusions, which praise the gods or the sacral king. To the last a number of texts, which treat his birth and his ascension to the throne, are dedicated. The famous texts in the temple of Queen Hatshepsut at Deir el-Bahri found the sacral kingship on the idea that the royal child is born from the marriage of the queen with the god Amon. Also in this case the pictures dominate.

A text from the Ramesseum describes the rite of the ascension to the throne. K. Sethe, who published this text, together with that of Shabaka, calls them: 'Dramatische Texte zu altaegyptischen Mysterienspiele.' This title is misleading. It is highly dubious whether the ascension to the throne can be characterized as a mystery play, in the strict sense of the word. The ancient Egyptians had no mysteries in the Hellenistic meaning of the word. Whether the qualification 'dramatic' is right, depends on the answer to the question whether the theatre already existed in ancient Egypt, also on the domain of the cult. The opinions of the Egyptologists differ.[21] I cannot dwell on this point at the moment. In my opinion it is preferable to call the text from the Ramesseum a royal ritual. The rituals, which were enacted in the cult of the gods, form a special category. We possess interesting texts which have the character of a book of liturgy. Let me mention the order of the daily service, the ritual for the hourly service in the cult of Osiris, the litany of the cult of Osiris, the descriptions of the festivals of Min and of Sokaris, both accompanied by pictures, which belong to the most beautiful products of Egyptian art, and the texts for the cult and the festivals of Hathor and Horus, to be found in the Ptolemaic temples at Dendera, Edfu, Philae and Esne. Special attention should be paid to the texts which describe the celebration of the so-called mysteries of Osiris. The principal documents are the report of Ichernofret, a courtier of king Sesostris III, about the rites fulfilled at Abydos, and a text from the small temple of Osiris on the roof of the temple at Dendera.

This enumeration, which does not pretend to be exhaustive, may be closed by mentioning the funerary texts. These texts form an age-long tradition, which extends from prehistory to the last period of the Egyptian civilization. Three collections of funerary texts have become famous: the pyramid texts, published by K. Sethe, the coffin texts, collected and edited by A. de Buck and the funerary papyri of the New Kingdom, in the publication of which E. Naville and Sir E. A. Wallis Budge served scholarship. The conclusion of this survey is, that in ancient Egypt several types of sacred and authoritative texts existed, but that none of them had the character of a holy book, in the sense of a book having a fixed shape and an unalterable wording.

VII

This thesis can best be substantiated by a further inquiry into the character and the structure of the funerary texts. For the first, the pyramid texts are collected from the tombs of six kings of the Vth and the VIth Dynasties, to wit Unis, Teti, Pepi I, Meryre, Merenre and Pepi II Neferkare. Sethe has in his edition arranged these texts in a chronological and at the same time synoptic order, in the sense that, starting with the spells of Unis, he put the parallel texts together consecutively in horizontal series. He translated the texts, and commented on them. To this publication he added two smaller volumes containing the epigraphic and critical apparatus. In this way one gets a clear picture of the original position of the texts in the pyramids and of their function. The edition of Sethe might give the impression that we have here a funerary book. Actually they represent complexes of texts, which apparently have arbitrarily or according to an unknown design been chosen from a richer oral tradition. The spells of the six kings do not form closed homogeneous wholes, and in each of the six collections smaller complexes can be distinguished. Moreover, after the publication of Sethe analogous spells have been discovered in other small pyramids. Meanwhile it cannot be doubted that they possessed high authority, because they serve to provide the Pharaoh with eternal life in the hereafter and they give by their sheer presence in the tombs the guarantee thereof.

The coffin texts continue this funerary custom. They are taken from a great number of coffins, dating from the Middle Kingdom. A. de Buck has arranged these spells in the seven volumes of his impressive publication in such a way that he first took the spells of which the most parallel texts were present. In opposition to Sethe, de Buck has put the texts in vertical columns, which is preferable in epigraphic and linguistic respects. These texts have not yet been thoroughly studied. A Dutch Egyptologist is preparing a translation and a commentary. The quoted monograph of Heerma van Voss has shown that it is not possible to arrange the spells in a pedigree scheme and to reconstruct the oldest text. This fact confirms the conception that the coffin texts are based on an oral tradition, which has been used according to the requirements. Neither can the coffin texts really be called books; they are complexes of texts.

In this respect the *Book of the Dead* has the best claim to the title 'book'. For it starts with the opening words: 'Here begin the spells of coming forth by day, of glorification and of coming forth from and of going into the nether world, which are to be recited on the day of the burial.' This superscription pertains to the whole collection. Moreover the spells are arranged by Lepsius in the order which in the Saitic time was more or less fixed. This does not mean that every funerary papyrus contains all and the same spells. This clearly appears from the publication of the *Book of the Dead* of the XVIIIth to the XXth Dynasty in two volumes by E. Naville. In the second volume Naville has placed one of the best papyri, i.e. No. 9900 of the British Museum, which he calls Aa, in the first vertical column, to which he added the variants of other papyri. Budge and other Egyptologists have later on published other papyri. A few years ago Th. G. Allen edited *The Egyptian Book of the Dead. Documents in the Oriental Institute Museum, The University of Chicago* in a publication of a high scholarly standard, which offers a very reliable translation of the spells. This critical edition of the funerary spells makes one more strongly aware than ever before of the fact that both the text and the contents of the so-called *Book of the Dead* fluctuated.

VIII

Next the question arises whether something is known about the way in which these sacred texts came about. Here an enigmatic term presents itself, namely 'the House of Life' (*pr ʿnḫ*). Some Egyptologists have argued that 'the House of Life' was a training college or even a kind of university, solely dedicated to the composition and the study of books. This proves to be a mistake.[22] The texts mention scribes of 'the House of Life'. Part of their duty must have been the composition of sacred books. They also took part in the learned discussions, which were held in the 'House of Life'. But their office was larger than that. They were consulted in questions of medicine and magic. They could decide how royal and divine titularies were to be worded. They gave interpretations and determined the conduct of festivals. However it is dubious whether 'the House of Life' had a library. On the other hand it is well known that some temples had libraries. The room of the library in the temple of Edfu even contained a list of books. Nearly all these books are of a magico-religious nature. So also about the composition and the storage of the sacred books uncertainty prevails.

IX

The conclusion of this argument is that the problem of scripture and tradition in the usual sense of the term is not to be found in ancient Egypt. There existed an oral religious tradition, which was widely ramified. Parts of it were put down in writing. So the religious texts came into being, which can be called books in a figurative sense.

However in this process of putting down in writing some factors were active, which lastly deserve our attention, because they are generally at work in the coming into existence of holy books. They are the following. It happened in ancient Egypt that texts were put out on the name of famous persons of former times in order to increase their authority. The same motive prompted the use of old-fashioned language. Furthermore, people were afraid to alter the text: apparently the text was sacrosanct. We learn that Pharaoh Shabaka, who had the document of the Memphite theology written on stone, was motivated to do this by the wish to preserve a very ancient text, which he held in high respect. We know that the priests kept sacred books in the libraries of the temple. Finally it is interesting to hear that funerary texts were sometimes so holy, that they were considered to be secret. In the literal sense of the word this is a fiction, but metaphorically understood it can be true, because it is a fact that the texts often refer to secret acts, which were enacted in the cult.[23] These peculiarities in the process of codification show that, though ancient Egypt knew no holy books in the ordinary sense of the word, there existed in any case a deep respect for the divine word, not only in its oral form, but also in its written shape.

NOTES

[1] E. Drioton, *Pages d'Égyptologie* (1957), pp. 29, 33, 37 f.

[2] H. Frankfort, *Ancient Egyptian Religion* (1948), p. 131.

[3] A. de Buck, *De Egyptische voorstellingen betreffende de oerheuvel* (1922).

[4] C. J. Bleeker, *Die Geburt eines Gottes* (1956).

[5] The author deals with Sokaris in a forthcoming study on Egyptian Festivals.

[6] A. H. Gardiner, 'Some Personifications, II', *Proceedings of the Society of Biblical Archeology*, xxxviii (1916); J. Zandee, 'Das Schoepferwort im alten Aegypten', in *Verbum, Essays on Some Aspects of the Religious Function of Words*, dedicated to Dr H. W. Obbink (1964).

[7] 17:29 f.

[8] C. J. Bleeker, *De betekenis van de Egyptische godin Ma-a-t* (1929), p. 33.

[9] K. Sethe, *Dramatische Texte zu altaegyptischen Mysterienspielen* (1928), pp. 50, 55.

[10] W. B. Kristensen, *Antieke Wetenschap* (1940).

[11] C. J. Bleeker, *De betekenis van de Egyptische godin Ma-a-t* (1929), p. 44.

[12] H. Bonnet, *Reallexikon der aegyptischen Religionsgeschichte* (1952), pp. 699 seq.

[13] H. Bonnet, op. cit., pp. 805 seq.

[14] A. H. Gardiner, 'The House of Life', *J.E.A.* xlii, pp. 167 f.

[15] A. de Buck, *Egyptische verhalen* (1938), p. 31.

[16] H. Frankfort, op. cit., p. 129.

[17] E. Naville, *Das aegyptische Todtenbuch der XVIII bis XX Dynastie, Einleitung* (1886), p. 30.

[18] M. S. H. G. Heerma van Voss, *De oudste versie van Dodenboek 17ᵃ, Coffin Texts spreuk 335ᵃ* (1963).

[19] J. Leipoldt und S. Morenz, *Heilige Schriften, Betrachtungen zur Religionsgeschichte der antiken Mittelwelt* (1953), pp. 40 f.

[20] H. Frankfort, op. cit., pp. 124 seq.

[21] E. Drioton, op. cit., pp. 217 seq.; G. Jéquier, 'Drames, mystères, rituels dans l'ancienne Égypte' in *Mélanges offerts à M. Max Niedermann* (1944).

[22] A. H. Gardiner, 'The House of Life', *J.E.A.* xlii.

[23] J. Leipoldt und S. Morenz, op. cit., pp. 16, 24, 55 f., 79, 89 f., 166.

III

Holy Book and Holy Tradition in Iran

THE PROBLEM OF THE SASSANID AVESTA

GEO WIDENGREN

I

The first scholar to draw attention to the problems presented by
Zoroastrian scriptures as a (holy) written canonical literature,
was Nyberg. In his book *Die Religionen des alten Iran* published in
1938 he emphasized the fact that the Zoroastrian so-called
Avesta is a comparatively late creation, dating from the Sasanian period. Nyberg insisted also on the long oral transmission
of the Avestic texts which were written down at such a late
time. And he also tried to explain the reason *why* the Zoroastrian
church in Sasanian times undertook to create a canonical
literature. He saw the reason for this in the fact that other religions, the Jewish, the Christian and the Manichaean, the
members of which were living inside the frontiers of the Sasanian
empire, all of them possessed canonical writings. Quite especially he wanted to explain the creation of a *written* Avesta
as a counter-move against Manichaeism which according to
him was the most serious rival of Zoroastrianism in the Sasanian
empire.

Bailey in his book *Zoroastrian Problems in the Ninth-Century
Books*, published in 1943, devoted a whole chapter to the problem of the transmission of the religious tradition, the so-called
patvand (in Pahlavi). This chapter is occupied with the passages in Pahlavi literature where the manner of transmission is
mentioned, and examines very carefully the Pahlavi expressions
of transmission. Bailey further investigated the passages in
Zoroastrian writings where a transmission of parts of Avesta is
mentioned. And lastly he also entered upon a discussion of the
two expressions *Apastāk ut Zand*, two expressions with which we
shall be occupied in the following pages. In this connection he

discussed the date of the composition of a written Avesta and the invention of a special alphabet, the Avestan script, for the very purpose of fixing the holy text in writing. Concerning this date he says (p. 169): 'The external evidence would not prevent us admitting the existence of a written text of the Avesta in Avestan script at a date about the middle of the sixth century A.D.' He actually then as a conclusion proposes (p. 176) 'to put the recording of the Avesta in written form about the middle of the sixth century A.D.'.

Nyberg had pointed out (p. 426) that the Zoroastrian notices associated the written revelation on the one hand with Šīz and on the other hand with 'the fortress possessed of an archive', as it is called.

These two places, Šīz and the *diz i nipišt*, as its name is in Pahlavi, were discussed by Wikander in his book *Feuerpriester in Kleinasien und Iran*, dating from 1946. This is the third book of fundamental importance to the problem of the Sassanid Avesta.

Wikander has first of all compared all the notices given in the Pahlavi compendium Dēnkart, Books III and IV, notices transcribed by Bailey in his book and partly translated by Nyberg. This comparison shows one fundamental thing: both Dēnkart III and IV describe the same course of events: the religious revelation, brought by Zoroaster, was put in writing in two copies, of which one was deposited in the treasury of Šīz and the other in the fortress with the archive, the *diz i nipišt*. They both met their fate, when Alexander, 'the accursed Alexander the Roman' as he is called, burnt the copy that was deposited in the imperial archive and brought the other copy to Greece. (Thus one copy was completely *destroyed* and consequently *disappeared*, an important fact to observe.) The notices where *the reconstruction* of the lost Avesta is mentioned may be quoted here, because they are of the greatest importance to our problem. Dēnkart IV, ed. Madan, p. 412:5–11 says as follows:

Valaxš, the Arsacid, commanded that a memorandum be made for the countries (of Iran) in order to pay attention to Avesta and Zand, as they had come down in an undefiled condition in all their totality, *i.e.* everything that after the damage and destruction wrought by Alexander and the pillage and looting of the Romans, in the country of Iran in scattered form was written down and that among the dasturs had remained preserved in oral tradition in the country, as it had come forth.[1]

Two things call for notice here: (1) both Avesta and Zand were to be carefully collected, *nikās dāštan* meaning 'to pay heed to', 'to give attention to'. (2) What was collected was brought together from what was 'in scattered form *written down*', *pargandakīhā nipištak*, *and* what had remained preserved *in oral tradition* among the dasturs, *če uzvān- aβspārišnīk pat dastaβar mānd ēstāt*. Avesta as collected and reconstructed in the Arsacid period accordingly was based on both *written* and *oral* tradition. The historical value of this notice we must leave undiscussed for the present and concentrate on the question of Avesta and Zand.

Here again Wikander has brought us a long way forward. Before him it was always taken for granted that in all passages where Avesta and Zand are mentioned together Avesta means the original canonical scripture in Avestic language and Zand the commentary in Pahlavi, or rather translation *and* commentary, both in Pahlavi. But Wikander observed that Dēnkart uses the terms *nipēk* (*nipēkīhā*) and *apastāk* in quite a special way, in so far that *nipēk* (*nipēkīhā*), the writing(s), denotes the tradition of Šīz, *apastāk*, however, the tradition of Istaxr. That in Sasanian times the *diz i nipišt* actually means Istaxr is perfectly clear from a passage in the Book of Ardā Virāz I.7 where it is stated that 'this Religion, namely the whole Avesta and Zand, had been prepared on ox-hides and written with golden ink, and was preserved in the Istaxr of Pāpak in the fortress with the archive'.[2] It is, however, extremely doubtful whether this Istaxr-tradition ever was existent in a written form before it was added to the Šīz-tradition. That such was the case is hinted at in Dēnkart III, p. 406:5–10 where it is said of the activities of Artaxšaθr (Artaxšēr) I, founder of the Sasanian dynasty, and the high-priest Tansar:

The whole writing he brought from (its) scattered condition to one place, and the ancient teacher, the righteous Tansar, who was a *hērbad*, came forth and added it again to the revelation from the Avesta, *apastāk* . . . he ordered to keep the splendid original in the treasury of Šīz, *ganž i Šēčīkān*, and to spread it in copies in a suitable manner.

Dēnkart (pp. 412:17–413:1) also states that the religious writings concerning different matters, which were widely scattered, were brought together and added to the Avesta.

The King of Kings, Šāhpuhr, son of Artaxšaθr, again brought together those writings from the Religion which were scattered among the Hindus and in Rome and other countries, treating of medicine, astronomy, movement, time, space and substance, creation, existing and passing away, change in quality and increase and other processes and organs and again added these to the Avesta, and ordered a reliable copy of all this to be deposited in the treasury of Šīz, *ganž i Šēčīkān.*

Accordingly, Dēnkart books III and IV are identical in their wording, telling us that the new collection, brought together from its scattered parts all over the world, was added to the Avesta, *apastāk*, and the original deposited in Šīz. It is because Dēnkart contrasts *nipēk* and *apastāk* that Wikander was able to identify *nipēk* with the Šīz-tradition. And it surely calls for notice that even *this* tradition of Šīz is called *nipēk*, *writing*, in opposition to the *apastāk*, the Avesta, which would seem to have been until this date preserved only in oral tradition. From here Wikander was able to proceed a step further. According to a passage in Bundahišn Alexander had seized the *Zand* and sent it to Rome, but burnt the *apastāk* (Bdhn., p. 214:12 f.). Again it is clear that *apastāk* disappeared completely. If we compare this passage with the notices of Dēnkart we see at once that Avesta, *apastāk*, has preserved its name, whereas *zand* here denotes the writing, *nipēk*. The conclusion therefore presents itself to Wikander: *apastāk* is the oral tradition, of a ritual character, attached to Istaxr, *zand* is the written tradition (cosmological, mythological etc.), concentrated at Šīz, the home of the Magians.

II

The name of *zand* did not lead Wikander to any further conclusions, but has been the starting point of my own research work. The Pahlavi form *zand* goes back to the Avestic *zainti*, meaning 'knowledge', and belongs to the north-western, Parthian dialect of Media Atropatene where Šīz was a political as well as a religious centre. Here the *Zervanite* type of religion had been a characteristic of the Magian priesthood already since pre-Achaemenid times. We must therefore ask ourselves two questions: (1) did there really exist in pre-Sassanid, i.e. Parthian times, a written religious literature among the Magians, and (2) if such is the case, did that literature bear the hallmark of Zervanism?

When trying to answer the first question we may first of all refer to the notice quoted from Dēnkart that Valaxš the Arsacid ordered to collect again both Avesta and Zand, both what was written, but scattered, *and* what was present among the dasturs, the priests, in oral tradition. One is generally agreed that the Valaxš alluded to must be the third Vologeses (A.D. 148–91).[3] Did there then, on the whole, exist any religious written literature in his time? Yes, there certainly did, though the material is scanty.

Pausanias in his well-known description of the fire-ritual of the Magians in Asia Minor actually tells us that the officiating Magian invokes a deity, reading out of a book (V. 27,6). This notice, from about A.D. 150, which would seem to be quite reliable, because there is no reason to doubt its historical truth, thus informs us that at the time of Pausanias a book was used among the Median Magians for ritual purposes and this date fits the reign of Vologeses III. It is probable that this ritual book contained invocations in the manner of the ancient Yašts. Further the so-called 'Oracles of Hystaspes', the authentic Iranian background of which is proved, would take us back to about 100 B.C., if it could be demonstrated that they originally were written down in a Middle-Iranian language. But we do not know anything about it and it seems more probable that these apocalyptic texts first were written down in Greek, having as their foundation only an *oral* Iranian tradition.

To the last period of the Parthian empire we are taken by no less a person than Mani himself, for he states in Kephalaia p. 7:27 ff. that 'Zarades did not write any books, but his disciples, after his death remembered and wrote [the books] which they read to-day'. Accordingly in the days of Mani certain religious writings were put in circulation in Iranian language under the name of Zoroaster.

With this conclusion agrees the well-known fact that among the Manichaean documents of Turfan, M 16 speaks of a

Zoroastrian book, *zarduštagān nibēg*. Mani obviously thought that he had incorporated with his own doctrine also the teachings of Zoroaster as well as those of Buddha and Jesus, as is stated in both T II D 126 and *Kephalaia*, Chapter 154. The famous text M 7 actually claims to be a word of Zoroaster himself. This is the so-called 'Zarathustra-Fragment'.

Also the Mithras mysteries, closely associated with Northwestern Iran and the Zervanism of the Median Magians, in the same period know of holy writings, for in the Dura Mithraeum the Mithras Magians are depicted in Parthian costume and holding in their left hand a scroll. We may also refer to a passage in *Ginzā*, p. 415:20 transl. Lidzbarski, where it is said that the Magians and scribes 'pervert the Nask and the Book'. Unfortunately this passage is next to impossible to date.

The term *nask* which we meet with here, is the special Zoroastrian name of the various books of the original Sassanid Avesta. *From Dēnkart VIII and IX we know that the Sassanid Avesta was divided into 21 nask-s.* Of these only one, *the 19th*, is preserved in the existing Avesta, the holy canon of the Parsi communities of our days. This is the Vendidad, i.e. *Vī-daēva-dāta*, the Law against the Demons. This nask certainly originated among the Median Magians as Moulton and Nyberg have shown. Other nask-s most probably also led their origin back to the same circles, e.g. the so-called Hādōxt Nask, a text chiefly occupied with the fate of the soul after death, of which a considerable part is preserved today. I have tried to demonstrate by means of a philological analysis that the language of Hādōxt Nask closely agrees above all with that of Vendidad. It is therefore highly probable that HN at least got its final redaction among the Magians of Media.

I have already spoken of the Pahlavi translation and commentary of Avesta. We may date the origin of a *written* Pahlavi translation to the later period of Sasanian times when the grammatical knowledge of the Avesta language had disappeared to a great extent. We may date it to before the reign of Xosrau Anōšurvān, if we suppose that the term *zand* used in the apocalyptic Pahlavi writing Bahman Yašt I. 7 here denotes the Pahlavi translation. This is, however, very uncertain, for from the context we would rather have to conclude that *zand* in this passage signifies some esoteric knowledge (cf. below, p. 51). At

D

any rate, at a given point in the history of the Canon, Pahlavi translations existed of all the extant Nask-s and they were now called *zand* which accordingly had acquired a new meaning.

III

This fact is all-important for the task of reconstructing the Sassanid Avesta. It has been calculated that today only the fourth part of the original Avesta is preserved. However, the missing three parts are partly possible to reconstruct. We possess a very comprehensive Zoroastrian Pahlavi literature, partly based on lost Avestic texts. The Apocalypse Bahman Yašt was just mentioned. According to the witness of that writing itself this Pahlavi text was based on the following Avestic texts: Vohuman Yasn, Hordāt Yasn und Aštāt Yasn. Two other very important texts are the Bundahišn, based on Dāmdāt Nask and Čihrdāt Nask, and the Selections of Zāt-spram. Both contain in certain parts Zervanite doctrines as was shown already some years ago.

How will it be possible then to say with some certainty whether these portions of the text characterized by Zervanite teachings are based on lost Avestic texts or not? Well, we have certain formal expressions in Pahlavi writings, indicating that what follows is a quotation from an Avestic text, now lost. Such expressions are the following (no exhaustive enumeration is intended, but only a selection giving some clear idea of how such quotations are introduced):

1. *pat vēh-dēn ōyōn paitāk ku*, 'in the Good Religion it is revealed in the following way that'
2. *(ēt) pat dēn ōyōn paitāk ku*, '(this)is revealed in the Religion in the following way that'
3. *ōyōn čiyōn pat dēn gōβēt ku*, 'in the following way as one says in the Religion that'
4. *čiyōn gōβēt pat dēn*, 'as one says in the Religion'
5. *gōβēt pat dēn ku*, 'one says in the Religion'
6. *andar dēn ōyōn nimūt ēstēt ku*, 'in the Religion is indicated in the following way that'
7. *ōyōn paitāk ku*, 'in the following way it is revealed'
8. *hač dēn paitāk ku*, 'in the Religion it is revealed'

There are also other expressions referring to the commentary

which, as we hinted at, often is given as interspersed with the
Pahlavi translation. I give here a sample of such exegetical indications:

1. *zand-ākāsih*, 'the Commentary-Knowledge', *zand* here accordingly indicating the *commentary*
2. *hač pōryōtkēš gōβišn, nikēž i vēh dēn*, 'from the sayings of the
   ancient teachers, the exposition of the Religion'
3. *hač nikēž i vēh-dēn*, 'from the exposition of the Religion' (*hač
   vēh-dēn nikēž, pōryōtkēšān cāštak*)
4. *pat zand i Vohuman Yasn paitāk ku*, 'in the Commentary to
   Vohu-Manah Yasna it is revealed'
5. *pat zand i Vohuman Yasn, Hōrdat Yasn, Aštāt Yasn paitāk ku*, 'in
   the Commentary to V. M. Yasna, H. Yasna, A. Yasna it is
   revealed'
6. *Māhvindāt guft ku*, 'Māhvindat said that'
7. *hast kē gōβēt* (*gōβēnd*) *ku*, 'some say that'

Such expressions tell us, that the sentence or portion of the
text in question is taken from the Avesta and especially commented on by the translators and exegetes. It is, however,
comparatively rare that the commentators are mentioned by
name, as is the case with Māhvindāt and Rōšn in Bahman Yašt
III. 3. The other extreme is that an exegetical gloss is introduced only by the word *ku* = i.e.

In the Zervanite texts mentioned in the following we meet
with the expressions *zand-ākāsih* (in Bundahišn) and *nikēž i vēh-
dēn* (in Dēnkart, where it is an ever-recurring formula).

There are, however, also certain linguistic and stylistic criteria. *Grosso modo* we might say that in an ordinary prosaic text
in Middle-Iranian language the verb comes at the end of the
sentence—with some easily explicable exceptions. If without
any special motivation the verb is placed at the beginning—and
this moreover in a section that we also for some other reason
would suspect to be Avestic—then we may say with a certainty
amounting to near one hundred per cent. that this part of the
Pahlavi text is a translation from Avesta.

Moreover we also meet with some peculiar syntactic constructions, especially relative clauses and constructions, characteristic of the extant Pahlavi translations from Avesta. By
comparing such a suspect passage with existing Pahlavi translations of Avestic texts it will be comparatively easy to state

whether the text in question is a translation or taken into the pen only in Pahlavi.

Much nonsense has been written by non-specialists about the late date of Pahlavi writings and the apparent impossibility of using them for comparative or historical purposes. I should like to draw attention to some well-known Pahlavi texts where the already presented observations are of the utmost importance for the history of Iranian religions and the comparative conclusions to be drawn from these writings. To mention but a couple of names I single out here for the apocalyptic literature Bahman Yašt, for cosmology, anthropology and apocalyptic speculation the two books Bundahišn and Zātspram, and for prophetology and the life of Zoroaster Dēnkart, Book VII.

In the *Festschrift for Wilhelm Eilers*[4] I concentrated on an analysis of two well-known Zervanite texts, namely Zātspram I and Bundahišn I, adding some observations on Zātspr. XXXIV. All three of them have at a recent date been edited by Professor Zaehner to whose lexicographical work I would like to pay a tribute here. However, from a grammatical point of view I do not think that he has been equally happy and for this reason I have analysed the translations anew in a *Festschrift* to be published by the Cama Oriental Institute in Bombay. There, however, my interest was chiefly concentrated on the syntactical questions, especially the use of the subjunctive in Pahlavi, so I can leave out of discussion these more technical philological problems.

Returning to our Zervanite texts it turned out that both Zātspram I and Bundahišn I go back to a common source—and this idea was expressed rather long ago.[5] But I hope to have proved by a philological analysis that it is beyond doubt that there once existed an *Avestic text of clear Zervanite type*, where the assault of Ahriman against Ōhrmazd and his heavenly abode was described. This conclusion has far-reaching consequences for the question of the Iranian background of similar gnostic descriptions, above all Mani's vivid relation of how the Prince of Darkness attempted an assault against the realms of Light. Already in my book *Mani and Manichaeism* I pointed to the description in Zātspram I as the only possible source of this part of Mani's system.

Here, however, we are not concerned with these consequences

but with other implications. In the first place we should notice that there are also in Zātspram XXXIV clear indications of an Avestic original in the paragraphs 8, 10, 12, 14, 16–20, accordingly in a considerable part of this chapter the content of which is apocalyptic-eschatological and, like Chapter I, possessed of a clear Zervanite character, as shown by Prof. Zaehner.

As to Bahman Yašt it is easy to prove that the quoted Avestic texts, i.e. Vohuman Yasn, Hordāt Yasn and Aštāt Yasn were utilized quite especially in the Book III, where quotations and exegetical glosses abound. To regain these Avestic passages from the Pahlavi text as it now stands I consider the next task to be carried out.[6]

IV

In one of the Syriac Acts of the Persian Martyrs we read a curious and very interesting notice about the Magians who are said to be organized in groups under the guidance of certain 'Masters', in Syriac rabbānē, the plural of rabbā, corresponding to the Pahlavi term ōstāt. These rather turbulent communities, we are told, were wandering around in Adhurbaidjan, obviously being *trained* by their 'masters', for we hear that they assemble from the whole kingdom of the Persians in order to receive here in Adhurbaidjan their training. And this instruction is characterized in a very peculiar way, for it is stated in this text that the Magians go there 'in order to learn the foolish murmuring of Zarduš, the Son of Spidtahman' (BKV[3] XXII, p. 204). What is called here in Syriac reṭnā, 'murmuring', is the special way of reciting the holy traditions, so characteristic of the Magians and their successors, the Mobads. This term reṭnā is used repeatedly in Syriac literature to denote the prayer or recitation of the Magians, what in Latin is called *magicum susurramen*. There are two Iranian terms for it: the first is Pahlavi dranǰēnītan 'to learn by heart', and Avestic drenǰaya-, from drang-, 'to learn by heart', 'to recite prayers in a murmuring manner', the Pahlavi verb continuing the Avestic linguistic usage. The Islamic authors too have noticed the special way in which the Mobads always used to recite their prayers. Wikander paid special attention to this art of recitation and for all details I refer to his book *Feuerpriester*. This recitation was combined with their method of learning their holy texts by heart. Bailey, who has the merit of having drawn attention to nearly all the relevant passages in Zoroastrian writings where the learning by heart of the holy tradition is referred to, established the meaning of *varm kartan* as meaning 'to memorize', and this is the second expression. We may start by quoting from the text *Husrav ut Rētak*, 'King Xosrau and his attendant-boy' where the page says in §§8–10:

In (due) time I was given to the School and in my work at School I was very diligent. I memorized the Yašt, the Hādōxt, the Bagān, and the Vīdēvdāt like a *hērbad* and passage by passage heard the Zand. My scribal ability is such that I am a good scribe and swift scribe, with keen understanding, successful, with skilful fingers.[7]

The page accordingly has learnt to recite by heart the Yašts, the Vendidad, the Hādōxt Nask and the Bagān Nask. This notice shows that these four nask-s, out of the twenty-one existing nask-s, obviously toward the end of the Sasanian period, let us say mid-sixth century and thereafter, constituted the essential part of the Sassanid Avesta. But before entering upon a discussion of this problem let us consider what is said about the *Zand*. It is stated that the page has 'heard the Zand passage by passage'. In this text it is obvious that Zand has acquired the meaning of 'Commentary'. At school the explanation was given, i.e. the Pahlavi translation with interspersed exegetical glosses as even today the Pahlavi translation of the Vendidad is before our eyes.

When the page, after telling this, boasts of having acquired a fine scribal ability, but does not say a single word about a writing down of the holy texts, we cannot evade the impression that at the priestly school, here called *frahangistān*, but later *hērpatistān*—we remember that he says that he memorized the four nask-s like a *hērbad*-priest—the canonical literature, what is called the Avesta, was still transmitted in oral tradition. In the passage from *Husrav ut Rētak* just quoted the Pahlavi expression for memorizing a sacred text is *varm kartan* and this is the technical expression used in several other passages as Bailey has pointed out. Among the five virtues of the priest is, e.g., 'the memorizing of the nask-s', *varm-naskīhā* (*PT*, pp. 129 f.). The ideal priest would be capable of memorizing not only four

nask-s, as the page did, but all the twenty-one nask-s. Such a
priest was said to be 'one who had memorized the *whole Apastāk
and Zand*', thus not only the Avesta, but also the Zand, in this
case obviously the translation and commentary. There is another
expression for the same ideal for it is said of the sisters of Ardā
Virāz that 'they had memorized the Dēn and had performed the
Yašt' (AVN II. 3). The expression 'to perform the Yašt', used
also in Syriac literature, denotes the recital of the sacrificial
prayer, *yašt*, and accordingly means a performance of the ritual.

The word *Dēn* which is used in the Ardā Virāz Nāmak to
signify not 'Religion', but 'religious tradition', as we remember
is used in the Pahlavi texts to indicate the Avesta as the source
of a quotation or statement. For the present I cannot give any
passage where instead of *Dēn* the word *Apastāk* is used. This is
a curious fact which needs an explanation, especially curious
because in the Syriac Acts of the Persian martyrs the Christian
martyrs when arguing with the Magians often say: 'it is said
in your Avesta', *aβastāg*, as the form is there, a form of the word
reflecting the real pronunciation of the word. In one passage in
the Syriac literature *aβastāg* is mentioned together with the *dēn*,
and in at least two passages, AVN XIV. 3 and MX IV. 5, it is
spoken of people who are able to recite (or perform) the whole
religious (ritual) tradition, *hamāk dēn yaštan*. In Pahlavi writings
we therefore meet with the following expressions for memorizing
the holy tradition in general:

1. *dēn varm kartan.*
2. *hamāk dēn yaštan.*
3. *hamāk apastāk ut zand varm kartan.*

Quite provisionally I would propose the explanation that *dēn*
as constantly used in Pahlavi literature for the holy tradition is
the older expression, later specified as *apastāk ut zand*. Here we
should note the expression *dēn-dipīrīh*, 'religious writing', for the
Avestan script.[8]

V

Wikander, by locating the original *zand* in its meaning of 'sacred
knowledge', not 'commentary', at Šīz in Adhurbaidjān, the
religious centre of the Median Magians, was also able to

associate the *zand* with the *Mobads*, the heirs of the Magians (*mōbad* < *mōpat* < *mōvpat*: *mōγpat* < *mayu-pati*). For the *apastāk* being located at Istaxr, he assumed the Herbads to be the up-holders of the tradition. We remember that he explained the origin of the Avesta as a collection of *apastāk* and *zand*, the written traditions of the mobads, and the oral tradition memor-ized by the *hērbads*.

When did that fusion take place? In other words: when did the Canon we call 'Avesta' originate?

The answer given by Dēnkart implies that Avesta was there from the time of Zoroaster. He brought the Religion, *dēn*, and engraved and wrote the 1,200 chapters of it in the Avestan script on tablets of gold, as it is said in the text called 'The Provincial Capitals of Ērān', §4. The same idea is underlying the relations given in Dēnkart III and IV. That this is completely un-historical is shown by the Syriac passages once quoted and analysed by François Nau. He was able to show that in the Syriac texts it was *never* spoken of Avesta as a ('holy') *Book*, but as a ('holy') Tradition. From this fact he wanted to draw the conclusion that the Mobads after the Arabian conquest of Iran in all haste produced a book out of their oral traditions in order to be accepted as a people with a Scripture, *ahl al-kitāb*. During the Sasanian period there was according to Nau no *written* Avesta at all. But this conclusion was far too rash and did not even take into account two passages where mention is made of the *sefrā damǧūšūṭā*, 'the literature of the magianhood'. Because of the clear meaning of the word *sefrā* it is hardly possible to understand this expression otherwise than denoting a *written literature*. Actually we have already seen that the Magians of Šīz must have been in possession of a written religious tradition *before* the Sasanian period and I have tried to show here that this literature to a great extent was coloured by Zervanite ideas. The Zoroastrian tradition concerning the origin of the Sassanid Avesta is contradictory. The Ardā Virāz Nāmak says that there was a general confusion and many religious opinions until the time of Šāhpuhr II (309–79) when Aturpāt i Mah-raspandān made an end of this deplorable state. Nothing is said of Artaxšēr I or Šāhpuhr I. Dēnkart III mentions Artaxšēr I and his collection of the scattered writings while Dēnkart IV mentions both Artaxšēr I and Šāhpuhr I and

their efforts to collect the canonical writings. These notices
have been criticized by Nyberg and Wikander. With Āturpāt i
Mahraspandān we are more on sure ground than in the case of
Tansar who is altogether a legendary personality. Dēnkart IV
relates how Šāhpuhr put the whole oral tradition, called *gōβišn*,
to a critical test and examination, *hamāk gōβišn ō uskār ut vičūδišn
āβurt*. Āturpāt testified to its truth by means of undergoing an
ordeal whereupon Šāhpuhr declared that he would not allow
any more people of bad religion, now that the Religion had
been acknowledged by him in the world. Here the *aydēnīk*, he
who belongs to the bad religion, is put in contrast to the
vēhdēnīk, he who belongs to the Good Religion of the Zoroastrians,
vēh-dēn i mazdēsnān.

The final process according to Dēnkart IV takes place in the
reign of Xosrau Anōšurvān (531–79). This is the latest possible
date of the creation of an Avestic canon and Bailey accepts the
middle of the sixth century A.D. as the date of 'the recording of
the Avesta in written form'.[9]

According to Dēnkart IV, p. 413:13 ff., Xosrau I had published a proclamation in which it was declared *inter alia*:

In such a way is in the whole quantity what belongs to the word of
the Avesta preserved *in pure oral tradition*, or *adorned by writing* by
means of *the creation of a Book* and *Memorial*, or *in the language of the
common people* by means *of oral transmission*, accordingly the whole
source-knowledge of the Religion of the Mazdā-worshippers.

The conclusion to be drawn from this proclamation is that
Avesta is on the one hand still preserved by means of oral transmission, on the other hand recorded in a written form, both the
oral and the written traditions being transmitted in the Avestic
language, and moreover that Avesta was handed down in oral
tradition in the Pahlavi language, for 'the language of the
common people' could be nothing but the Middle-Iranian
language. This again means that what we now call the Pāzand,
i.e. the Pahlavi as written in phonetic transcription without the
learned Aramaic ideograms, dates from the time of Xosrau
Anōšurvān as the latest possible date. We draw attention to the
fact that according to Bahman Yašt II. 55 both *zand* and *pāzand*
had to be repeated and memorized.

VI

From Nyberg on it was seen that the creation of an Avestic canon was intimately bound up with the creation of a Sasanian State Church. And these two processes were conditioned by the necessity to draw as sharp limits as possible against other religions whose adherents were found within the frontiers of the Sasanian empire.

If we then try to take a survey of the whole historical development we will obtain the following picture:

Artaxšēr and Šāhpuhr I cannot be called strict Zoroastrians in any sense of the word, even if Artaxšēr—probably for political reasons—was a convinced adherent of the religion of the Magians and undertook some measures against the Christians. His son Šāhpuhr I was the protector of Mani and likewise his son Ohrmazd I. It is typical that Dēnkart only speaks of a written copy deposited in Šīz by Šāhpuhr I. The turning point comes with Bahrām I under whose reign Kartēr, the real creator of a Sasanian State Church, starts his career as the most influential ecclesiastic dignitary of the empire under the three Bahrāms, Bahrām I, II and III as well as Narsē. A fusion between the two priest-classes, the Mobads of Šīz and the Herbads of Istaxr is brought about and this implies as we have seen that the *written* religious tradition of Šīz, the *zand*, is added to the oral tradition, of the *herbads* of Istaxr, the *apastāk*. At the same time Kartēr starts some whole-scale persecutions against *all* religious minorities of Iran, including Jews, Christians, Manichaeans, Nasoraeans (i.e. Mandaeans) and Buddhists and Brahmins. Under Šāhpuhr II (309–79 A.D.) start the most determined persecutions of the Christians ever heard of. He also at the same time accepts after examination *hamāk gōβišn*, the whole word, as brought by Āturpāt i Mahraspandān, and declares that he acknowledges the Religion, *dēn*, in the world. He declares himself unwilling to tolerate people belonging to any other religion.

Xosrau Anōšurvān (531–79) brings about a new collection of religious writings, both as written and oral Avesta, and as a Pahlavi translation. At the same time he starts the wholesale massacre of the Mazdakites, a communistic-gnostic sect of

Manichaean origin of real danger to the feudal society of the empire.

We may thus state that the decisive events in the history of the creation of a Sasanian Church, the fusion of the Mobads and Herbads, the fusion of their traditions, and the writing down of the whole religious tradition, are coupled together with severe measures against heretics and foreign minorities. The Canon, the Avesta, really is the *canon* of this State Church.

But the Avesta as accepted in the time of Šāhpuhr II (mid-fourth century) still contained a lot of Zervanite doctrines and myths. This fact is perfectly clear from those Acts of the Persian martyrs that we are able to date to his time and a century later. The passion of Pethion, a martyr in the year 447, contains a Christian polemical argument against the religion of the Mobads as found in the Avesta, *aβastāg*. This religion is the most pure Zervanism to be found. Accordingly the Avesta of the fifth century was still characterized by a great many Zervanite dogmas. This agrees perfectly with what we know from other sources about the Iranian religion of the period of Yazdagird II (439–57), especially from the proclamation of his leading minister Mihr Narsē, a famous Zervanite document.

With the time of Xosrau I the situation is altogether changed. The polemical arguments in the Acts of the Martyrs are no longer directed against Zervanism, but above all against fire-worship. In this connection the notice Bahman Yašt I. 7 is again seen to possess some importance, for it is prescribed by Xosrau Anōšurvān not to teach the *zand—bē pat patvand i šmāh* which I previously have translated 'except in the circle of your relatives'.[10] But perhaps it would be better to translate 'in the circle of your transmission'. I think *zand* here denotes some esoteric knowledge rather than the ordinary Pahlavi translation. If Zervanite teachings were included in this commentary, emanating from the *zand* of Šīz, this could perhaps explain why *zand* changed its meaning to denote ultimately the Pahlavi translation and commentary, a change in meaning which otherwise seems inexplicable. From the time of Xosrau Anōšurvān we have to count with the so-called 'orthodox Zoroastrianism', i.e. a Zoroastrian Avesta without Zervanism and other heretic ingredients.

Two types of religion were confronted with each other and

this was seen quite clearly by Nyberg. The Christians always fall back on their Holy Book whereas the Magians invoke the Avesta, but do not regard it as a 'Holy' Book but as a 'Sacred' Tradition in oral transmission. The scribal culture of the ancient Near East meets the methods of oral transmission, so well preserved in Indo-Iranian culture. The same opposition is found between Zoroastrianism and Manichaeism, for Mani's religion was above all a religion based upon canonical writings, the works of the founder himself. The Jews occupied the same position as the Christians, but there was not much polemic between them and Zoroastrians. When the Arabs conquered Iran it was of fundamental importance to the Zoroastrians to produce a Holy Book and presumably it was only then that they started thinking of Avesta as a *Book*, containing the Revelation received by Zoroaster from Ōhrmazd, and presented in *a Book, called Avesta*. Now the existent pattern found in many types of religion in the ancient Near East, and above all in Gnosticism and Islam, had ultimately emerged the victor also on Iranian soil.

The Avesta as the Zoroastrians were able to produce it was only a poor ruin of the Sassanid Avesta. The few existing copies had obviously been destroyed and the carriers of the oral tradition scattered all over Iran. This deplorable state of things was in the historical legend projected back in time to explain the loss of so many Avestic texts. The task will be to reconstruct as much as possible of the Sassanid Avesta. I do not think, however, that when this task is carried out in the future our picture of the historical process will be essentially changed.

The rôle of the king is to be emphasized. Tradition was of course preserved by the priests, the dasturs, including the Mobads and the Herbads, but the king obviously took the initiative of collecting the sacred traditions.

NOTES

[1] My translation is based on the German one given in *Iranische Geisteswelt* (Baden-Baden, 1960), p. 311, with some revision. It differs both from that of Zaehner, *Zurvan* (Oxford, 1955), p. 8, and that of Nyberg, op. cit., p. 416. The text: *Valaxš i Ašakānān apastāk ut zand, čēyōn apēčakīhā andar āmat ēstāt, hamōk-ič i hač-aš, har čē hač vizand ut āšuft-kārīh i Alaksandar ut ēvār ut rōp i Hrōmāyān andar Ērān šaϑr pargandakīhā apar nipištak, ut čē uzvān-aβspārišnīk pat*

dastaβar mānd ēstāt andar šaϑr, cēyōn frāč mat ēstāt, nikās dāštan, ō šaϑrīhā aβyātkār kartan framūt.

[2] Cf. Widengren, *Iranische Geisteswelt*, pp. 309 f.

[3] Nyberg, op. cit., p. 417.

[4] *Zervanitische Texte aus dem 'Avesta' in der Pahlavi-Überlieferung.*

[5] Cf. Schaeder and Zaehner.

[6] I propose to do this in a *Festschrift* dedicated to Prof. Kerenyi.

[7] Cf. Bailey, *Zoroastrian Problems in the Ninth-Century Books* (1943), p. 160 and Widengren, op. cit., p. 250.

[8] Cf. Bailey, op. cit., p. 153 with n. 3.

[9] Bailey, op. cit., p. 176.

[10] Cf. *Die Religionen Irans*, p. 256.

Oral Torah and Written Records

J. WEINGREEN

I

During the past few years I have been engaged in a major study aimed at presenting a case for the continuity of tradition from at least the latter historical period of the Old Testament to that of early Rabbinic times. In a number of scattered articles, to some of which I shall make reference, the following general conclusion has been reached. Certain institutions, regulations and religious concepts which are usually associated with the Rabbinic mode of thinking and, therefore, designated as being Rabbinic, not only in character but also in origin, are, in fact, to be detected, in rudimentary forms, in the Pentateuch and in the other books of the Old Testament. I have found this to be the case in the spheres of law-making, history-writing, folk-lore, authoritative exposition and devotional literature. It may be said that some, at least, of the Halakic and Midrashic formulations which are to be found in the Mishna in mature forms may be traced back to their emergent beginnings in the Old Testament records. Instead of following the conventional practice of moving forward from the Old Testament to post-biblical literature, I have adopted the method of looking back from the Rabbinic to pre-Rabbinic, i.e. post-exilic times and, on occasion, still further back to pre-exilic times. In this exercise I have come across what I have termed Rabbinic-type situations recorded in the pages of the Old Testament. Broadly speaking, my investigations may be described as the search for the materials with which to reconstruct the bridges linking the Old Testament with the Mishna.

In this paper dealing with the relationship between the oral Torah and the authoritative written records 1 shall be concerned with both the Mishna and the Old Testament and I propose employing the same methods which have guided my earlier studies. It will be necessary, in the first instance, to point out the recognized method of preserving the vast amount of Mishnaic material adopted by the Rabbis before the compilation of the Mishna by Rabbi Judah at the beginning of the third century C.E. This will enable us to see whether or not there were parallel factors, both explicit and implicit, in the Old Testament literature which preceded and contributed to its compilation. If such points of contact emerge—and it is my purpose to try to find them—then these would indicate a continuity of pattern in the preservation of sacred Jewish literature and thus support the case for a direct line of tradition, linking the Old Testament and the Mishna.

In this connection I should like to refer to Professor Geo Widengren's 'Concluding Remarks' with which he rounds off his very instructive book *Literary and Psychological Aspects of the Hebrew Prophets*.[1] In this erudite work the author draws a comparison between the methods adopted by the Arabs in the transmission of their sacred literature and corresponding Hebrew modes. His final judgment is summed up in these words: 'the literary analysis of the Pentateuch and the Books of Joshua-Judges is completely to be revised in the light of comparative research, where corresponding Arabic literature must serve as the *only* accurate guide' (italics mine). While accepting the thesis that the history of Arabic sacred literature has much to offer as a reliable guide in the study of the history of sacred Hebrew literature, I would venture to add the following consideration. If it is possible to sustain firmly the contention that there is an unbroken continuity of tradition from the Old Testament to the Mishna, then a search through Mishnaic records might provide fresh light, in retrospect, on the influences which contributed to the compilation of the Massoretic Hebrew Old Testament. This is an avenue of approach which has not hitherto attracted adequate attention. I hope that this paper, in addition to dealing with the immediate problems inherent in its title, may, at the same time, serve to indicate the value of this line of research for the study of the Old Testament, as a picture of a living culture in ancient Israel.

It is always tempting to place one's researches within a neat chronological framework and thus present an orderly progression of ideas and movements. However, it will suit our purpose equally well if, while recognizing that references to historical settings may be desirable, we merely indicate these loosely, for the conclusions we hope to reach for Old Testament times are not subject to strict chronological control. The date of the final compilation of the Mishna by Rabbi Judah is the beginning of the third century C.E., but this date does not imply the sudden initiation of such editorial activity. It marks, rather, the culmination of a cultural process which stretches far back into the history of Israel. While it is not possible to fix a *terminus a quo* for this cultural development, the indications are, as we shall attempt to demonstrate, that this Mishnaic-type tradition is consistent with the functioning of an organized social, political and religious order, that is to say, during the pre-exilic period.

I might mention, in passing, that I am not unaware of the relevance of the literature of the apocrypha for this study, nor do I overlook the importance of the writings of the Qumran community. In this paper, however, I am confining myself to Rabbinic sources for the materials required in attempting to establish points of comparison between early Rabbinic writings and the Hebrew Scriptures. On a broader canvas, the above mentioned post-biblical literary sources would, of course, have their place.

II

Let us now turn to an examination of the information supplied by the Talmud on the subject of the oral Torah, with regard to its development, preservation and transmission. The Mishna *Sanhedrin* iv. 3[2] gives the following description of arrangements and procedures at the judicial sessions of the Sanhedrin: 'The Sanhedrin was arranged like half of a round threshing floor, so that they might all see one another. Before them stood the two scribes of the judges, one to the right and one to the left, and they wrote down the words of them that favoured acquittal and the words of them that favoured conviction.'[3] We need not concern ourselves here with a variant statement appended to this Mishna that there were, in fact, three and not two clerks of the court. The central item of information which this Mishna provides is that official records of the deliberations of the Sanhedrin court and the verdicts reached by the judges were recorded by professional court clerks. Such records must surely have been the basis of much of the Tannaitic teaching in the academies of legal disputations and of the Halakic summaries which formed much of the Mishna. On this point Julius Kaplan is firmly convinced that 'while recording the different opinions of the judges, the clerks were writing Halakah pure and simple'.[4]

We note, then, that fresh Halakic material was being continually developed as the result of court proceedings and that the preservation of this ever-growing bulk of juridical decisions was not consigned to the memory of succeeding generations of scholars but, on the contrary, records of the proceedings were made for future reference. One may now pose the question: 'Were these accumulated written Halakic summaries at all used by the teaching authorities of the academies?' The answer is given by Talmudic references to the preservation in private of such recorded Halakic material by these authorities, while lectures on the Halakic decisions, as well as on the variant views of the leading jurists, were given in the academies orally. That such, indeed, was the general practice among the Talmudic Rabbis is borne out by a ruling recorded in *Temurah* 14b and elsewhere that 'matter which is of the oral category must not be recited from a written record and matter which is of the written category must not be recited orally'.[5] One may observe, in passing, that the second half of this directive carries with it the plain warning that too much reliance should not be placed upon memory, when the sacred Scriptures are to be quoted. Those scholars who draw analogies from other cultures and advocate the view that, with regard to the sacred writings of the Israelites, memory was a much more reliable mode of preservation than written records, might give some thought to this Talmudic directive. It might even conceal a tradition of some antiquity. However, for our immediate concern, it is the first of these two prohibitions which is of special interest, for it forbids the reciting of 'oral' material from a written record. Here, then, is clear evidence that what is designated as 'oral' matter actually existed in written form. Otherwise the prohibition would have been directed against a non-existing situation. We conclude, then, that the adjective 'oral' refers not to the means of preserving authoritative Rabbinic legalistic material, but only to their circulation and transmission. It

E

seems that, though summary records were made in writing, pre-
cautions were taken against copies being made for circulation.

The view expressed by Rabbi Yoḥanan, as stated in the above
quoted reference in *Temurah* 14b, is of relevance in this connection. He is reported as saying that 'those who write down
Halakot are like those who burn the Torah and anyone who
studies from them (i.e. from written Halakot) will not receive
any reward'.[6] At first sight it might appear that Rabbi Yoḥanan's
view was in protest against the generally accepted practice in
the academies of recording Halakot. Yet, a close examination
of his statement, particularly in the light of his condemnation
of the study of Halakot from a written document, reveals his
fear that the practice of recording the oral Torah, restricted to
the recognized authorities and kept in strict privacy, might
become widespread. The temptation to provide written textbooks of the oral Torah for the use of students must have been
ever present and, in fact, in the course of time the pressure of
this need eventually resulted in the circulation of the written
Mishna. The motive behind the restriction which prohibited
the circulation of recorded oral material may have been to
prevent the oral Torah being accorded the status of the written
Torah. It is interesting to note, incidentally, that when the
Mishna was circulated in written form it did, in fact, compete
with the Old Testament in authority, as evidenced by the
statement in the Mishna *Sanhedrin* xi. 3: 'Greater stringency
applies to (the observance of) the words of the Scribes than to
(the observance of) the words of the (written) Torah.'[7]

A direct reference to the existence of written Halakic material,
kept in strict privacy, is made in *Shabbath* 6b and elsewhere.
Rab, an early third century Amora and a pupil of Rabbi
Judah, states that, in the house or, most likely, in the academy,
of his uncle Rabbi Ḥiyya he found what he describes as a
מגילת סתרים, i.e. a scroll of hidden literary material and from
this he quotes some Halakic rulings.[8] The word מצאתי could
imply either that this scroll was mislaid and discovered by Rab
or, simply, that it was deposited away secretly and that he
came across it. However, his statement indicates that, at the
close of the Tannaitic period, written Halakic summaries existed,
but these had been hidden away and thus the possibility of their
being circulated prevented. Kaplan interprets Rab's remark

as follows: 'while it implies that written documents were used as a means of preserving Halakic matter, it also indicates that these were secreted and withdrawn from view'.[9] It thus becomes clear that, when the Mishna was being compiled, the compiler did not have to search his memory or tap the memories of his contemporaries for the numerous items he selected for inclusion in his collection. It was the written records of 'oral' material preserved privately in the academies, such as the hidden scroll of Rabbi Ḥiyya, which provided the substance of the Mishnayot which have come down to us.

Finally, I would refer to a tradition mentioned by Maimonides in the Introduction to his Yad Haḥazakah, the compendium of Halakah. He wrote that 'from the time of our master Moses till (the time of) our holy Rabbi (i.e. Rabbi Judah, the Prince), no written compositions were made for the purpose of teaching them publicly as the oral Torah. In each generation, however, the president of the law-court, or a prophet who lived in a particular generation, made for himself a written record of the information he had received from his masters and he taught them in public orally.'[10] Maimonides, then, confirms the fact that, before the final compilation of the Mishna by Rabbi Judah, it was customary for the judicial authorities and accredited scholars to make written records of any fresh material which would be added to the growing bulk of the oral Torah. Such documents were kept in strict privacy, but their contents were communicated to students orally. In the light of the Talmudic references to this phenomenon, this statement by Maimonides is, simply, a restatement of a well-attested tradition which goes back into early Mishnaic times.

Two further points about the final compilation of the Mishna are relevant before we attempt to ascertain whether this tradition may be traced back to the processes which produced our Massoretic Hebrew Bible. Rabbi Judah's compilation of the Mishna marks the culmination of a series of similar attempts which had been made in the decades preceding him. He was anticipated in this venture by Rabbi Akiba and by the latter's pupil Rabbi Meir. There are, in fact, even references to a Mishna which existed earlier than the time of Rabbi Akiba. The Mishna *Sanhedrin* iii. 4 mentions, in the name of Rabbi Jose, that the list of kinsmen not qualified to be witnesses or judges given in that Mishna agreed with the Mishna of Rabbi Akiba, but the First Mishna had a longer list.[11] The need for a systematic presentation of Rabbinic rulings and traditions found practical expression early in the Tannaitic period and the contribution by Rabbi Judah marks the end of a period in which attempts had been made progressively to produce a standard Mishna. Secondly, Rabbi Judah did not include in his Mishna every item in the mass of material available to him. He deliberately selected what he considered as being of high merit or importance and left a great deal outside his collection. Hence the supplementary collections under the titles of Tosephta and Baraita. In adopting the principle that an authoritative religious work should contain selected items culled from a larger body of literature, Rabbi Judah was following a time-honoured tradition, going back to the compilation of the Old Testament itself.

III

Turning now to the Old Testament to examine the relationship between oral tradition and written records, it would be useful if, in the first place, we were to define, even loosely, the nature and scope of the extra-biblical literature which co-existed along with the Old Testament, during the latter's phases of development. In broad terms we would define this oral Torah as being a body of authoritative legalistic, historical, folkloreistic and expositional literature which was external to, but which in effect supplemented and often modified, the basic biblical text. There are two main areas to which this definition may be applied: (*a*) the mass of ever-growing matter which remained permanently outside the Scriptures, but was operative in the religious life of the people and (*b*) such material which had been originally external to the text, but which was subsequently incorporated into it, either by the design of the redactors or through the inept work of copyists. It is our purpose to demonstrate that, in both these categories of the oral Torah, as we have defined them, we find modes of interpretation which are the same as those of the Mishna and we therefore describe them as Rabbinic-type formulations. Thus the present study may be seen in a wider context of a continuously evolving pattern, traceable in discernible emergent forms in the

Old Testament and carried through to maturity in the Mishna. The possibility then presents itself that the practice of recording summaries of what later became the standard Mishna and of preserving them privately may not be a Rabbinic innovation, but a continuation of the means of preserving early extra-pentateuchal authoritative matter of the two categories described above. Our first task now is to adduce the evidence for the existence and growth of a Rabbinic type of extra-biblical literature which co-existed with the basic Scriptures and we shall here confine ourselves to the sphere of law-making.

There is, firstly, the *a priori* assumption which postulates the progressive growth and operation of a wide range of law in ancient Israel beyond the scope of pentateuchal legislation. It might be fair to argue that, just as the historical narratives in the Book of Kings represent but meagre selections from fuller extant written secular histories, so the pentateuchal legislation is, likewise, a small portion of law, selected from a wide corpus of jurisprudence which was operative and of which there were written records. Legalistic formulae and rules, some based purely upon experience, must have evolved to meet the needs of an ordered society. Yet we do not have to rely entirely upon either an *a priori* assumption or upon general deductions, for the Old Testament itself provides us with examples of creative legal activity.

There are three fully documented examples, two in Numbers and one in Leviticus, of the introduction of novel legal rulings and, in two cases, of fresh legislation to meet situations for which no provision had been made in the Mosaic code. They are (1) the case of the man found gathering wood on the Sabbath (Numbers 15:32–8), (2) the case of the daughters of Zelophehad, who claimed the legal status of heirs to their deceased father's property, in the absence of a natural male heir (Numbers 27:1–11) and (3) the case of the blasphemer (Leviticus 24:11–16). In each of these three cases Moses did not know how to adjudicate and they were referred to divine ruling. Apart from the legal decisions attributed to divine directive, two new laws were consequently promulgated covering the right of daughters to their deceased father's property, where there was no son, and also laying down the penalty for any future cases of blasphemy. Since these new laws were not listed in the tabulated Mosaic laws, where the statement of the laws is made without any reference to immediate situations, they may be described as addenda to the Mosaic code.

We can scarcely regard these two cases as isolated instances of fresh legislation resulting from novel situations. Rather should we see them as being but rare examples of what was the general pattern of the development of a category of law which was dictated by experience. In other words, we have here two examples of what may be termed the growth of case-law in ancient Israel. As in any socially regulated nation, novel cases must have, from time to time, come before the judicial authorities for judgment, decisions were taken and sometimes, in consequence, resultant legislation enacted. We have but two examples of this kind of law-making in ancient Israel selected by the pentateuchal compiler for inclusion in the Pentateuch as addenda to the Mosaic code by some principle known to him. The bulk of this continuously developing body of law, keeping pace with successive novel cases, belongs to the extra-pentateuchal jurisprudence, that is, the oral Torah.

1 Kings 21 provides us with an example of the trial and conviction of an individual on a criminal charge and the enforcement of the penalty laid down for the crime, though nowhere in the Pentateuch is there any mention of such a criminal offence. It will be recalled that King Ahab coveted the property of a peasant named Naboth and, when the latter refused all tempting offers by the king, it was left to the crafty Queen Jezebel to gratify the king's desire through ostensibly legal means. She arranged that witnesses should come forward and testify, quite falsely, that Naboth had cursed God and the king. When the judges had heard and admitted the evidence of these false witnesses, their verdict was that Naboth should be executed and his property confiscated by the crown. This story clearly points to a law which was operative and which laid down that anyone convicted of the crime of open treason against divine and royal authority was to be executed and his property seized by the crown. That this was an established law is confirmed, indirectly but positively, by the case of the daughters of Zelophehad referred to earlier. In presenting their claim to the right of inheritance because there was no primary male heir, they included in their plea the statement that their father had not

been implicated in the plot of Korah and his confederates against the authority of Moses. The implication is that, had he been involved in any such treasonable conspiracy, his property would have been liable to seizure. However, since he was free from any such suspicion, there was no legal restraint upon his property and this could be passed on to his legal heirs, which status his daughters claimed. The insertion in their plea of the statement that Zelophehad had not engaged in treasonable activities testifies to the existence and operation of a law, or laws, relating to treasonable acts and actually enforced in the case of the unfortunate Naboth. This legal provision is not part of the pentateuchal legislation, but belongs to the corpus of law outside it, i.e. to the oral Torah.

We now proceed to give examples of religious regulations first mentioned in prophetic literature and apparently derived, in Rabbinic fashion, from authoritative interpretations of a basic Mosaic law. Amos 8:5 indicates that the conducting of commercial transactions on the Sabbath (and, curiously enough, on New Moons also) was prohibited. In Jeremiah 17:21, 22 reference is made to the prohibition of carrying any burden on the Sabbath. Literary critics say that this section, attributed to Jeremiah, is more in keeping with the religious reform so vigorously enforced by Nehemiah, who insisted upon the stringent observance of the Sabbath. However, even if this Jeremiah text is to be relegated to the post-exilic period, it by no means follows that this date marks the initiation of this regulation. It could well reflect a pre-exilic rule which was being ignored and therefore specially emphasized at this time. Yet, the conclusions of literary critics as to the date of this passage do not affect the point we wish to make. The prohibitions against the transaction of business on the Sabbath and the carrying of burdens on the Sabbath are not, strictly speaking, new extra-pentateuchal laws. They look rather like Rabbinic-type extensions of the basic pentateuchal law forbidding work on the Sabbath. They specify two types of activity which are to be considered as work and, therefore, forbidden on the Sabbath.

The Mishna *Shabbath* vii. 2 gives a list of forty minus one, that is thirty-nine modes of activity which are considered major forms of work and therefore prohibited on the Sabbath,[12] and thus interpreting the phrase 'all manner of work'. It is suggested here that the references in Amos and Jeremiah mention two forms of activity which come under the general heading of 'all manner of work'. These prohibitions may be described as being Rabbinic in character and are to be assigned to the body of extra-pentateuchal laws derived from authoritative exposition, that is, to the oral Torah.

Curiously enough, these two samples of what is considered work are anticipated by two other activities which are considered work by the compiler of the Pentateuch. In Exodus 34:21 we read: 'Six days shall you work, but on the seventh day you shall rest; in ploughing time and in harvest you shall rest.' Furthermore, in Exodus 35:2, 3 we read: 'Six days shall work be done, but on the seventh day you shall have a holy Sabbath of solemn rest to the Lord; whoever does any work on it shall be put to death. You shall kindle no fire in all your habitations on the Sabbath day.' These specified activities which are phases of work, namely ploughing or harvesting and the making of fire, look like later additions, derived by way of exposition, and attached to the statement of the basic law and could be termed Rabbinic-type. If this is so, then we would say that they were originally extra-pentateuchal and, at some point in the history of these two texts, were incorporated into these passages. These two specified forms of work, along with the two mentioned in the prophetic writings cited above, are part of the elaborate Rabbinic list of activities prohibited on the Sabbath as given in the Mishna and represent a Rabbinic type of exposition of the basic law. Is it then extravagant to suggest that these biblical examples of work forbidden on the Sabbath point to a continuing process of exposition, discernible already in biblical times and elaborately developed in the Mishna?

What is rather startling is the explanation offered in Genesis 32:32, in pure Midrashic fashion, to account for the abstention of the Israelites from eating a certain sinew in the thigh of an animal. This dietary rule is associated with the story of Jacob's struggle with the angel and the injury the patriarch received by the angel touching him on this spot in his body. The inclusion of such a peculiar expository note in the text suggests that, at the time of its final editing at least, it was already well established in the text. This points to a specific kind of Midrashic literary activity which was already current in ancient Israel and flourished in the Rabbinic era, by which extra-pentateuchal regulations are midrashically derived from a scriptural passage. Such additional expositional material I would consider as having been originally in the oral Torah, i.e. external to the basic text, and as having been, at some period, attached to the biblical text.

The view put forward here, then, is that Rabbinic modes of interpretation are to be found in certain scriptural passages and, on that account, are to be considered as having been originally within the category of the oral Torah. To indicate that this is the case also with regard to non-legalistic Rabbinic-type exposition, I refer very briefly to a short study of mine entitled 'Exposition in the Old Testament and in Rabbinic Writings'.[13] In the Decalogue, following upon the basic law to honour one's parents, there is an exhortatory note which promises 'that your days may be long'. Apart from the judgment that this note represents what we would now call a sermon, the Deuteronomy version has an additional note which says 'that it may be well with you'. This latter note interprets the long life promised as being a happy one and may be identified with one of Rabbi Ishmael's thirteen principles of exposition, דבר הלמד מעניגו, that is, an extension of the sense which is inherent in the text.

IV

The final question which now confronts us is this. Was the oral Torah which co-existed with the sacred Scriptures in the monarchial period preserved by memory or are there indications that important elements were reduced to writing and preserved in written form? The presence in the pentateuchal writings of Rabbinic-type expository notes is highly suggestive of the possibility that they existed in written form prior to their being incorporated into the text. However, a more positive answer might be supplied by the study of, what I have elsewhere termed 'Rabbinic-type Glosses in the Hebrew Old Testament'.[14] After defining glosses as being obvious intrusions of foreign matter into the text, I was able to classify glosses into recognizable categories, such as interpretative variant readings and even one example of a Massoretic-type note. Since many of these glosses appear in the LXX version, one concludes that, at the time that this translation was made, they were already firmly established in the text and that they are, therefore, considerably older. These glosses appear to be standard, authoritative, though terse, notes or comments on the words affected. Since they are intrusions in the text, they were originally extra-biblical and they thus belong to the category of the oral Torah.

The phenomenon of glosses appearing in the Hebrew Old Testament suggests that it was the practice among the scholarly to write terse standard expository notes over the words expounded, but only in manuscripts which were in private possession and not intended for the public reading of scriptural lessons in the synagogues. This practice must have been general and the notes uniform, so that the continuous association of the notes with the words expounded must have led to their being read as an integral part of the text and thus, ultimately, copied into the text. These standard expository notes, which we recognize as being a manifestation of the operation of the oral Torah, as we have defined it, were not preserved by memory, but by written records. How far back this process goes one cannot tell. What does appear likely is that the study of sacred texts, from the time of their availability, must have involved official exposition. Traces of this have persisted in the supplementary notes on passages scattered throughout the Old Testament and in glosses. They are of the same character as the later Rabbinic forms of exposition and thus indicate a direct line of continuity between the Old Testament and the Mishna in this kind of literary activity.

The question as to whether or not the oral Torah in general was preserved in written summary records cannot be answered conclusively from direct evidence. However, in addition to the inferences given above, there are further considerations which, at least, do not rule out the likelihood of the practice of recording the essentials of extra-biblical authoritative directives in law and in pure exposition. Even in the early monarchial period there was no physical impediment to writing by individuals. The Gezer Calendar assigned to the tenth century B.C., the Samaria ostraca of the eighth century B.C. and the Lachish letters of the sixth century B.C. all testify to the use of writing for secular purposes. The annals of the kings of Israel and Judah were recorded in writing and there were such compositions as the Book of Yashar and the Book of the Battles of Yahweh. Why, then, should one postulate that the oral Torah, which had a direct impact upon the religious life of the people, should have been the exception and the mode of preservation relegated to feats of memory and not to the practical method of written records?

The compilation of the Mishna closed a long period in the history of the oral Torah and we have shown, I hope, that the adjective 'oral' must be redefined as referring only to its circulation and transmission and not as the means of preservation. It seems plausible that such, indeed, was the case with the oral Torah which flourished alongside the sacred Scriptures. That is to say, that the expository notes which were attached to the text by the redactors and the glosses incorporated by copyists could have come from the written records of originally extra-biblical sources.

NOTES

[1] Geo Widengren, *Literary and Psychological Aspects of the Hebrew Prophets* (Uppsala and Leipzig: Uppsala Universitets Årsskrift, 1948), p. 122.

[2] All Talmudic references are to the Babylonian Talmud.

[3] The Mishna reads:

ושני סופרי הדיינים עומדים לפניהם אחד מימין ואחד משמאל וכותכין דברי המזכין ודברי המחייבין

The translation given is that of H. Danby, *The Mishna, translated from the Hebrew with Introduction and brief explanatory notes* (Oxford University Press, 1954 edition), p. 387.

[4] Julius Kaplan, *The Redaction of the Babylonian Talmud* (Bloch Publishing Co., New York, 1933), p. 266.

[5] דברים שבעל פה אי אתה רשאי לאומרן בכתב ושבכתב אי אתה רשאי לאומרן בעל פה.

[6] כותבי הלכות כשורפי תורה והלומד מהן אינו נוטל שכר.

[7] חומר בדברי סופרים מבדברי תורה.

[8] אני מצאתי מגילת סתרים בי רבי חייא וכתוב בה.

[9] Julius Kaplan, op. cit., p. 263.

[10] ומימות משה רבינו ועד רבינו הקדוש לא חברו חבור שמלמדין אותו ברבים בתורה שבעל פה אלא בכל דור ודור ראש בית דין או נביא שהיה באותו דור כותב לעצמו זכרון השמעות ששמע מרבותיו והוא מלמד על פה ברבים.

[11] זו משנת רבי עקיבה אבל משנה ראשונה.

[12] אבות מלאכה ארבעים חסר אחת.

[13] A contribution to *Promise and Fulfilment*, Festschrift to Professor S. H. Hooke, ed. F. F. Bruce (T. & T. Clark, Edinburgh, 1963), pp. 187–201.

[14] *J.S.S.* Vol. ii, No. 2, April 1957, pp. 149–62.

V

Scripture and Tradition in the New Testament

F. F. BRUCE

I

In the Editor's Foreword to the recently published English version of *The Jerusalem Bible*, Fr Alexander Jones speaks of 'Christianity's adopted child, which is the Old Testament, and her natural child, which is the New'.[1] Without commenting on the aptness or otherwise of the epithet 'natural', one may ask what the situation was with regard to these two children in the earliest days of Christianity.

Early Christianity possessed many strands of tradition. We may think of preaching,[2] ethical catechesis,[3] confession of faith,[4] liturgical practice,[5] hymns and spiritual songs,[6] and so on. There are the early layers of 'tradition' which can be traced behind our written Gospels, even behind the earlier documentary sources which Gospel criticism has uncovered.[7] There are those forms of oral tradition whose familiarity to the original readers of the several writings (especially the epistles) which came in due course to constitute the New Testament is presupposed by the writers. The knowledge of these forms of oral tradition is not so immediately accessible to us as it was to them, and must be reconstructed by inference and careful comparative study; this raises questions (not necessarily unanswerable questions) for those who adhere to the theological principle of *sola scriptura*.[8] So far as the New Testament is concerned, here is tradition that precedes scripture;[9] so far as the Old Testament is concerned, it is a tradition that follows scripture, a tradition by means of which the Old Testament is so reinterpreted as to become a new book.

For the church of the apostolic age inherited a holy book, the Jewish Bible in its Hebrew or Greek form, which Christians call the Old Testament. It also quickly acquired a holy tradition—or rather several strands of holy tradition—one of the uses of which was to enable them to read their holy book aright. The church shared its holy book with the commonwealth of Israel, but because the main lines of its interpretative tradition were so different from those of Jewish tradition, it was almost as if the two communities read two different holy books. When asked how their understanding of the holy book was so different from that of the synagogue, the early Christians were wont to reply that the mind of the synagogue was blinded, that between its face and the sacred text was interposed a veil which could be removed only when it turned to Christ;[10] then it would read and understand clearly in all the scriptures the things concerning Jesus as the Christ.

Of the various kinds of tradition mentioned in the New Testament, some are approved and some disapproved. Among the latter are the 'tradition of the elders'—the growing accumulation of oral law—by which Jesus said the scribes had nullified the plain sense of the Word of God,[11] and the 'tradition of men'[12] attacked in the Epistle to the Colossians, an incipient gnosticism which threatened to transform apostolic Christianity into something of a different order. To this 'tradition of men' is opposed the true tradition of Christ: 'as therefore you received (παρελάβετε) Christ Jesus the Lord, so live in him, rooted and built up in him and established in the faith, just as you were taught'.[13] The verb παραλαμβάνειν, 'to receive by tradition', is the correlative of παραδιδόναι, 'to deliver, transmit' (the two correlative verbs corresponding to Heb. qibbēl and māsar).

When Paul uses the verb παραδιδόναι or its cognate noun παράδοσις, he sometimes makes it plain that what he is transmitting to others was similarly delivered to himself. Thus in 1 Corinthians 11:23 ff. and 1 Corinthians 15:3 ff. the account of the institution of the Eucharist and the skeleton of the kerygma which he delivered (παρέδωκα) to the Corinthians are things which he claims in the first instance to have 'received' (παρέλαβον) himself.[14] But on other occasions, as when he charges the church of Thessalonica to hold fast the traditions (παραδόσεις) which, he says, 'you were taught by us, either by word of mouth or by letter',[15] it is not necessary to confine them to things which he himself first learned from those who were in Christ before him.[16] Tradition must start somewhere, and while the bulk of apostolic tradition stemmed, like the words of institution, 'from the Lord' (ἀπὸ τοῦ κυρίου),[17] it does not follow that Christian tradition in the New Testament is invariably a synonym for κύριος.[18]

The possession of a common holy book, as has been said, does not guarantee religious unity. The interpretation of the holy book—and this will at first take the form of tradition—is important;[19] and divergent interpretations tend to produce religious divisions. In the period with which this paper is concerned this tendency is particularly prominent where the divergent traditions have to do with the observance of the law and religious practice in general—pre-eminently where those who embrace one line of interpretation band themselves together in ḥᵃḇūrōṭ, like the Pharisees, or in covenant-communities, like the men of Qumran. It is in complete accordance with this general pattern that the first really serious external threat to the life of the Christian church should be bound up with the charge that Stephen understood Christianity to involve changing 'the customs which Moses delivered (παρέδωκεν) to us',[20] and that the first internal threat to the unity of the church should be posed by sharply divergent views on the necessity for Gentile converts to be 'circumcised according to the custom of Moses' and so undertake an obligation to keep the Jewish law.[21]

As against those who took the latter line ('believers who belonged to the party of the Pharisees') the narrative of Acts represents Paul and the Jerusalem leaders as sharing substantially the same tradition.[22] But a hint is given of another tradition, perhaps as far to the 'left' as the Pharisaic believers were to the 'right', represented by Apollos of Alexandria, who was an expert in biblical exegesis, well versed in the story of Jesus, so that he could argue powerfully from the Old Testament that Jesus was the Messiah—yet his understanding of the Way deviated so much from the tradition which Acts presents as the main stream that by the standard of the latter it was positively defective.[23]

In one of his 'Father Brown' stories (*The Sign of the Broken Sword*), G. K. Chesterton describes one General Sir Arthur St Clare as 'a man who read his Bible'. 'That', remarks Father Brown, 'was what was the matter with *him*. When will people understand that it is useless for a man to read his Bible unless he also reads everybody else's Bible?' The point—a characteristically propagandist point—is that when a man reads 'his' Bible he tends to find there what he is looking for, and what he is looking for will be determined by a wide background of presupposition, temperament, interest, motive and the like.[24] Through General St Clare's reading of 'his' Bible, the story goes on, he was able to justify many a dubious activity by saying 'that he did it to the glory of the Lord'. 'My own theology', comments Father Brown, 'is sufficiently expressed by asking which Lord?'[25]

Chesterton's lesson receives copious illustration in the period of our present concern.

II

Jesus and his Jewish contemporaries shared the same sacred scriptures, the same divinely-given law, the same written sabbath commandment.

On the sabbath day, the Israelite was enjoined in that commandment, 'thou shalt not do any work'.[26] But what was the precise meaning of 'work'? Which activities counted as work, and which did not? In a simple agricultural community the answer was relatively easy: 'work' consisted of those activities which made up the daily routine of labour. But in the Pentateuchal legislation itself we have evidence of rulings on the question whether this or that more occasional activity constituted work within the meaning of the commandment. What of those special agricultural activities which recurred season by season, and not day by day? The ruling was plain: even 'in ploughing time and in harvest you shall rest'.[27] What of lighting a fire? Was that permissible or not? The answer was 'No'.[28] What about gathering fuel to light a fire? Again the answer is 'No'—and in this case we have the ruling embodied in a narrative: a man who was found gathering sticks on the sabbath was kept in custody until a divine response was secured.[29] In the time of Nehemiah the importation of wares into Jerusalem on the sabbath, already forbidden under the monarchy in terms of a ban on commercial transactions and the carrying of burdens on that day,[30] was effectually prevented by the governor's order that the city gates be closed and guarded by Levites from sundown on Friday till after sundown on Saturday[31]—but those Levites, be it noted, were not deemed to violate the sabbath by standing on guard over the gates.

The thirty-nine categories of work defined in the traditional sabbath regulation of the rabbis[32] no doubt reflect an interpretation current in the school of Hillel. The school of Shammai, we may surmise, had an even stricter interpretation. Yet both of these schools would probably have agreed that a domestic animal might be rescued from a pit on the sabbath without detriment to the sanctity of the day—a situation which must have called for a ruling quite early in a pastoral or agricultural community. Jesus assumes that no objection to an action of this kind will be raised by any of his Pharisaic hearers.[33] But the community of Qumran, to judge by the sabbath *halakhah* of the Zadokite work, would apparently have disagreed: 'Let no one help an animal in birth on the sabbath. Even if she drops [her young] into a cistern or a pit, let him not lift it out on the sabbath.'[34]

It was evidently accepted from early times that the ban on sabbath work did not apply to the sacrificial services in the sanctuary or to certain other ceremonial obligations. Jesus in debate appeals to this fact. 'The priests in the temple "profane" the sabbath with impunity',[35] he says—that is, by doing their regular work on it (in fact, probably by doing more work on it than on other days). The implication is: if one form of serving God is permissible on the sabbath, why not others (which from certain points of view might be considered more important, such as healing)? Again, if the eighth day from a Jewish boy's birth coincided with the sabbath, he must be circumcised on that day, sabbath or no. Hence the argument in John 7:23, 'If on the sabbath a man receives circumcision [undergoes an operation affecting but one small part of his body], so that the law of Moses may not be broken, are you angry with me because on the sabbath I made a man's whole body well?'[36]

But Jesus' basic principle of interpretation of the sabbath law appears not so much in these *ad hominem* arguments with doctors of the law as in those Synoptic passages where he appeals to the primary intention of the sabbath institution. 'The sabbath was made for man, not man for the sabbath'[37] —more particularly, the sabbath was instituted for men's rest and relief, not to be a burden to them. Therefore, any action which promoted the divine intention in instituting the sabbath was appropriate for that day. The satisfaction of normal human need, he held, takes precedence over ceremonial requirements or the rulings of the schools. The bread before the altar in the sanctuary might be reserved by sacral law for the priests alone, but the scriptures do not censure David and his company for eating it when he was hungry.[38] As for the sabbath law, others might concede that in a case of extreme urgency, a matter of life and death, remedial measures might be applied on the sacred day—but as an exception to the general rule. If there was no great urgency, then, in the words of a synagogue official who was annoyed by an act of healing in his synagogue on the sabbath, 'there are six days on which work ought to be done; come on those days and be healed, and not on the sabbath day'.[39] A woman who had suffered from *spondylitis deformans*[40] (if that is what it was) for eighteen years could easily wait another day, he reckoned. But Jesus in effect said 'No; she has waited long enough, and the sabbath is the most fitting day for her to be released from her trouble. If on the sabbath you untie your ox or ass as a matter of course and take it off to be watered, how much more should this daughter of Abraham be relieved on the sabbath?'[41]

If we turn from the sabbath law to the law of divorce, a comparable situation meets us. Jesus, together with the Qumran community, the schools of Hillel and Shammai and the Jews in general, read the same wording in the Deuteronomic legislation where it is recognized that a man is entitled to divorce his wife if, after marrying her, he finds in her 'some unseemliness' ('*erwaṯ dāḇār*').[42]

But here too the question of definition arose. What constitutes '*erwaṯ dāḇār*? The school of Shammai, as we know, limited it to unchastity: if a man found that his bride was not a virgin, as he might reasonably expect her to be, he was entitled to dismiss her. The school of Hillel, commonly credited with milder interpretations than the school of Shammai, manifested its 'mildness' here in the husband's interest: he might divorce her (so its leaders expounded the law) for practically any feature or practice which he found displeasing.[43] But when Jesus was asked to say whether a man might put away his wife for any cause, he did not deal with the exegesis of Deuteronomy 24:1–4; however

F

'*erwaṭ dāḇār* might be interpreted, that whole provision, he said, was a modification of the original principle, introduced later because of the hardness of men's hearts.[44] The original principle was disclosed by the Creator's intention in instituting marriage, as laid down in Genesis: 'From the beginning of creation he "made them male and female"; this is why a man will leave his father and mother and be joined to his wife, so that the two become one flesh.'[45] From this Jesus deduced that in the original institution man and woman were made for each other, being joined together by God, and divorce was not contemplated; divorce, in fact, was an attempt to undo the work of God. The practical implication of this ruling—although it is not explicitly attributed to Jesus—would have been a redressing of the unequal balance in favour of the wife, who under Jewish law could not take the initiative in divorcing her husband and who had little opportunity of defending herself against such initiative on his part.[46]

Paul underlines the tradition of Jesus in this matter not only in Ephesians 5:22 ff., where the marriage relationship, expounded in the light of Genesis 2:24, is treated as a 'mystery' setting forth the relationship between Christ and the church, but in 1 Corinthians 6:15 f., where he uses the Genesis language about 'one flesh' to insist that even a man's casual intercourse with a harlot establishes a vital bond between the two, and thus 'displays a psychological insight into human sexuality which is altogether exceptional by first-century standards'.[47]

But such is the hardness of men's hearts that before the gospel tradition was stereotyped Jesus' ruling was modified by the reintroduction of the '*erwaṭ dāḇār*. The two exceptive clauses in the First Gospel[48] may indeed represent an adaptation of his ruling to the conditions of the Gentile mission, in which a couple might before their conversion have cohabited within forbidden degrees of affinity, so that their union constituted a form of πορνεία.[49] But the history of canon law shows how the kind of approach which Jesus was careful to avoid has tended to obscure the spirit of his liberating pronouncement by treating it woodenly as a piece of legislation.[50]

Yet this principle of legal interpretation, rejecting an existing tradition and establishing a new one, is not the most distinctive form of the Christian interpretative tradition. For this we find

the readiest analogy not in rabbinical jurisprudence but in the
literature of the Qumran community.

III

The community of Qumran read for the most part the same
sacred scriptures, so far as we can judge, as many of their
fellow-Jews; but they read them through spectacles of quite a
different sort and therefore understood them quite differently.
Their interpretation of the Torah, if we may make an inference
from the Zadokite work, was different in a number of respects
from that of the Pharisees (although the Pharisees were not in
themselves entirely agreed on the application of many of the
laws).

It is in the interpretation of the Prophets and Psalms, and
of prophetic oracles and hymnic passages found *passim* in other
Old Testament books, that we find the really distinctive 'tradition' by which the scriptures were understood at Qumran. This
'tradition', by the testimony of the Qumran texts themselves,
was established by the Teacher of Righteousness, whom God
raised up to lead the faithful remnant 'in the way of his heart,
and to make known to the last generations what he was about
to do to the last generation—the congregation of deceivers'.[51]
This man taught his followers how to interpret the prophetic
writings, and enabled them to see their own duty and prospects
written clearly there. To the prophets much had been revealed,
but not everything. One thing in particular had been withheld
from them—the *time* at which their oracles would be fulfilled
—and the withholding of this meant that their oracles remained
mysteries, both to the prophets themselves and (even more so)
to their readers. But when the time of their fulfilment was at
last revealed, the mystery was a mystery no longer: with this
further revelation its solution was imparted. The man chosen
by God to be the recipient of this further revelation was the
Teacher of Righteousness. Of the oracle of Habakkuk, for
example, the Qumran commentator on that prophet says: 'God
commanded Habakkuk to write the things that were coming
on the last generation, but the fulfilment of the epoch (*g^emar
haqqēṣ*) he did not make known to him. And as for the expression, "that he may run who reads it", its interpretation

concerns the Teacher of Righteousness, to whom God made known all the mysteries (*rāzē*) of the words of his servants the prophets.'[52]

There are, of course, exceptions to the rule that the prophets were not told when their predictions would be fulfilled. We may recall passages in Isaiah, Jeremiah and Ezekiel where periods of between forty and seventy years from the prophet's time are prescribed for the accomplishment of certain events, such as Jeremiah's fixing of seventy years as the epoch of the desolations of Jerusalem.[53] But the 'epoch' (*qēṣ*) which the Qumran interpreters had in mind was that which marked the end of the current age. In this respect they had only one canonical predecessor, Daniel. When Daniel reinterprets Jeremiah's seventy years as seventy sevens of years, the terminus of the period is not now a return from exile but the inauguration of the age to come, with the putting an end to sin and the bringing in of everlasting righteousness.[54] Josephus remarks that Daniel alone among the prophets of old was able to state the *time* of the fulfilment of his oracles;[55] in Qumran terminology, which is in essence that of the book of Daniel, his visions embrace both mystery (*rāz*) and interpretation (*pēšer*). Indeed, there is probably a closer relation between Daniel and the Teacher of Righteousness than can be established thus far by detailed evidence; it is somewhat surprising that, so far as I know, no one has thought of identifying the two (not that I myself have any idea of doing so).

At any rate, instructed by the Teacher of Righteousness and the men who learned from him their principles of biblical exegesis, the members of the Qumran community found the sacred scriptures an open book. The interpretative 'tradition' which they 'received'—a 'tradition' which to their minds was as fully the product of divine revelation as were the written oracles themselves—embodied a few simple principles.

1. God revealed his purpose to the prophets, but the relevance of his purpose could not be understood until the *time* of its fulfilment was revealed to the Teacher of Righteousness.

2. All the words of the prophets referred to the time of the end.

3. The time of the end is at hand.

It was in the eschatological situation which the rise of the Teacher of Righteousness showed to be imminent that the true context of any oracle was sought; the text was atomized, regardless of what *we* call context, so as to fit here or there into the eschatological situation. Variant readings were selected so as best to serve the interpreter's purpose. Where a relation could not otherwise be established between the text and the eschatological situation, allegorization was employed.[56]

The men of Qumran, properly instructed in these principles, had no difficulty in understanding passages like Psalm 37:32, 'the wicked watches the righteous and seeks to slay him',[57] or Habakkuk 1:4, 'the wicked surrounds the righteous'.[58] Language like this infallibly points to the attacks made on the Teacher of Righteousness by his inveterate enemy, the Wicked Priest. References to the overthrow of Israel's enemies—the 'sons of Sheth' in Balaam's oracles,[59] the Assyrians in Isaiah,[60] the Chaldaeans in Habakkuk[61] and Gog in Ezekiel[62]—were understood not of nations contemporary with these prophets but of the last Gentile oppressors of the people of God, the 'Kittim' of the commentaries and of the War scroll.

Again, references to the building of a wall or a city were understood of the building either of the righteous community or of some rival enterprise, political or religious, according as the building was spoken of in terms of approval, promising success, or in terms of reprobation, portending destruction. 'Samaria' in Micah 1:5 is interpreted of the 'Spouter of falsehood, who led the simple astray' (perhaps some early leader of the group that developed into the party of the Pharisees), while 'Jerusalem' is related to 'the Teacher of Righteousness, who expounded the law to his council, to all who voluntarily pledged themselves to join the elect of God'.[63] The builders of the unstable wall in Ezekiel 13:10 ff. are similarly the 'Spouter of falsehood' and his associates;[64] on the other hand, the wall of Micah 7:11 is the fence (the rule of life) which keeps the righteous community insulated from the contamination of evil.[65]

The members of the righteous community are not only the builders of the well-founded wall; they are also the diggers of the well of Numbers 21:17 f.: '*the nobles of the people* are those who have come to dig the well with the staves which the lawgiver (*mᵉḥōqēq*) appointed for them to walk withal during the whole epoch of wickedness'.[66]

And so on. Grasp the basic principles of the interpretative tradition, and the sacred text becomes luminous.

IV

We revert now to the parallel situation in the Church. 'One of the extraordinary features of the early Church', it has been said, 'is the number of men who were converted by reading the Old Testament'[67]—converted, that is to say, from paganism to Christianity. It does not appear that these men had any antecedent conviction of the authority of the Old Testament, but as they read it, it 'found' them (in Coleridge's sense of the word).[68] One wonders, however, if they were completely ignorant of a 'tradition' which helped them to read the Christian gospel in those pre-Christian scriptures.

A good example is provided by Tatian in an autobiographical section of his *Address to the Greeks*. After unsatisfying experience of Greek philosophical and legal literature and of mystery religions, he says:

> I withdrew by myself and sought how best to discover the truth. While I was giving earnest attention to this, I happened to light upon certain barbaric writings, too old to be compared with the opinions of the Greeks and too divine to be compared with their error. I found myself convinced by these writings, because of the unpretentious cast of the language, the unstudied character of the writers, the ready comprehension of the making of the universe, the foreknowledge of things to come, the excellence of the precepts and the placing of all things under the rule of one principle. My soul being thus taught by God, I understood that the pagan writings led to condemnation, whereas these put an end to the slavery that is in the world, rescuing us from many rulers (ἄρχοντες), yes, from ten thousand tyrants. These writings do not indeed give us something that we had not received before, but rather something which we had indeed received but were prevented by error from making our own.[69]

These last words suggest that Tatian's reading of the Old Testament books was preceded or accompanied by some awareness of the kind of 'tradition' which enabled him to understand them in a Christian sense.

What can be said of such a 'tradition'?

That the Old Testament prophecies were 'mysteries' whose interpretation was concealed from the prophets themselves is a theme common to Qumran and the early church. The prophets, according to one New Testament writer, foretold the advent of the Christian salvation, but they did not grasp the full purport of their own predictions; they 'searched and inquired diligently' in order to discover who was the person and what the time pointed to by the Spirit of messianic prophecy within them when bearing witness in advance to 'the sufferings of the Messiah and the glories that were to follow'.[70] But the writer and his readers had no need to search and inquire diligently; they knew that the person was Jesus and the time was now. 'This is that which was spoken through the prophet'[71]—Peter's message on the day of Pentecost—is writ large over the New Testament writings; it is plainly affirmed in the gospel tradition itself. Jesus congratulates his disciples because they see and hear things to which prophets and righteous men had looked forward with longing expectation, but which they did not live to witness.[72]

Occasionally the very word 'mystery', in the same sense as *rāz* in Daniel and the Qumran texts, is used in this regard. 'To you', says Jesus to his disciples, 'the mystery of the kingdom of God has been given, but to outsiders all these things come as riddles; they see without perceiving, and hear without understanding, otherwise they would turn back and receive forgiveness'.[73] And one aspect of the gospel—the manner and purpose of its communication to the Gentile world—is treated in the Pauline corpus as a mystery 'which was not made known to the sons of men in other generations as it has now been revealed to Christ's holy apostles and prophets in the Spirit'.[74] That the Gentiles would place their hope on the Davidic Messiah and rejoice in Israel's God was foretold in the Old Testament, as Paul emphasizes in a catena of quotations in Romans 15:9–12, but the implications of this hope were not appreciated until the time of its fulfilment.

This interpretative tradition pervades all the strata of the New Testament. We find it in the Synoptic records and in the Fourth Gospel, in Paul and Peter, in the Alexandrian Epistle to the Hebrews and the Hebraic book of the Revelation. The various writers have their distinctive hermeneutical principles and methods, it is true. Matthew records how this or that incident in the life of Jesus 'took place in order that it might be fulfilled which was spoken through the prophet'.[75] Paul sees the temporary and partial setting aside of Israel as clearly in the Law, the Prophets and the Psalms, as he finds the in-gathering of the Gentiles adumbrated there.[76] He is careful withal to distinguish his Old Testament authors—Moses, David, Hosea, Isaiah[77]—unlike the writer to the Hebrews who, true to his Alexandrian heritage, ignores such details for the most part, since to him all scripture is oracular in character.[78] John the Evangelist portrays Jesus as the fulfiller of a number of Old Testament motifs, such as the *dābār*, the *kābōd* and the *miškān*;[79] the bread of life, the water of life, the light of life;[80] while the Apocalypse, in Austin Farrer's words, is 'a rebirth of images' from the Old Testament and other ancient lore[81]—some of them remarkably recalcitrant to a Christian purpose,[82] yet all pressed into service to depict the triumph of Christ. But, how-ever variously the interpretative tradition be treated by the different New Testament writers, the core of the tradition is common property: the central subject of the Old Testament writings is Jesus; he is the one to whom they all bear witness.

The analogy of Qumran would lead us to the conclusion which is in any case the plain testimony of the gospel record: that the main lines of this tradition were laid down by Jesus himself. It is not necessary here to repeat the arguments to this effect so cogently deployed by my distinguished predecessors C. H. Dodd and T. W. Manson.[83] The insistence that 'so it is written' is too deeply imbedded in all the gospel strata to be reasonably suspected of being an accretion, due to reflection in the post-Easter church on the events of the ministry and passion of Jesus. I have elsewhere[84] drawn attention to the way in which the visions and oracles of Zechariah 9-14 have influenced the passion narratives, and this, I believe, stems from Jesus himself —from his deliberate choice of 'a colt, the foal of an ass'[85] to ride into Jerusalem on Palm Sunday, and his reference, an hour or two before his arrest, to the words of Zechariah 13:7, 'Smite the shepherd and scatter the sheep.'[86]

This reference to Zechariah 9-14 reminds us of a feature of New Testament interpretation of the Old Testament which to a large degree distinguishes it from the *pēšer* interpretation of

Qumran: the New Testament interpretation of a few words or sentences from the Old Testament which are actually quoted very often implies the context in which these words or sentences occur—we may think of such contexts as Zechariah 9-14; Isaiah 40-66, Psalm 69 and so forth. Moreover, different New Testament writers will quote different words or sentences from the same context in a manner which suggests that the complete context had received a Christian interpretation before these writers quoted from it. For example, C. H. Dodd points out that from Psalm 69:9 ('zeal for thy house has consumed me, and the insults of those who insult thee have fallen on me') the former part is applied to Christ in John 2:17 and the latter part in Romans 15:3. While no one is likely to maintain that the one writer has influenced the other, 'it would be too much of a coincidence if the two writers independently happened to cite the two halves of a single verse, unless they were both aware that at least this whole verse, if not any more of the Psalm, formed part of a scheme of scriptural passages generally held to be especially significant'.[87] This implies something more substantial in the way of primitive Christian exegesis of the Old Testament than a catena of more isolated proof-texts or 'testimonies' such as J. R. Harris envisaged.[88]

Alongside this contextual element in the interpretative tradition there is another, which (unlike the former) does have an analogue in the Qumran literature (as also in rabbinical literature). This is the bringing together and giving a unified exegesis to widely separated scriptures which have a significant term in common.[89] Perhaps the most prominent example in the New Testament is the widespread evidence for an integrated messianic interpretation of various 'stone' passages in the Old Testament—the stone which the builders rejected in Psalm 118:22, the stone in Nebuchadnezzar's dream which pulverized the great image (Daniel 2:34 f.), the tested corner stone of sure foundation in Isaiah 28:16 and the rock of refuge amid the flood waters in Isaiah 8:14 which proves a stone of stumbling to those who refuse to take refuge upon it.[90] Again, we find the 'one like a son of man' of Daniel 7:13 brought into close relation with the 'son of man' of Psalm 8:4 beneath whose feet all things have been placed and possibly also with the 'son of man' of Psalm 80:17 whom God makes strong for himself;[91] or we find

the deliverance from death of God's *ḥāsīḏ* (ὅσιος) in Psalm
16:10 linked in Acts 13:34 f. with the promise of the *ḥasḏē*
(ὅσια) of David in Isaiah 55:3 to provide a joint *testimonium* of
the resurrection of Christ.

It is not surprising that the Psalter as well as the Prophets
should be expounded thus. In addition to those royal psalms
which were commonly acknowledged in the first century A.D.
as 'messianic',[92] and whose fulfilment Christians naturally recognized in Jesus, there are many psalms in which a righteous
sufferer raises his plaint to God, and which were equally naturally
interpreted of Jesus. Indeed, had not Jesus confirmed this
interpretation by making the language of one of these psalms
his own in the bitterness of dereliction on the cross?[93]

But if the righteous sufferer was recognized as Jesus, the per-
secutors of the righteous sufferer were identified with Jesus'
enemies,[94] and with none more freely than with Judas Iscariot.
Here again the cue appears to have been given by Jesus himself; there is no good reason for doubting that at the Last
Supper he used the words of Psalm 41:9, 'he who ate of my
bread has lifted his heel against me', to indicate to his companions that he knew there was a traitor in the camp.[95] It was
no difficult matter to find other passages in the Psalter which
could be similarly applied to Judas; the quotation in this connection of Psalms 69:25 and 109:8 in Acts 1:20 is a case in point.
The tradition still flourishes vigorously in circles less severely
academic than ours; I have known it to be seriously argued that
since Psalm 109:8 (applied by Peter to Judas in the form, 'his
office let another take') is followed immediately by the words,
'May his children be fatherless and his wife a widow' (Psalm
109:9), Judas was therefore a married man with a family.

With such dominical and apostolic precedent, the Christian
church was able so to read the Old Testament writings that
they supplied not only an increasing store of christological
testimonia but additional factual evidence about New Testament
events. This tendency we find well established in Justin and the
Cyprianic *Testimonia adversus Iudaeos*; it was carried to excess in
the Middle Ages. The passion narrative in particular was em-
bellished by mediaeval piety by the liberal importation of Old
Testament *motifs* divorced from their context as well as elements
from other sources; striking examples are provided in the

fourteenth-century German mystical treatise now called *Christi Leiden in einer Vision geschaut*[96] or in the fifteenth-century poem quoted by G. L. Prestige where the words of Canticles 2:5, *quia amore langueo*,[97] are pressed into service as a passion theme. Even today this tendency is strong enough in much traditional Christian piety to be the cause of some uneasiness when it is found that several modern versions of the Old Testament exhibit readings and renderings which do not lend themselves so readily to this kind of traditional interpretation as older versions did.[98]

V

One important phase of the early Christian interpretative tradition is the tracing of a recurrent pattern in the story of God's dealing with his people. For instance, New Testament writers view the history of Israel in the Old Testament, with special emphasis on the course of events from Egypt to Canaan, as recapitulated either in the personal experience of the Messiah or in the corporate experience of the church.[99]

Recapitulation in the Messiah's personal experience (perhaps by way of applying Isaiah 63:9, 'In all their affliction he was afflicted'),[100] appears especially in the Old Testament quotations in Matthew's nativity narrative where, for example, the reference to the Exodus in Hosea 11:1, 'out of Egypt I called my son', is said to be fulfilled in the Holy Family's flight into Egypt and return thence to Judaea.[101] It is not that the Evangelist arbitrarily detaches a sentence from its context in order to apply it to an event with which it has nothing to do; it is rather that he sees the fortunes of the messianic people as re-enacted by the Messiah himself. Something of the same sort may be implicit in the parallel between Jesus' forty days in the wilderness and Israel's forty years of wilderness wandering (cf. Deuteronomy 8:2 f.), both periods of 'testing' coming as the sequel to a 'baptismal' experience.[102]

As for the recapitulation of the Egypt-to-Canaan sequence in the life of the church, this pervades the major epistles of the New Testament, Pauline and non-Pauline alike, and must be an extremely primitive Christian tradition.

Israel had the paschal lamb; 'Christ our passover was sacrificed for us', says Paul[103]—'a lamb without blemish and with-

out spot', says Peter.[104] Israel passed through the Red Sea, says
Paul, being thus 'baptized unto Moses'[105] (baptized without
being immersed, as a Scots divine once pointed out, whereas
the Egyptians were immersed without being baptized);[106]
Christians for their part are baptized εἰς Χριστόν.[107] Israel had
manna from heaven and water from the rock to sustain and
refresh them in the wilderness;[108] Christians too have their
supernatural food and drink.[109] But for all these privileges, the
generation that left Egypt died in the wilderness because of
rebellion against Israel's God; Christians should take due warning lest disobedience on their part brings them into comparable
disaster.[110] And here the writer to the Hebrews takes over from
Paul: the Israelites in the wilderness had a promised rest before them, but failed to enter into it because of unbelief; so
Christians may miss the rest that remains for the people of God
if they in their turn cherish 'an evil heart of unbelief, in falling
away from the living God'.[111]

Then there is the interpretative principle which A. T. Hanson
has called the 'real presence' of Christ in Old Testament
history.[112] He sees it in places where it is not properly to be
found, to the point where it becomes the central principle of
Old Testament interpretation in the New Testament, but in
certain forms it is plain enough.

In a Pauline passage already alluded to, it is stated that the
'rock' which accompanied Israel in the wilderness was Christ[113]
—that it was from Christ that they drew their 'spiritual' re-
freshment, just as Christians do. But a clearer instance still is
provided by the *lectio difficilior* in Jude 5: 'I desire to remind you,
though you were once for all fully informed, that Jesus, who
delivered a people from the land of Egypt, later destroyed those
who did not believe.' In place of 'Jesus' various authorities for
the text have 'the Lord' or 'God' or the Greek definite article.
But on the principle *praestat lectio ardua* 'Jesus' is the preferable
reading.[114] What, then, can 'Jesus' mean in this context? It does
not mean the Old Testament leader Joshua, as it does in Acts
7:45 and Hebrews 4:8. Joshua led Israel into the promised land
(thus providing the basis for a rich Joshua-Jesus messian-
ology),[115] but he did not deliver them from the land of Egypt.
No; Jude's point is that it was Jesus the Son of God who, centuries before his incarnation, delivered Israel from Egypt. The

fact that Yahweh was commonly rendered κύριος in the Septuagint, and that Jesus was called κύριος in the church, made it the easier to identify Jesus with 'the Lord' who went before Israel in a pillar of cloud and fire,[116] who rescued them from the hand of the Egyptians,[117] who healed them in the wilderness.[118] It was even easier to identify Jesus with the covenant-messenger, Yahweh's 'angel' or 'presence', who led them under Moses towards the land of rest.[119]

This goes farther than either Paul or the writer to the Hebrews goes; it is, however, adumbrated in Stephen's speech in Acts, where—by implication, though not expressly—Jesus is 'the angel' who appeared to Moses 'in a flame of fire in a bush'[120] and later on the day of the assembly at Mount Sinai;[121] it appears in full development in the second century, not least in Justin's *Apology*[122] and *Dialogue with Trypho*.[123] Justin criticizes the Jewish belief that the one who said to Moses in the bush, 'I am the God of Abraham and the God of Isaac and the God of Jacob', was 'the Father and Creator of the universe'.[124] No, says Justin, they are wrong (as the spirit of prophecy says, 'Israel does not know me, my people have not understood me');[125] it was the Son of God who spoke those words. Here the exegesis does not depend on the ambiguity of κύριος (it is not κύριος but θεός who calls to Moses out of the bush); it depends on the statement that 'the angel of the Lord' (ἄγγελος κυρίου) appeared to Moses in the burning bush, and it is the Son of God, says Justin, 'who is called both angel and apostle'.[126] Justin was manifestly acquainted with the Synoptic incident in which these words from Exodus 3:6 are quoted by Jesus himself with unambiguous reference to 'the Father and Creator of the universe'.[127] But that could not outweigh in his mind the force of the interpretative principle that where ἄγγελος κυρίου appears in the Old Testament narrative—especially in passages where the phrase alternates with θεός or κύριος—the pre-incarnate Christ is indicated. In fact, Trypho's exegesis of Exodus 3:6 is more in line with that of Jesus than Justin's is: 'This is not what we understand from the words quoted', says Trypho in reply to Justin, 'but we understand that, while it was an *angel* that appeared in a flame of fire, it was *God* who spoke to Moses'.[128] Justin and Trypho read (substantially)[129] the same Bible, so far as the Old Testament books are concerned, but in another sense they read different Bibles, because their respective 'traditions' were so different.

By the same process Justin argues that it was Christ who announced the birth of Isaac to Abraham and Sarah,[130] who overthrew the cities of the plain,[131] who spoke to Jacob in his dreams at Bethel and Padan-aram and wrestled with him at Peniel,[132] who appeared to Joshua as captain of the Lord's host,[133] and so forth. This line of interpretation has passed into traditional Christian theology; in its main features, however, it is post-apostolic and goes far beyond the interpretative tradition of the New Testament.

Quite apart from the differences between the Septuagint and Massoretic texts, Jews and Christians could no longer be said to read the same scriptures in a material sense, in view of the divergent 'traditions' by which they understood them. The accepted Christian tradition became more sharply anti-Judaic, and the Jewish tradition in turn became increasingly careful to exclude those renderings or interpretations, previously quite acceptable, which now proved to lend themselves all too readily to Christian use.[134] So, despite the common heritage of the holy book, the two opposed traditions hardened. Only in more recent times, with the acceptance on both sides of the principle of grammatico-historical exegesis, have their hard outlines softened, so that today Jews and Christians of varying traditions can collaborate happily in the common task of translating and interpreting the Bible.[135]

NOTES

[1] *The Jerusalem Bible* (London, October 21, 1966), p.v.

[2] Cf. C. H. Dodd, *The Apostolic Preaching and its Developments* (London, 1936).

[3] Cf. A. Seeberg, *Der Katechismus der Urchristenheit* (Leipzig, 1903); G. Klein, *Der älteste christliche Katechismus* (Berlin, 1909); P. Carrington, *The Primitive Christian Catechism* (Cambridge, 1940); E. G. Selwyn, *The First Epistle of Peter* (London, 1946), pp. 363 ff.; C. H. Dodd, *Gospel and Law* (Cambridge, 1951).

[4] Cf. O. Cullmann, *The Earliest Christian Confessions* (London, 1949); R. P. Martin, *An Early Christian Confession* (London, 1960); *Carmen Christi* (Cambridge, 1967).

[5] Liturgical practice is one of the most important elements in the development of religious tradition. In the New Testament we may think especially

of baptism and its accompanying words, τῷ λουτρῷ τοῦ ὕδατος ἐν ῥήματι (Ephesians 5:26), and the Eucharist with its accompanying words (1 Corinthians 11:24 f.). Cf. O. Cullmann, *Baptism in the New Testament* (Eng. trans., London, 1950) and *Early Christian Worship* (Eng. trans., London, 1953); A. J. B. Higgins, *The Lord's Supper in the New Testament* (London, 1952); R. P. Martin, *Worship in the Early Church* (London, 1964).

[6] Cf. Colossians 3:16 and Ephesians 5:19; these found an early place in the context of sacrament (cf. ἔγειρε ὁ καθεύδων . . . in Ephesians 5:14) and liturgy (cf. the canticles of Revelation).

[7] Cf. the recurrence of the word 'tradition' in the titles of works on Gospel criticism, especially form criticism; e.g. R. Bultmann, *Die Geschichte der synoptischen Tradition* (Göttingen, 1921; Eng. trans. of 3rd edition, *The History of the Synoptic Tradition* [Oxford, 1963]); M. Dibelius, *From Tradition to Gospel* (London, 1934, Eng. trans. of *Die Formgeschichte des Evangeliums* [Tübingen, ¹1919, ³1959]); V. Taylor, *The Formation of the Gospel Tradition* (London, 1933); H. Riesenfeld, *The Gospel Tradition and its Beginnings* (London, 1957); J. W. Doeve, 'Le rôle de la tradition orale dans la composition des Évangiles Synoptiques', in J. Cambier *et al.*, *La formation des Évangiles* (Bruges, 1957), pp. 70 ff.

[8] Thus proponents of *sola scriptura* may well ask what elements of tradition have been preserved from the apostolic age to our day apart from those which have been recorded in extant writings. See pp. 129, 163.

[9] See pp. 3, 99 f., 160. On the relation of the New Testament canon to the tradition which preceded it, cf. pp. 183, 189, below; also E. Flesseman-van Leer, 'Prinzipien der Sammlung und Ausscheidung bei der Bildung des Kanons', *Zeitschrift für Theologie und Kirche*, lxi (1964), pp. 404 ff. See too on the general theme her *Tradition and Scripture in the Early Church* (Assen, 1955).

[10] Cf. the sculptured portrayal of the church and the synagogue in Strasbourg and Rochester Cathedrals. The *motif* goes back to Paul's application of Exodus 34:29 ff. in 2 Corinthians 3:12 ff.

[11] Mark 7:1 ff. and Matthew 15:1 ff.

[12] Colossians 2:8.

[13] Colossians 2:6 f.; cf. Philippians 4:9.

[14] Cf. 1 Thessalonians 2:13, discussed by R. Schippers, 'The Pre-Synoptic Tradition in I Thessalonians II 13–16', *Novum Testamentum*, viii (1966), pp. 223 ff. One occasion on which Paul could have 'received' these things is indicated in Galatians 1:18 ff. On the sense in which he asserts that he did not 'receive' (οὐδὲ . . . παρέλαβον) his gospel from any human source (Galatians 1:11 f.) as contrasted with the sense in which he did so receive it, see H. Lietzmann, *Handbuch zum Neuen Testament: An die Korinther I–II²* (Tübingen, 1923), p. 58 (*ad* 1 Corinthians 11:23), quoted p. 97 below.

[15] 2 Thessalonians 2:15. Here παράδοσις covers both spoken and written instruction. Compare the evidence of Papias (*apud* Euseb. *Hist. Eccl.*, iii. 39. 3 f.) for the availability of both oral and written tradition in his day; he himself regarded the former as the more valuable, 'for I did not suppose that what I could get from books would help me so much as what came from a living and abiding voice' (cf. H. D. Lockett, 'The Growth of Creeds', in

Inaugural Lectures delivered by Members of the Faculty of Theology, ed. A. S. Peake [Manchester, 1905], pp. 235 ff., especially p. 251). The gnostics also appealed to oral and written tradition; hence arose the question which Irenaeus set himself to answer, how to distinguish true from false tradition.

¹⁶ Cf. G. Widengren, 'Tradition and Literature in Early Judaism and in the Early Church', *Numen*, x (1963), pp. 42 ff., especially pp. 79 f.

¹⁷ I Corinthians 11:23. See p. 95.

¹⁸ Cf. O. Cullmann, '*Kyrios* as Designation for the Oral Tradition concerning Jesus (*Paradosis* and *Kyrios*)', *Scottish Journal of Theology*, iii (1950), pp. 180 ff.; 'Scripture and Tradition', *Scottish Journal of Theology*, vi (1953), pp. 113 ff. (with reply by J. Daniélou, 'Réponse à Oscar Cullmann', *Dieu vivant*, no. 24 [1953], pp. 107 ff.); 'The Tradition', Eng. trans. in *The Early Church* (London, 1956), pp. 55 ff.

¹⁹ So important, indeed, that it may become an integral part of the holy revelation; cf. the rabbinical dictum in TB *Qiddušin* 49b, '*mā'ī tōrāh? midraš tōrāh*' (quoted by J. Weingreen, 'Old Testament and Rabbinical Exposition' in *Promise and Fulfilment* [ed. F. F. Bruce, Edinburgh, 1963], p. 192).

²⁰ Acts 6:14.

²¹ Acts 15:1, 5.

²² Cf. Acts 15:22 ff.; 21:17 ff.

²³ Acts 18:24 ff.; cf. G. Widengren, *Numen*, x (1963), p. 78 (art. cit., n. 16 above).

²⁴ I recall a Scots lady, member of a church which confined its hymnody to the Old Testament Psalter and which eschewed the use of any musical instrument, who on being asked how she could intelligently sing words about praising God on a ten-stringed instrument (e.g. Psalm 33:2) replied that this, of course, was a reference to the Ten Commandments and showed surprise that anyone should be ignorant of so elementary a truth. Here church practice controlled the interpretative tradition.

²⁵ G. K. Chesterton, *The Father Brown Stories* (London, 1929), pp. 266 f.

²⁶ Exodus 20:10; Deuteronomy 5:14.

²⁷ Exodus 34:21.

²⁸ Exodus 35:3.

²⁹ Numbers 15:32 ff. Thus we trace the growth of case-law (see p. 61).

³⁰ Cf. Amos 8:5; Jeremiah 17:22 ff. (see p. 63).

³¹ Nehemiah 13:19 ff.

³² Mishnah *Shabbath* vii. 1 ff. (see p. 67, n. 12).

³³ Cf. Matthew 12:11; Luke 14:5.

³⁴ CD xi. 13 f. Compare Josephus's statement that the Essenes 'are stricter than all Jews in abstaining from work on the seventh day' (*BJ*, ii. 147).

³⁵ Matthew 12:5.

³⁶ On such characteristic samples of rabbinical argument in the Fourth Gospel cf. I. Abrahams, 'Rabbinic Aids to Exegesis', in *Cambridge Biblical Essays*, ed. H. B. Swete (Cambridge, 1909), pp. 159 ff., especially p. 181; *Studies in Pharisaism and the Gospels*, i (Cambridge, 1917), p. 12.

³⁷ Mark 2:27.

³⁸ Mark 2:25 f., referring to I Samuel 21:1 ff.

SCRIPTURE AND TRADITION IN NEW TESTAMENT 89

[39] Luke 13:14. Cf. TB *'Abodah Zārāh*, 27b–28a.

[40] Luke 13:11; cf. A. R. Short, *Modern Discovery and the Bible* (London, 1943), p. 91.

[41] Luke 13:15 f.

[42] Deuteronomy 24:1. The provision for divorce is assumed, not laid down *de novo*; the whole sentence consists of Deuteronomy 24:1–4 (cf. RSV) and the substantive provision is laid down in verse 4.

[43] Mishnah *Giṭṭin*, ix. 10; TB *Giṭṭin*, 90a. 'If she spoils his dinner', said the school of Hillel; 'if he sees a woman fairer than she', said Aqiba.

[44] Mark 10:2 ff.

[45] Genesis 1:27 with 2:24. Genesis 1:27 is quoted with a similar rubric (*yᵉsōd habbᵉrīʾāh*; cf. ἀπ᾽ ἀρχῆς κτίσεως in Mark 10:6) in CD iv. 21, but there not to forbid divorce but to forbid bigamy. Genesis 2:24 is quoted as a divine utterance in Matthew 19:5.

[46] Mark 10:12 seems to contemplate the wife's initiation of divorce proceedings, but this may refer to Herodias, who as a Roman citizen could do so under Roman law (Josephus, *Ant.*, xviii. 136); cf. her grand-aunt Salome (Josephus, *Ant.*, xv. 259 ff.).

[47] D. S. Bailey, *The Man-Woman Relation in Christian Thought* (London, 1959), p. 10.

[48] παρεκτὸς λόγου πορνείας (Matthew 5:32); μὴ ἐπὶ πορνείᾳ (Matthew 19:9).

[49] Cf. the force of πορνεία in the Jerusalem decree (Acts 15:20, 29; 21:25) and in 1 Corinthians 5:1, and the force of the corresponding Hebrew *zᵉnūt* in CD iv. 20 (similarly the rabbis understood the *zōnāh* of Leviticus 21:7 of a woman who had contracted a union within forbidden degrees; cf. C. Rabin, *The Zadokite Documents*[2] [Oxford, 1958], p. 17).

[50] On Jesus' procedure in delivering 'tradition' to his disciples for preservation and transmission see B. Gerhardsson, *Memory and Manuscript* (Lund and Copenhagen, 1961); *Tradition and Transmission in Early Christianity* (Lund and Copenhagen, 1964). Cf. T. W. Manson, *The Teaching of Jesus*[2] (Cambridge, 1935), pp. 237 ff., for the view that Jesus would have called one of his disciples *šᵉwilyī* ('my apprentice') rather than (like a rabbi) *talmīdī*.

[51] CD i. 11 f.

[52] 1QpHab. vii. 1–5, on Habakkuk 2:1 f.

[53] Jeremiah 25:11 f.; 29:10. Cf. the sixty-five years of Isaiah 7:8; the seventy years of Isaiah 23:15 ff.; the forty years of Ezekiel 29:11 ff.

[54] Daniel 9:2, 24 ff.

[55] Josephus, *Ant.*, x. 267.

[56] Cf. K. Elliger, *Studien zum Habakuk-Kommentar vom Toten Meer* (Tübingen, 1953); O. Betz, *Offenbarung und Schriftforschung in der Qumransekte* (Tübingen, 1960); F. F. Bruce, *Biblical Exegesis in the Qumran Texts* (London, 1960).

[57] Cf. 4QpPs. 37, frag. 2, lines 1–4.

[58] Cf. 1QpHab. i. 12 f.

[59] Numbers 24:17, quoted in CD vii. 20; 1QM xi. 6; 4Q *Testimonia* 13.

[60] Isaiah 31:8, quoted in 1QM xi. 11 f.

[61] Habakkuk 1:6 ff., quoted in 1QpHab. ii. 11 ff.

G

[62] Ezekiel 38:2 ff., mentioned in 1QM xi. 16.

[63] 1QpMic., frags. 8–10.

[64] CD iv. 19, viii. 12 f.

[65] CD iv. 12. Compare the rabbinical depiction of teachers and scribes as builders in passages quoted by Strack-Billerbeck i, p. 876 (on Matthew 21:42).

[66] CD vi. 3 ff.

[67] W. Barclay, *The Making of the Bible* (London, 1961), p. 41.

[68] S. T. Coleridge, *Confessions of an Inquiring Spirit*[2] (London, 1849), pp. 11, 13.

[69] Tatian, *Address to the Greeks*, 29. Cf. Justin, *Dialogue* 8:1; Theophilus, *To Autolycus* i. 14. See E. Flesseman-van Leer, *Zeitschrift für Theologie und Kirche*, lxi (1964), p. 407 with n. 14 (art. cit. p. 88, n. 9 above).

[70] 1 Peter 1:10 f.

[71] Acts 2:16, introducing the quotation from Joel 2:28 ff. about the eschatological outpouring of the Spirit.

[72] Matthew 13:16 f. and Luke 10:23 f.

[73] Mark 4:11 f., quoting Isaiah 6:9 f.

[74] Ephesians 3:4 f.; cf. Colossians 1:26 f.; Romans 16:25 f.

[75] Matthew 1:23, etc.

[76] Romans 9–11, *passim*; cf. 2 Corinthians 3:14 f.

[77] E.g. Romans 10:5, 19; 11:9; 9:27; 9:25.

[78] Cf. Philo, *passim*. An exception is Hebrews 3:7, 'saying through David', where it is of the essence of the argument that the words of Psalms 95:7 ff. were spoken 'so long after' the entry into Canaan under Joshua.

[79] All three motifs are combined in John 1:14.

[80] John 6:35 (cf. Psalm 78:24 f.); 4:10 ff. and 7:37 ff. (cf. Psalm 78:15 f., 20; 105:41; Ezekiel 47:1 ff.; Zechariah 14:8); 8:12 (cf. Psalm 56:13; 1QS iii. 7). These motifs, of course, were widespread in antiquity beyond the Old Testament. Cf. R. A. Henderson, *The Gospel of Fulfilment* (London, 1936); J. G. H. Hoffman, 'Le quatrième Évangile', *La Revue Réformée*, iii (1952), pp. 1 ff.; and pre-eminently C. H. Dodd, *The Interpretation of the Fourth Gospel* (Cambridge, 1953).

[81] A. M. Farrer, *A Rebirth of Images* (London, 1949). The motif of the heavenly book, familiar in other settings (cf. G. Widengren, p. 211 below; also *The Ascension of the Apostle and the Heavenly Book* [Uppsala, 1950]), has its New Testament representation not surprisingly in the Apocalypse. This work is introduced by the words, 'the apocalypse of Jesus Christ which God gave to him' (Revelation 1:1), and we actually see God giving it to him in Revelation 5:7, in the form of the seven-sealed scroll of destiny. The fulfilment of the divine purpose written down there in advance (cf. the 'writing of truth' in Daniel 10:21) is launched by the unsealing of the scroll and divulging of its contents. Yet the rich pre-history of the Apocalypse is plain to read even on its surface.

[82] E.g. the use of Isaiah 63:1 ff. in Revelation 19:11 ff.

[83] C. H. Dodd, *According to the Scriptures* (London, 1952); T. W. Manson, 'The Old Testament in the Teaching of Jesus', *BJRL*, xxxiv (1951–2), pp. 312 ff. Manson finds that 'our Lord's treatment of the Old Testament

is based on two things: a profound understanding of the essential teaching of the Hebrew Scriptures and a sure judgment of his own contemporary situation,' thus providing 'the standard and pattern for our own exegesis of the Old Testament and the New' (p. 332).

[84] F. F. Bruce, 'The Book of Zechariah and the Passion Narrative', *BJRL*, xliii (1960–1), pp. 336 ff.

[85] Zechariah 9:9, quoted Matthew 21:5; John 12:15; cf. Mark 11:1 ff.; Luke 19:29 ff.

[86] Mark 14:27.

[87] C. H. Dodd, *The Old Testament in the New* (London, 1952), p. 8; cf. *According to the Scriptures*, p. 57 ('it is more probable that both writers were guided by a tradition in which this psalm was already referred to Christ'). Cf. further quotations from Psalm 69 in Matthew 27:34; Mark 15:36 (with John 19:28); John 15:25; Acts 1:20.

[88] J. R. Harris, *Testimonies*, i (Cambridge, 1916), ii (Cambridge, 1920). On this subject see also B. Lindars, *New Testament Apologetic* (London, 1961).

[89] The rabbinical principle of $g^e z\bar{e}r\bar{a}h$ $\check{s}\bar{a}w\bar{a}h$.

[90] Cf. Mark 12:10 f. and more particularly its parallel Luke 20:17 f.; Acts 4:11; Romans 9:32 f.; 1 Peter 2:6 ff.

[91] E.g. in Hebrews 2:5 ff.; also in 1 Corinthians 15:25 ff.; Ephesians 1:22; 1 Peter 3:22.

[92] E.g. Psalms 2 (Luke 3:22 D; Acts 13:33; Hebrews 1:5; 5:5, and, in an extended application, Revelation 2:26 f., etc.) and 110 (Mark 12:35 ff.; 14:62; Acts 2:34 f.; Hebrews 1:13; 5:6, etc.).

[93] Psalms 22:1, quoted in Mark 15:34; cf. an extended application of the psalm in Hebrews 2:12.

[94] So too in a 'messianic' psalm the enemies of Yahweh and his Anointed are interpreted as the enemies of Jesus; cf. Acts 4:25 ff., where the nations, the peoples, the kings and the rulers of Psalms 2:1 are identified with 'Herod and Pontius Pilate, with the Gentiles and the peoples of Israel' (cf. also Tertullian, *de resurr. carn.* 20).

[95] John 13:18 (cf. John 17:12, 'that the scripture might be fulfilled'; and Matthew 27:9 f. for Zechariah 11:12 f. as a Judas *testimonium*).

[96] Cf. editions by R. Priebsch (Heidelberg, 1936) and F. P. Pickering (Manchester, 1952). An example is the expansion as a historical incident in Jesus' arrest of Isaiah 50:6, 'I gave my back to the smiters, and my cheeks to those who pulled out the beard' (ed. Pickering, pp. 65 f.); this passage in the third Isaianic Servant Song, incidentally, may have provided scriptural support for the figure of the bearded Christ discussed in Professor Brandon's article, p. 10 above. See also F. P. Pickering, *Literatur und darstellende Kunst im Mittelalter* (Berlin, 1966), especially the section on 'Christi Kreuzigung' (pp. 146 ff.).

[97] G. L. Prestige, *Fathers and Heretics* (London, 1954), p. 195 ('its whole contents', says Prestige, 'are permeated with the spirit and language of Bernard's exposition of the Song of Songs'). Chapter 1 of Prestige's book, entitled 'Tradition: or, The Scriptural Basis of Theology', is germane to our general theme.

[98] E.g., although the last clause of Psalm 22:16, which RSV (following

LXX, Peshitta and Vulgate, and the earlier English versions) translates 'they have pierced my hands and feet', is not quoted in the New Testament as a *testimonium* of the crucifixion of Christ, this rendering lends itself so compellingly to such use that any deviation from it (as in *The Jerusalem Bible*, 'they tie me hand and foot') is bound to arouse misgivings.

⁹⁹ Cf. J. R. Harris, 'Jesus and the Exodus', *Testimonies*, ii (Cambridge, 1920), pp. 51 ff.; E. Käsemann, *Das wandernde Gottesvolk* (Göttingen, 1938); H. Sahlin, 'The New Exodus of Salvation according to S. Paul', in A. Fridrichsen *et al.*, *The Root of the Vine* (London, 1953), pp. 81 ff.; J. Daniélou, *From Shadow to Reality* (Eng. trans., London, 1960); S. H. Hooke, *Alpha and Omega* (London, 1961), *passim*; R. E. Nixon, *The Exodus in the New Testament* (London, 1963); D. Daube, *The Exodus Pattern in the Bible* (London, 1963); H. H. Rowley, 'The Authority of the Bible', *From Moses to Qumran* (London, 1963), pp. 3 ff. The Exodus pattern had been used already in the history of Israel as a mode of portraying the return from the Babylonian exile, especially in Isaiah 40–55.

¹⁰⁰ So MT; LXX renders differently, 'Not an ambassador, nor a messenger, but he himself saved them' (this wording has echoes in later Jewish literature as also in the language of Christian confession; see p. 196 below). The LXX reading presupposes Hebrew *lô ṣîr* ('not a messenger') as against MT *lô ṣar* (lit. 'to him affliction').

¹⁰¹ Matthew 2:15.

¹⁰² Or we may compare the reference to Jesus' death as his 'exodus' in Luke 9:31.

¹⁰³ 1 Corinthians 5:7.

¹⁰⁴ 1 Peter 1:19. Cf. Melito, *Paschal Homily*, especially § 69.

¹⁰⁵ 1 Corinthians 10:2.

¹⁰⁶ Neil Macmichael, *apud* J. Macleod, *Scottish Theology* (Edinburgh, 1945), pp. 253 f.

¹⁰⁷ Galatians 3:27, etc.

¹⁰⁸ 1 Corinthians 10:3 f.

¹⁰⁹ 1 Corinthians 10:16.

¹¹⁰ 1 Corinthians 10:5 ff.

¹¹¹ Hebrews 3:12 in the context of 3:7–4:11, where the words of Psalm 95:7–11 are applied to the current situation.

¹¹² A. T. Hanson, *Jesus Christ in the Old Testament* (London, 1965), p. 7 *et passim*.

¹¹³ 1 Corinthians 10:4. A halfway stage towards Paul's statement that 'the Rock was Christ' may have been the identification of the rock with divine wisdom, attested in Philo, *The Worse attacks the Better*, 115 (cf. Wisdom 11:4).

¹¹⁴ The latest edition of *The Greek New Testament*, edited by K. Aland, M. Black, B. M. Metzger and A. Wikgren (Stuttgart, 1966), commendably prints 'Ἰησοῦς in the text. But see M. Black, 'Critical and Exegetical Notes on Three New Testament Texts', in *Apophoreta: Festschrift für Ernst Haenchen* (Berlin, 1964), pp. 39 ff., especially pp. 44 f.

¹¹⁵ Cf. Barnabas 6:8 f.; Justin, *Dialogue*, 113, 132; see J. R. Harris, *Testimonies*, ii (Cambridge, 1920), pp. 51 ff.

[116] Exodus 13:21.

[117] Exodus 14:30.

[118] Exodus 15:26 (for the use of 'The LORD thy healer' in Judaism cf. Mishnah *Sanhedrin* x. 1).

[119] Exodus 14:19; 23:20 ff.; 32:34; 33:2, 14 ff. Cf. Justin's exegesis of 'my name is in him' (Exodus 23:21) in *Dialogue* 75.

[120] Acts 7:30.

[121] Acts 7:38.

[122] *First Apology* 63.

[123] *Dialogue* 59 f.

[124] *First Apology* 63:11; *Dialogue* 60:2, 3.

[125] *First Apology* 63:12.

[126] *First Apology* 63:5.

[127] Mark 12:26; Matthew 22:32; Luke 20:37. Justin quotes Luke 20:35 f. in *Dialogue* 81:4.

[128] *Dialogue* 60:1.

[129] Where their received texts of Scripture diverged, as in the famous question of the insertion or omission of ἀπὸ τοῦ ξύλου in Psalm 96:10 (LXX 95:10), Trypho's was the more accurate (*Dialogue* 41;73).

[130] *Dialogue* 56:6 ff. (on Genesis 18:9 ff.).

[131] *Dialogue* 56:18 ff. (on Genesis 19:1 ff.).

[132] *Dialogue* 58 (on Genesis 31:10 ff.; 32:22 ff.; 35:6 ff.; 28:10 ff.).

[133] *Dialogue* 62:4 f. (on Joshua 5:14).

[134] See Professor Simon's reference to the removal of the Decalogue from the daily liturgy (p. 110). We may instance also the Jewish rejection of the Septuagint (e.g. *Sopherim*, i. 8 f.) or the shocked surprise of Aqiba's hearers when he appeared still to accept the messianic identification of the 'one like a son of man' in Daniel 7:13 (TB *Ḥagigah* 14a, *Sanhedrin* 38b).

[135] A good example of this cooperation is *The Anchor Bible*, edited by W. F. Albright and D. N. Freedman (Doubleday, New York). The validity of the christological *sensus plenior* in the church is something which elsewhere I have already defended and hope to defend more fully, but to be valid it must be based on grammatico-historical exegesis of the text. Cf. p. 181 below; also H. Cunliffe-Jones, *The Authority of the Biblical Revelation* (London, 1945), pp. 93 f.

VI

The Ancient Church and Rabbinical Tradition

M. SIMON

I

There is, at first sight, a striking analogy between the rabbinic conception of tradition and that which gradually developed in the Christian Church and eventually characterized Catholicism as opposed to the various Protestant denominations and their *sola Scriptura* principle. What *The Catholic Encyclopaedia* writes on this subject could just as well have been written by a rabbi: 'Holy Scripture is . . . not the only theological source of the Revelation made by God (to his Church). Side by side with Scripture there is tradition, side by side with the written revelation there is the oral revelation.'[1] In both cases, tradition, by which is meant oral revelation, is considered as explaining and complementing Holy Scripture, and therefore invested with an authority equal, or almost equal, to that of Holy Scripture. This is made very clear, in the case of Judaism, by the fact that the same word Torah applies to both aspects of divine revelation: there is on the one hand the written Law, *Torah she-bi-ketav*, on the other hand the oral Law, *Torah she-be'al-peh*. The second term is used—I quote from *The Jewish Encyclopaedia*—'to denote the laws and statutes which, in addition to the Pentateuch, God gave to Moses'.[2] But even as in the Catholic Church the teaching of the *magisterium* through the centuries is included in tradition considered as a source of doctrinal authority, similarly, in the rabbinic conception—and I resume my quotation from the *Jewish Encyclopaedia*—'in a wider sense, *Torah she-be'al-peh* includes all the interpretations and conclusions which the Scribes deduced from the written Torah as well as the regulations instituted by them (*Yoma* 28 a, b) and therefore comprises the entire traditional teaching contained in the Mishnah, the Tosephta and the halachic midrashim, since these were taught only orally and were not committed to writing'.[3] This distinction is made by the author of the article for clarity's sake. The Talmud and other rabbinic sources would probably not adopt it without some qualification. In fact, according to these writings, every point of traditional teaching, far from representing a late and more or less arbitrary addition to divine revelation, either was explicitly delivered by God to Moses, who transmitted it orally to his successors, or is at least implied in the written Torah. Likewise, Tradition, in the Catholic perspective, claims apostolic origin. It goes back, ultimately, just as the written revelation recorded in the books of the New Testament, to the teaching of the Apostles and thus to Christ: it is the apostolic tradition, handed down from one generation to another by the apostolic succession of bishops.

Since Christianity is an offspring of Judaism, claims to be the new and only legitimate Israel of God, and, at least in some quarters of the Church, kept in close contact with Judaism and its schemes of thought for a considerable length of time, there is a strong *a priori* likelihood that the pattern provided by the rabbis should have been present, in this case as in many others, to the mind of the Christian thinkers and that the Christian conception of tradition should have been, to a certain extent, influenced by the Jewish one and shaped in reaction against it.

This process is made perfectly clear from the outset if one compares the classical formulation of rabbinic doctrine about tradition given in the treatise *Pirke Aboth* with the earliest formulations of the Christian idea of tradition, as they appear in I Corinthians. I quote the two texts in succession:

Aboth 1:1: 'Moses received (*kibbel*) Torah from Mount Sinai and delivered it (*umesarah*) to Joshua, and Joshua to the Elders, and the Elders to the Prophets, and the Prophets to the Men of the Great Synagogue.'

I Corinthians 11:23: 'I have received of the Lord, that which also I delivered unto you' (ἐγὼ γὰρ παρέλαβον ἀπὸ τοῦ κυρίου ὃ καὶ παρέδωκα ὑμῖν).

Παρέλαβον corresponds very precisely to *kibbel* and παρέδωκα to *mesarah* and it is, I think, quite safe to assume that ἀπὸ τοῦ κυρίου is the equivalent, in Paul's perspective, of *miSinai*. There can be little doubt that Paul, Pharisee of the Pharisees, took over and adapted the scheme which must have been familiar to any pupil of rabbinic schools.

The sentence of 1 Corinthians introduces the tradition about the Last Supper. Paul, eager as he always is to emphasize his complete autonomy vis-à-vis the first disciples, tends to present himself as the first and so far the only witness to this tradition. It is clear, however, that he does not seriously mean to rule the Jerusalem disciples out altogether from this scheme of transmission of the Christian tradition. The disciples, though not mentioned, are indeed implied. They are explicitly mentioned in the other, more developed, Pauline formulation of tradition, 1 Corinthians 15:3, regarding the death and resurrection of Christ: 'I delivered unto you first of all that which I also received, how that Christ died for our sins . . .' The various links in the chain of witnesses are then mentioned in succession, in the chronological order of the appearances of the risen Christ: Cephas, the Twelve, five hundred brethren, James, all the apostles, Paul.

As regards Paul, we could speak here of a twofold revelation: through oral teaching, and through the vision he himself had of Christ. The tradition about the resurrection is rooted in the first appearance, to Peter, who was thus able to preach, out of personal experience, the good news of the resurrection to the Jerusalem Church. The members of this Church, in their turn, having already received the message, were granted a personal confirmation of their belief. Paul does not claim to be an exception in this respect. He underlines the fact that he was the last to see Jesus, being the least of the apostles. In his case, however, it was the experience of the vision which created and founded the belief, and made him a Christian. But he too, though at that time still an unbeliever, had already heard of the Christian kerygma before his vision. He knew of the existence of the Church and, though he rejected it, of the meaning of its message. The content of the tradition, as it is handed down from Peter to the other apostles and disciples and to Paul himself, is in this case the fact of the Resurrection. In the previously quoted chapter it is the institution of the Eucharist. There can be little doubt that the scheme of transmission is the same in both cases. Paul could not possibly maintain, momentous though his vision was in his eyes, that all he knew of Christianity was revealed to him directly by the Lord on this unique occasion. Sure, ἀπὸ τοῦ κυρίου is to be contrasted with παρὰ ἀνθρώπου in Galatians 1:12, where Paul affirms that he neither received his gospel of man, nor was taught it, but received it from the revelation of Jesus Christ. The contradiction between the two passages, however, is only apparent. Lietzmann has, I think, struck the right note when he writes: 'As he owes his Gospel in its entirety, in the last analysis, to a revelation of the Lord, he says ἀπὸ τοῦ κυρίου (*vom Herrn her*) coming from the Lord, who delivered it to him in a mediate way (*mittelbar*). In his mind, all that he has heard about Jesus before and after his conversion springs from the revelation at Damascus as its unifying source.'[4]

This element of personal, mystical experience implied in the visions is of capital importance in the shaping of a Christian tradition and represents, in a sense, its very foundation. It must be noted that it is not completely absent from the Jewish conception either, since Moses experienced something similar on Sinai: though hidden in a cloud, God revealed Himself to him before He revealed Torah; a vision, a theophany—however we may interpret it—is at the root of the Jewish as well as of the Christian tradition. But once Moses had received the written and the oral Law, no further vision was required to make it accepted by the subsequent generations in Israel. Moses stands from this point of view isolated: none of his people was granted the privilege of sharing his experience on the mount. The Christian tradition on the contrary, at least as regards the central affirmation of the faith, the Resurrection, rests on the experience of a number of eye-witnesses, ending with Paul. It could be said that the part played by Moses only on the Jewish side is played by the whole primitive community on the Christian side, and more precisely by the apostles in the wider meaning of the term, those who have seen the Lord. But already within this group there is a chronological sequence, as indicated in 1 Corinthians 15, which is not unlike the one indicated in *Aboth*, with this important difference, however, that the Jewish tradition is centuries old, and is handed down from one generation to another by a considerable number of exponents, while the Christian tradition is still at its beginnings when Paul mentions it.

But once the apostolic age is over, the further transmission takes place exactly according to the Jewish pattern. If we consider that the apostolic group, including Paul, corresponds to Moses, it is perhaps legitimate to look for a sort of equivalent of the subsequent exponents of the Jewish tradition, or at least of some of them, as presented by *Aboth*. I am thinking in particular of those mysterious elders mentioned by Papias, and whom he distinguishes from the apostles. The order of succession is clearly indicated by Eusebius: 'Papias himself, in the preface to his discourses, makes it plain that he was in no sense a hearer and eye-witness of the holy apostles, but tells us, by the language he uses, that he had received the things pertaining to the faith from those who were their pupils.' And then comes a quotation from Papias: 'But I will not hesitate also to set down for thy benefit, along with the interpretations, all that ever I carefully learnt and carefully recalled from the elders guaranteeing its truth.'[5] This group of elders or presbyters, 'distinct from the apostles but apparently direct successors to them in the function of handing on the original tradition'[6] is mentioned not only by Papias, but also by Irenaeus, who includes Papias himself and Polycarp among them, by Clement of Alexandria and perhaps also, in a controversial passage, by Hippolytus.[7] R. P. C. Hanson, commenting on these texts, has this interesting remark: 'It is quite possible that this group of "the presbyters" never existed as a formal body, but are the result of an assumption made widely in the Church of the second century that there must have existed such a group in order to bridge the gap between the deaths of the apostles and the universal recognition of their written tradition in the New Testament, much as Rabbinic Judaism believed vaguely in the existence of the men of the Great Synagogue.'[8] In both cases the phrase probably means no more than 'the men of old'.

The parallel is thus pretty close between the two conceptions of tradition. But once we leave the period of Christian beginnings, there appear important differences. While in Judaism tradition rests on the teaching of individual rabbis, whose names are given in *Aboth* after the mention of the Prophets, elders and men of the Great Synagogue, and has therefore a more personal or, one might also say, academic character, tradition in the ancient Church, as formulated for instance by Irenaeus, becomes an essentially ecclesiastical, that is institutional or collective business: it is the magisterium of the Church, as exerted by the hierarchy, which is the bearer of tradition. And also what is perhaps more important still, while Rabbinic Judaism draws a clear dividing line between written and oral Law, between Scripture and Tradition, the early Christian conception of tradition is of a less precise nature. At the initial stage of its development, Christian tradition is oral. But it soon came to express itself in written documents as well. Once the writings, whether *logia*, Gospels or Epistles, which were to be assembled in the New Testament, began to circulate, tradition assumed two different but closely interrelated aspects. The written text, just as, later on, Mishnah and Talmud, represents, in a sense, but the fixation of the underlying oral tradition. But while the codification of the Mishnah comes after centuries of oral transmission in the schools, only a few years separate the beginnings of Christian preaching and its writing down in the oldest parts of the New Testament. The two stages are almost simultaneous: this is expressed very clearly in 2 Thessalonians 2:15: 'Hold the traditions (παραδόσεις) which ye have been taught, whether by word (διὰ λόγου) or our epistle (δι᾿ ἐπιστολῆς ἡμῶν).'

One might think, at first sight, that the mutual relation of written revelation and oral tradition, as Rabbinic Judaism sees it, is, from a chronological point of view, inverted in the early Christian conception. In the opinion of the rabbis, the written Torah comes first and provides the point from which oral tradition takes its start and develops. Even those rabbinic texts which affirm that the oral Law was revealed to Moses none the less emphasize the fact that the written Law came first: 'When the Holy One, blessed be He, revealed Himself on Mount Sinai in order to give Torah to the people of Israel, he dictated it to Moses in the following order: first *mikra* (reading = written Law), then *Mishnah, Talmud, Agada*.'⁹ But we ought not to forget that the Sinaitic legislation in its turn represents but one stage, the most important one by far, in the unfolding, throughout the centuries and from the very beginnings of mankind, of a divine revelation imparted to Adam, Noah, Abraham, the other patriarchs and which, up to Moses, remained unwritten. Seen in this wider perspective, oral tradition, even from a Jewish point of view, precedes written revelation. And some among the ancient Christian writers based on this fact an argument against the Jews, and interpreted the pre-Mosaic period in the religious history of mankind as the initial form of perennial Christianity.[10]

But conversely, the early Christian conception of tradition is to be understood not only in relation to the revealed Scripture of the New Testament, whose canonical authority was established when the oral tradition had already been in existence for a certain length of time, but also and even more in the light of the Old Testament. For the early Church, Holy Scripture is, first of all, the Jewish Bible. In the Christian tradition the person and message of Christ are, of course, central, since it consists, as we may, I think, safely assume, in its earliest form, of the kerygma, the logia, and narratives about certain facts of the life of Jesus. But at the same time it takes its stand on the Old Testament. It provides the only valid interpretation of it and the key to its understanding. It is significant that in his account of the tradition about the death and resurrection of Christ, Paul appeals not only to the eye-witnesses, but also to the testimony of Holy Scripture: 'I delivered unto you . . . that which I also received, how that Christ died for our sins according to the Scriptures; and that he was buried, and that he rose again the third day according to the Scriptures'. Christian tradition is thus in the same relation to the Old Testament as Jewish rabbinic tradition. It complements it and makes it explicit, with this fundamental difference, however, that it is concerned mainly with historical facts, announced by the Prophets or prefigured typologically in the Bible, and with doctrinal statements, while the Jewish tradition deals above all with legal ordinances.

In the Epistle to Diognetus we have this interesting passage: 'Now (in the Church) the fear of the Law is exalted, the grace of the Prophets is acknowledged, the faith in the Gospels is strengthened, the tradition of the apostles (ἀποστόλων παράδοσις) is kept' (11:6): obviously, in the writer's view, Law, Prophets, that is to say the basic elements of the Old Testament, and the Gospels, representing the New Testament, are the chronologically successive foundations on which the tradition is built (we are at a time when oral tradition and Christian Scripture are clearly distinguished). The same idea is expressed more clearly still by Clement of Rome: 'The apostles were sent by the

Lord Jesus Christ to preach the Gospel, and Jesus Christ was sent by God. Christ therefore comes from God (ἀπὸ τοῦ θεοῦ) and the apostles come from Christ. . . . They went preaching through towns and country and they established their first fruits as bishops and deacons to the believers. And this was by no means a new use. For already a long time ago bishops and deacons were mentioned in Holy Scripture, which says: I shall establish their bishops in justice and their deacons in faith' (Corinthians 42). In this passage of Isaiah 60:17, the Septuagint reads in fact ἐπισκόπους, but where Clement reads διακόνους it has ἄρχοντας. Clement's misreading of the text makes his attempt to found the Christian hierarchy and, through it, that Christian tradition handed on by the clergy, on the Old Testament all the more significant.

II

Since the two conflicting traditions both claimed to be firmly rooted in the Old Testament, and since they could not both be authentic, each of them was led to refute the other one. While the Christian Church accepted the Jewish Bible, without the slightest hesitation, as inspired Scripture, and even vindicated it as its own property, it could not possibly accept the validity of the oral Torah. In fact, it denied it any vestige of authority from the very beginning.

In the early Christian use, the first word which describes the Jewish oral tradition or traditions is *paradosis*. It appears several times in this acceptation in the New Testament. Paul speaks of himself before his conversion as 'zealous of the traditions of my fathers' ζηλωτὴς τῶν πατρικῶν μου παραδόσεων (Galatians 1:14). Likewise the Gospels speak of the tradition of the elders, τὴν παράδοσιν τῶν πρεσβυτέρων (Mark 7:3; Matthew 15:2). Jesus asserts his own position on the subject by speaking of 'your tradition' or 'the tradition of men' (Matthew 15:3; Mark 7:8–9), which he sets over against the commandments of God: this amounts to a very definite condemnation of the Pharisaic view of tradition.

Justin Martyr still applies the same term to Jewish teaching, and asks Trypho to despise 'the tradition of your rabbis' (τῆς παραδόσεως τῶν ὑμετέρων διδασκάλων), 'since they are unable to grasp the word of God and cling to the teaching of their own doctrines' (*Dialogue*, 38:2).

But at the same time the word *paradosis* was becoming a sort of technical term with a merely Christian meaning, and applied more and more commonly to the teaching of the Church, whether written down in the New Testament and the works of the Fathers, or transmitted orally by ecclesiastical authority. We have seen this process already initiated in the Pauline Epistles, where the verbs παραλαμβάνω, to receive, and παραδίδωμι, to transmit, as well as the noun παράδοσις, describe the Christian message as preached by the apostle.

'If we consider,' writes Cullmann, 'how Jesus radically and completely rejected the *paradosis* of the Jews, we are surprised to note that Paul could, without further explanation, apply this concept, discredited as it was, to the moral precepts and to the doctrines to which the primitive Church attributed a normative value.'[11]

I see no real contradiction or problem in the fact that Paul takes over the word *paradosis* to describe Christian realities. For the term in itself does not imply a disparaging nuance or a judgment of value. There can be and indeed there is a true divinely inspired tradition and a false and merely human one. Just as Christianity is, in Paul's eyes, the true Israel, likewise Christian tradition, rooted in Holy Scripture and centred on Christ, who gives it its unique value, is the authentic tradition, whereas Jewish tradition is a human extension or rather distortion of divine revelation. It could however be somewhat confusing to use one and the same word to describe these two traditions. Once *paradosis* had been adopted by the early Church for its own teaching, it became increasingly difficult still to use the term for Rabbinic teaching. This certainly accounts for the fact that subsequent ancient Christian writers do not, as a rule, apply *paradosis* to the Jewish tradition and replace it, for this purpose, by another term, namely *deuterosis*: 'The traditions of the elders (παραδόσεις τῶν πρεσβυτέρων)', writes Epiphanius, 'are called δευτερώσεις among the Jews' (*Haer.* 33:9).

This word as used by ancient Christian writers has an interesting history. If we trust several of them, it was coined by the Greek-speaking Jews themselves, obviously as a translation of the word *Mishnah*, of which it represents the exact equivalent. It seems that, in its Jewish use, it was intended to describe, just as the Hebrew *mishnah*, a method of teaching by repetition, 'as it was only by dint of repetition that an oral teaching, transmitted without the aid of a written text, could have been imparted and fixed in the memory'.[12] In fact, the Hebrew verb *shanah* as well as the Greek δευτερῶ means to repeat; and the noun δευτερωταί, which is sometimes mentioned by Christian writers as a name given by the Jews to their rabbis,[13] is nothing else, originally, than a translation of *Tannaim*, the name, built from an Aramaic root corresponding to the Hebrew *shanah*, of those rabbis who specialized in teaching Mishnah and, more precisely, whose opinions are quoted in the written Mishnah. Something of the original meaning of the verb still appears in the following quotation from St Jerome: 'Si quando certis diebus traditiones suas exponunt discipulis suis, solent dicere οἱ σοφοὶ δευτεροῦσι, id est Sapientes docent traditionem.'[14] The fact that here, as in a number of other cases, Latin writers quote Greek words seems sufficient proof that these were indeed coined and used by the Jews which, by the way, testifies to the existence, as late as the end of the fourth century, even in Palestine if we follow Jerome, and probably also, *a fortiori*, in the Dispersion, of rabbinic schools where Greek along with, or in the place of, Hebrew or Aramaic was the usual academic language.[15]

But as the terms *deuterosis, deuterotes, deuteró* were adopted by Christian writers to describe Jewish traditional teaching, they were given a meaning very different from its original Jewish one. It is quite certain that in the mind of the Christians it had a disparaging nuance, which reflected anti-Jewish polemics. The meaning 'repetition' is lost sight of, and the emphasis is laid on the word *deuteros* implied in each of these terms. *Deuterosis* thus comes to mean that which is second, or secondary, from the point of view of both chronology and importance, as contrasted with the authentic Law of God, as it is written down in the Pentateuch and particularly in the Decalogue. *Deuterosis* represents a mere human addition to Torah: 'Contemnentes legem Dei, et sequentes traditiones hominum, quas illi *deuteroseis* vocant', says St Jerome.[16] Applied to either the oral teaching of the rabbis, or its written codification in the Mishnah, the term amounts to denying it any link with the revealed will of God.

It is possible that this change of meaning goes back to pre-Christian controversies within Judaism. It is a well-known fact that the question of tradition versus Scripture was a bone of contention between Pharisees and Sadducees. The Pharisees, writes Josephus, 'have transmitted to the people certain uses which came from the traditions of the fathers, but which are not written down in the Law of Moses';[17] the Sadducees on the contrary 'maintain that only the written law is to be regarded as binding, whereas one should not keep that which is pre-scribed only by the tradition of the fathers'.[18] It is therefore not unlikely that already the Sadducees should have based an argument on the ambiguity of the term *deuterosis*, which they would interpret as meaning that which comes second or later. Or more probably, since Greek was not their more familiar language, they may have made a play on words in Hebrew, and connected *mishnah* with *mishneh*, that which comes next, or later, a double or second, a law that is which is of subordinate value and, in the opinion of the Sadducees, altogether valueless. However this may be—and I shall come back to the rabbinic use of *mishneh* later on—the Christian interpretation of the word *deuterosis* at least is quite clear. It implies that, despite the Jewish claim to the contrary, the Mishnah cannot be traced back to the divine revelation on Mount Sinai and is a merely human addition to the authentic Law. It is interesting, in this connection, to quote a curious passage where Epiphanius maintains that there are four different and successive Jewish *deuteroseis*. The first one is attributed to 'Moses the prophet', the second to 'their teacher Akiba', the third to one Andas or Annas, who is also called Judah, and the last to 'the sons of Assa-monaios' (τοὺς υἱοὺς Ἀσσαμωναίου).[19] It is certainly wise not to put too much trust, here as in a number of other instances, in the information provided by Epiphanius. As regards the fourth *deuterosis*, there might well be some queer confusion with the Asmoneans: the sons of Assamonaios could, if any-thing at all, mean the Maccabaean dynasty, taken out of its normal chronological location. That Judah, whom our writer also calls Andas or Annas, might well be Judah ha-Nasi, the editor of the Mishnah. It is only natural that he should be named here as the father of one of the *deuteroseis*. As for Akiba, he was sufficiently known, even outside Jewish circles, to be mentioned too in this connection. It is interesting to note this saying of his, as recorded in the *Pirke Aboth*: 'Masorah is a hedge around Torah' (*masoreth seiag la-torah*).[20] *Masorah* here quite certainly means not what we usually mean by that term in relation with the written text of the Bible, but, according to etymology, tradition, and in this case oral tradition, considered as complementing, and providing the correct interpretation of, the written Law. As for the attribution of the first *deuterosis* to Moses, I see two possible explanations. Either we have here an echo, as it were, of the rabbinic contention that the whole oral Law, as well as the written Law, was revealed to Moses by God. Or Epiphanius is to be understood in the light of another use of the word *deuterosis* in the ancient Church, that which is found in the third-century Syrian *Didascalia Apostolorum*.[21]

By *deuterosis* the *Didascalia* does not mean the oral tradition of Pharisaic Judaism, but a part of the Mosaic legislation itself. It makes an interesting distinction between the two successive codifications of the Covenant. Only the first one really deserves the name of law, as expressing God's authentic and immutable will. Its commandments, as summarized in the Decalogue, are simple and true and mild, and are to be kept also by the Christians, since they are of an essentially ethical character. In so far as this first legislation includes ritual commandments, these are by no means compulsory and are to be interpreted typologically as the image of things to come.[22] The second codification, which was promulgated after the Israelites had worshipped the Golden Calf, is a punishment for that sin of theirs. It consists of the ritual and ceremonial legislation summarized in what is sometimes called the cultic Decalogue,[23] and developed at great length in the Pentateuch, particularly in Leviticus and Deuteronomy. This part of the Mosaic legislation, though indeed of divine origin, was imposed upon the Jews as a burden and intended for them only. For God 'justly laid upon them the bonds, as they deserved'.[24] It is the instrument of divine reprisals upon the unfaithful people. God enforced it upon the Jews almost against his will; it certainly was no part of his own original plan: 'The Lord was angry and in his hot anger He bound them with the second legislation and laid

H

heavy burdens upon them, and a hard yoke upon their neck.'[25] It does not in the least concern the Christians, 'for in the Gospel Jesus renewed and fulfilled and affirmed the Law; but the second legislation He did away and abolished. For indeed it was to this end that he came, that he might affirm the Law and abolish the second legislation.'[26]

This is a very interesting, though as far as I know, completely isolated acceptation of the word *deuterosis*. Although the *Didascalia* is earlier than all the other Christian texts where *deuterosis* applies to the oral Jewish tradition,[27] there can be little doubt that the usual meaning is the original one, since the term, as already noted, was certainly coined by the Jews as an equivalent of *mishnah*, considered both as a method of teaching and, later on, as a book. How the transition was made from this meaning to the very peculiar one which appears in the *Didascalia* is not absolutely clear. It seems however, once more, to be in some way related to the rabbinic contention that the oral tradition was imparted to Moses by God. The *Didascalia*, written in a milieu where the Christians still were in close contact with the Jews, knows this claim and rejects it. But it agrees with the rabbis in finding in the revelation on Mount Sinai the roots of Jewish tradition: they are to be found in the second legislation, subsequent to the episode of the Golden Calf, of which the Mishnah, concerned as it is with ritual regulations, provides the explanation and represents the development. The *Didascalia* feels therefore entitled to apply to those parts of the Mosaic legislation this name of *deuterosis* which emphasizes their secondary and superadded character.

If the notion of *deuterosis* as understood by the *Didascalia* had been commonly accepted in the ancient Church, this would have logically entailed the rejection of those parts of the Old Testament where the *deuterosis* is recorded. In fact, to the *Didascalia* they are of no value whatever, nor are they, even typologically or allegorically interpreted, of any help to a Christian: 'When thou readest the Law, beware of the second legislation, that thou do but read it merely; but the commands and warnings that are therein much avoid, lest thou lead thyself astray and bind thyself with the bonds which may not be loosed of heavy burdens.'[28]

The *Didascalia*, however, does not go so far as explicitly to exclude *deuterosis*, as it understands it, from canonical Scripture. The anti-Jewish polemical treatise known as *The Dialogue of Timothy and Aquila* takes this step and denies the book of Deuteronomy, which the author apparently considers as synonymous with, or representing the most important part of, *deuterosis*, the character of a revealed writing: 'The fifth book is Deuteronomy, which was not dictated by the mouth of God—but [adds one of the manuscripts of the *Dialogue*] deuteronomized (δευτερονομισθέντα) by Moses. This is the reason why it was not laid down in the ark of the covenant.'[29] This statement stands, I think, quite isolated among ancient Christian writers.

All these Christian interpretations are to be understood against the background of theological discussions with the rabbis. It must be kept in mind that in some parts of rabbinic literature Deuteronomy is sometimes called *mishneh Torah*, the second (edition of the) Law. This might provide the starting-point, as already noted, for the disparaging nuance of *deuterosis* as applied by Christian writers either to the oral tradition or to those parts of Mosaic Law related to the second covenant, subsequent to the worship of the calf. It might also explain the position taken by the *Dialogue of Timothy and Aquila* vis-à-vis the book of Deuteronomy. It is perhaps possible, as regards this last point, to go one step further. In the book of Joshua, 8:32, we read that when the Israelites had ascended mount Ebal, 'Joshua wrote upon the stones (of an altar) a copy of the law of Moses which he had written for the children of Israel'. The Hebrew text reads: *mishneh torath Mosheh 'asher katav lifne bene Israel*. The modern translators usually agree on *mishneh torath Mosheh* meaning a copy of the Law of Moses. It is interesting, however, to note that Luther translates 'das andere Gesetz, das Mose den Kindern Israel vorgeschrieben hatte'. He had perhaps in mind, and was misled by, the rabbinic use of *mishneh Torah* to describe Deuteronomy. It is, for our purpose, much more interesting still to note that the Septuagint provides a rather queer translation for that passage: καὶ ἔγραψεν ᾽Ιησοῦς ἐπὶ τῶν λίθων τὸ δευτερονόμιον νόμον Μωυσῆ ἐνώπιον τῶν υἱῶν ᾽Ισραηλ. Certain manuscripts add ὃ ἔγραψεν between Μωυσῆ and ἐνώπιον, thus making the translation more literal. The strange thing about this passage is the translation τὸ δευτερονόμιον νόμον Μωυσῆ for *mishneh torath Mosheh*. Apparently the translator already

knew the two different meanings of *mishneh torah* and was, just
as Luther—or maybe Luther followed the Septuagint and not
the rabbis—misled by this knowledge. To a Christian reader of
the Septuagint, in this case the author of our *Dialogue of Timothy
and Aquila*, the curious phrase τὸ δευτερονόμιον νόμον Μωυσῆ
could easily be understood as stating that Moses, not God, was
the author of Deuteronomy. The phrase 'Law of Moses' is used
elsewhere in the Old Testament, but in most cases with some
addition probably intended to prevent any misinterpretation
of the sort; thus for instance in Nehemiah 8:1: 'And they spake
unto Ezra the scribe to bring the book of the Law of Moses,
which the Lord had commanded to Israel.'[30] And the Midrash
knows that it is owing to this unequalled devotion to Torah that
Moses was granted the privilege to have it named after his own
name. This shows, at the very least, that some rabbis were
puzzled by the expression 'Law of Moses' and attempted to find
an explanation of it. It might well imply also that some Christians made of the phrase an argument for denying the divine
authorship of at least Deuteronomy and that their objections
had to be refuted.

The Church could not possibly adopt a conception which
questioned the divine authorship and the unity of the Old
Testament. It came back to the original meaning of *deuterosis*
and was thus able to safeguard the integrity of Biblical revelation, of which it considers itself the only legitimate trustee.
There can be no opposition between two parts of Holy Scripture, two strata, as it were, of Mosaic legislation. The opposition
is between Holy Scripture, which is in its entirety inspired, and
the arbitrary accretions imposed upon it by the rabbis.

As for the *Dialogue of Timothy and Aquila*, its position is
undoubtedly related to that of the *Didascalia*. It only goes one
step further in attributing to Moses and not to God the initiative of the second code of the covenant as developed in Deuteronomy, which appears therefore, just as the Mishnah, as a
merely human work. It thus shows some affinity with the
Gnostic *Letter of Ptolemaeus to Flora* which distinguishes, within
Torah, three different sorts of commandments: those which are
of divine origin, although the Legislator is only the Demiurge,
not to be identified with the supreme God; those which were
invented by Moses and are imperfect, if not exactly bad; and

those which were imagined by the Elders.[31] While, according to the letter of Ptolemaeus, the work of the Elders can be traced in the Old Testament itself, the *Dialogue of Timothy and Aquila* attributes all that which, according to its views, is of human origin in the Pentateuch, the written *deuterosis* and mainly Deuteronomy, to Moses only, and would probably consider that the work of the Elders is limited to post-canonical oral *deuterosis*.

But despite these differences in detail, it is perfectly clear that each of these three writings, *Didascalia, Dialogue of Timothy and Aquila* and *Letter of Ptolemaeus*, starts from the Jewish contention that *deuterosis*, even in its oral form, *Torah she-beʿal-peh*, was imparted to Moses by God and is therefore to be put on exactly the same level as the written Law. Each of them aims, in its own way, at refuting the position of the rabbis.

III

Conversely, a number of rabbinic statements about oral tradition are of a polemical character. They are intended not only to meet possible objections formulated by the pupils of the rabbis, but to establish the legitimacy of the Pharisaic position against adversaries who hold opposite views. It is not altogether impossible that in some cases we have an aftermath, as it were, of controversies with the Sadducees. This, however, is certainly rather exceptional, since there was hardly anything left of the Sadducean school of thought after A.D. 70, let alone when Midrash and Talmud were written down. By that time, the major adversary of the rabbis was Christianity, and there is abundant proof on both sides, in rabbinic as well as in patristic literature, that numerous discussions actually took place and that the Jews had to vindicate their position against Christian attacks.[32] It is no longer possible to believe, as Harnack and a number of other outstanding scholars of the previous generations believed, that Church and Synagogue left sight of, and contact with, each other at a very early date, soon after the appearance of Christianity on the stage and the Palestinian catastrophes. The simple fact that Christianity claimed the Old Testament as its own exclusive property and built all its apologetic system on it implied that it had to refute, time and again, the Jewish claims.

And as it went on, at least in some quarters, attempting to gain the Jews as well as the Gentiles to its message, as, on the other hand, Judaism had not yet given up completely its missionary activities, the rabbis must, of necessity, take into account the arguments and objections of the rival faith. They could not possibly ignore them. Though in the present state of our information, rabbinic texts do not mention Christianity by its name, there can be little doubt that in a number of cases, whether under the name of *minim* or in a completely anonymous way and by mere allusion, the Christians are indeed present in the mind of the Jewish doctors and in rabbinic literature. This is true in particular of the passages concerning the Law and its perennial validity, the election of Israel, monotheism and those who profess 'another God'—in some cases perhaps Gnostics, in most cases Christians—and oral tradition, *mishnah, deuterosis*.[33] I must be content here with a few examples.

When a rabbi maintains that 'even what a disciple is going to teach in the presence of his master was already delivered unto Moses on mount Sinai',[34] this can perhaps be explained in the light of diverging opinions within Judaism itself. But if we remember the Christian attacks on *deuterosis*, it might just as well represent the answer to some fundamental objection formulated by the Church: the whole complex of rabbinic oral teaching is a late and merely human addition to revelation. When we hear that the Ten Commandments, which had first been recited daily, were taken out from the daily liturgy of the Synagogue, in order to refute the objection of those who say that only these commandments, and not the complete codification of ritual Law, let alone oral tradition, were given to Moses by God,[35] it can hardly be doubted that this explanation is intended for some Christian adversary. The following passage is more illuminating still: 'After he had taught Moses the oral Torah, the Holy One—blessed be He—said unto him: teach it to Israel. Moses answered: Lord of the Universe, I shall write it down for them. But God replied, saying: I do not want you to write it down, for I know that the nations of the world will rule over Israel and attempt to take it from them. I give Israel *mikra* in written form, but I give them *Mishnah*, Talmud and Agada orally, and thus will Israel be distinguished from all other nations.'[36] A parallel passage makes it even clearer that the Christians are meant. It says that Moses was forbidden to write the Mishnah down because God knew that the nations would translate Torah into their language and then say 'we are Israel, we are God's own children'.[37] Possessing Mishnah is thus made a touchstone: those who have it are the true people of God.

It is, I think, quite clear, and I would just like to underline it by way of conclusion, that the Christian and the rabbinic Jewish conception of tradition have, to a large extent, been developed in reaction against each other. Of course, the rabbinic doctrine of tradition already existed when Christianity appeared on the stage. But we have probably to take Christianity into account if we want to explain in detail its final formulation. And conversely, the ancient Christian thinkers could not possibly avoid the Jewish patterns when they began to formulate their own faith and teaching in terms of Tradition *versus* Scripture.

NOTES

[1] *The Catholic Encyclopaedia*, art. *Tradition*.

[2] *Jewish Encyclopedia*, art. *Law (oral)*.

[3] Ibid.

[4] *An die Korinther* I–II (*Handbuch zum Neuen Testament*, 9)² (Tübingen, 1923), p. 58.

[5] Eusebius, *Eccl. Hist.*, 3, 39:2–3.

[6] R. P. C. Hanson, *Tradition in the Early Church* (London, 1962).

[7] *Apostolic Tradition*, 36:12.

[8] Op. cit., p. 44.

[9] *Midr. Exod. rabba*, 47.

[10] On this point, cf. M. Simon, *Verus Israel*² (Paris, 1964), pp. 105 ff.

[11] *La Tradition* (Neuchâtel-Paris, 1953), p. 11.

[12] I. Epstein, *Judaism, A Historical Presentation* (London, 1959), p. 114.

[13] Eusebius, *Praep. Evang.*, 11:5; Jerome, *in Habac.*, 2:15.

[14] Ep. 121, 10, *ad Algasiam*.

[15] On the use of Greek among the Jews cf. S. Liebermann, *Greek in Jewish Palestine* (New York, 1942), and *Hellenism in Jewish Palestine* (New York, 1950).

[16] *In Is.* 59:12.

[17] *Ant.*, 13, 10:6.

[18] Ibid.

[19] *Haer.* 1:15.

[20] *Aboth*, 3:13.

[21] English Translation from the Syriac, with the Latin fragments, by R. H. Connolly, *Didascalia Apostolorum* (Oxford, 1929).

[22] The developments on *deuterosis* are mainly in chapter 26 of Connolly's edition. On the problem of *deuterosis*, cf. Connolly's introduction, pp. lvii ff.

[23] Exodus 34:10–28.

[24] Connolly, op. cit., p. 14.

[25] Ibid., p. 222.

[26] Ibid., p. 224.

[27] Connolly, however (p. lix), has a quotation from Rufinus' translation of Origen's Commentary on Canticles where the word *deuterosis* appears: GCS (Berlin Corpus), vol. 8 of Origen's works, p. 62.

[28] Connolly, p. 12.

[29] *Dialogue*, 77a, edited by F. C. Conybeare, *Anecdota Oxoniensia* (Oxford, 1898).

[30] Other instances Joshua 23:6; 1 Kings 2:3; 2 Kings 14:6; 23:25; 2 Chronicles 23:18; 30:16; 34:14; Ezra 3:2; 7:6; Daniel 9:13.

[31] Cf. G. Quispel's introduction to his edition of the Letter in *Sources Chrétiennes* (Paris, 1949); also J. Héring, 'Dieu, Moïse et les Anciens', in *Revue d'Histoire et de Philosophie Religieuses*, 1941, pp. 192 ff.

[32] On this point, M. Simon, *Verus Israel*² (Paris, 1964), chap. 5–7.

[33] M. Simon, op. cit., pp. 214 ff.

[34] *Jer. Pea*, 11:4.

[35] *B. Berach.*, 3c.

[36] *Midr. Exod. rabba*, 47; cf. *Jer. Pea*, 11:6.

[37] *Tanh. B. Gen.* 44b; *Pes. Rabb.* 14b; *b. Ber.* 5a.

VII

Scripture, Tradition and Sacrament
in the Middle Ages and in Luther

B. MOELLER

I

My subject is: 'Scripture, Tradition and Sacrament in the Middle Ages and in Luther'. Many of you will probably have received such an announcement with a certain scepticism. How can all these important things be put into the 'nutshell' of one single lecture—if not at the price of problematical simplifications and extravagances, or at the expense of prolonging this paper endlessly? I cannot pretend to dispel these fears if I give the two reasons which have caused me to bring together the five dimensions mentioned in the title of this paper, without any thought of exhausting the theme. Firstly: I dare to speak about the thousand years of troubled history which we call the Middle Ages because in my opinion this remarkable period in Western history with all its varied layers and dramatic turbulence, seen as a whole, was a period of signal compactness, because all the opposing and disparate lines remained within the firm framework of what was in the end a single understanding of the world and of life, and because in the question of the connection between Scripture, Tradition and Sacrament we can hope to grasp in its centre the peculiar self-understanding of the age. Secondly: this compactness of the Middle Ages on the other hand is best recognizable, I believe, to the person who seeks to understand Luther against his historical background; in the confrontation with Luther who, Heimpel says, perhaps did not indeed end the Middle Ages, but made them 'impossible',[1] the Middle Ages draw together, and their peculiar self-understanding becomes visible.

Before we take up this inner compactness of the centuries of the Middle Ages, let us inquire into the reasons for it.

Normatively they may be sought in the historical presuppositions of the Middle Ages. It grew up, of course, out of the meeting of younger races with an ancient culture, out of the irruption of the Germanic peoples into the ancient world. The fusion of Antiquity and Germanic culture (*Germanentum*), which came about as a result, constituted the 'Middle' Ages, and in this period there happened for the third time in Western history what Horace observed when the Romans came into contact with the Greeks: just as then the conquered and chained Greece spiritually overcame victorious Rome, just as conquered Palestine has also since done in another way, a similar thing happened to victorious Germany.[2] The Middle Ages became a 'daughter-culture' of the Ancient World.[3]

The spiritual, cultural and religious realms of the Ancient World were normative for its life—and indeed it lived as if it were the young daughter, born later—or perhaps better, as the foreigner who has become heir. Already the physical frontiers which enclosed the world of the Middle Ages were extensively the same as those of Antiquity. Also when the centre of gravity of mediaeval history moved from the Mediterranean world into the area north and west of the Alps; also when the East, Byzantium and the Islamic kingdoms were, if only spasmodically, in the age of crusades, a stronger and more integrating part of the mediaeval understanding of the world; and other places, especially Scandinavia, had recently been included— nevertheless, Thule and India still counted in the Middle Ages as the distant fairy-tale borders of the world. The urge to explore them filled only a few; and when that changed, the Middle Ages came to an end. But still—and with this we shall be especially occupied today—the Middle Ages was conscious of its time, knowing the past and its value, selecting the things it esteemed significant and enlivening, completely under the spell of Antiquity and its decisions.

That Antiquity could exercise a spell of such a strong kind, she did not owe only to her great spiritual strength as such. Rather it worked out in this way, that the German peoples— very different from the Arabs, the second heirs of Antiquity— made Christianity their own, viz., not only the culture but also the religion of moribund Antiquity, and in that way the orientation to the past received a religious-spiritual basis. Especially as it was not a question of just *any* religion, but of one which with peculiar power, unlike any other, by its nature is historically determined. The Middle Ages became a period of Christian history and was fixed in its way on an event of the past and a historical context.

And this event and this historical context by which one lived in the Middle Ages certainly belonged to *ancient* history, and one therefore faced it in the situation of heirs who had remained foreigners. One lived in a new scene and, above all, one lived with Christ, Peter and Paul, with Jerome and Augustine, no longer in the same time, no longer speaking the same tongue. The ancient language, Latin, was and remained in the Middle Ages, however widespread it was, a foreign language; salvation-history was and always remained, however holy it was, the history of another time. The historical self-understanding of the Middle Ages and of mediaeval Christianity had, from the first, peculiar characteristics.

One was certainly scarcely conscious in the Middle Ages that it was so, and in any case it was hardly felt to be a problem. This is not finally explained by the fact that the Christian tradition to the Middle Ages was mediated with peculiar signs. For this it is especially significant that already in the later part of the ancient period (*Spätantike*) a reduction of Christian, especially theological, thought-formation had taken place. Men began to be tired of spiritual effort: the exposition of scripture, i.e. access to that event and that historical context in the past, was regulated; theological teaching, pondering over the revelation, had at any rate in the questioning circles which moved Christianity along been fixed in dogma and made sacrosanct, and creative work was limited for the next five hundred years to the collection and preparation of florilegia, catenae and lexica. History, by which the Christian faith lives, was, when the Middle Ages began, already on the way to being transformed into a system of truth, and when Antiquity gave way to the Middle Ages, it was not so much the material for contemplation itself which changed, as the addition to it. Men no longer adopted the conservatism of tired, timid old age to which the material, however, still belonged, but rather the boyish uncomplicated respect of later-born youth.

Already in those collections of later antiquity, Christian-theological and pagan-profane communities of ideas had been joined together in varying degree. Christian truth and general truth had in the main begun to grow together into a unity. So Christian truth and general truth corresponded in structure to one another for the Middle Ages. Truth was for the Middle Ages a gift of overpowering fullness and grandeur. In music, say, melodies and rhythms were not invented (*erfunden*) but found (*gefunden*) in a treasure of tropes, which constituted *vera musica* never completely accessible to man. Likewise the law was not made, created or formed, but found. There was 'no written (*geschrieben*) but only copied (*aufgeschrieben*) law',[4] and when one wanted to insist upon new law, it could only be in the pretence and opinion that good ancient law was, in the light of the intervening breakdown of law, being reinstated. Also the unbelievably numerous forgeries in the Middle Ages, in part manufactured with masterly skill and in great numbers, went back normatively, it seems, with the intention of helping to carry through a good legal state of affairs of which one could be sure, on the single basis of an eternal legal order. Truth, as something given, therefore meant in practice *given in advance*. Truth was esteemed in its essence to be old, and access to it was only to be found when one turned to the past. To the term *modernus* was attached the reputation of deterioration and, in a measure, of being contemptible, until late in the Middle Ages. The famous saying of the *moderni*, that they were only dwarfs on the shoulders of giants, was coined in the twelfth century, the liveliest and most adventurous period in the Middle Ages, in the circle of the Chartres School which strove to reach new shores and reached them.[5] And if at the end of the Middle Ages, under the ideas of *via moderna* and *devotio moderna*, the adverse connotation disappeared, a modernistic pathos still remained foreign to those who called themselves such.

II

The ancestors of the Middle Ages, to whom one had to turn in the search for the truth, were in the first place the writings of Antiquity. They faced one as a self-contained collection, in the main separated from one's own time. The holy documents of

Christianity—the writings of Church Fathers, canons of synods (the tradition) and primarily the Holy Book (the Bible)—possessed the highest status and highest authority of them all; for there alone was the highest truth, which was about the life of man, his being, his salvation and his duties, and about the fate of the world.

Thus this truth, too (we concentrate now on the understanding of the Bible), was counted as something given. And indeed it rested properly and originally with God, in His knowledge and plans. But God has given man access to it and participation in it in those ancient and holy writings. So man could know how he was created, what he had to do and what lay before him and the world. And he had to know. Familiarity with those ancient Scriptures was necessary to him for life. The way which opened up truth to him, and thereby life, was their exposition. So every effort in the search for wisdom was concentrated in this place, and just as all knowledge, even all mediaeval culture was only in the end concerned with exposition, so especially was spiritual life and theology. The holy texts which one studied— and this follows from what has been said up to now—were characterized on the one side by their authority, on the other by their strangeness. The latter is new, I think, in respect to antiquity, and therefore it is possible to say that it was a new age of understanding the Bible, which began in the Middle Ages. It is clear that an historical attitude in our sense was outside their horizon. Their historical limitation was scarcely known, and the historical line which connected men with them was seen just as little. The ancient texts were not historical documents and historical reports, but books of truth.

One could track down the truth of these texts, it was believed, if one used the right exegetical method. The Middle Ages knew several such methods and did not feel their multiplicity to be a problem. The one amongst them which came nearest to the inner structure of the biblical texts must be the one which we, after the thoughtful analysis, which Erich Auerbach has given it, call 'figurative interpretation' (*Figuraldeutung*), and which may also be called 'typological' interpretation. Thereby is meant a way of understanding the history of salvation reported in the Bible, which was met already in the Early Church, even in the writings of Paul, and which had arisen in an attempt to link the Testaments and to point the way for the Church to enter the covenant-history of Israel. Happenings or people in the Old Testament were understood as anticipations of the New Testament; the Old Testament as a whole was made to be an obvious 'shadow of the future'. Therefore the historical reality of the occurrences considered together was not questioned, because of their meaning as prefiguration (*figura*) and fulfilment—the sacrifice of Isaac was treated as the promise of the crucifixion of Christ, just as an historical event like the crucifixion itself. But it is not this which was really important, but the wonderful spiritual sense, which the exegete found, and in which it became visible beyond and above the reality of the concealed plan of God. The peculiar difficulties of the biblical narratives, the volume of the ambiguous and impenetrable which lies beyond each of them, was support for figurative interpretation, and therefore, further, every single event of interpretation pointed beyond itself to the future, to a final fulfilment. Auerbach has observed that this method of exposition spread and gained assurance in an extraordinary degree between Antiquity and the Middle Ages, and he has given enlightening reasons for this. In the missionary situation of the early Middle Ages, the mysterious vista of history, which was opened here, must have had a stronger power of conviction with its glittering pictorial clarity than the simple history of the people of Israel. So the exposition of the figurative meaning of the Bible went far beyond the framework of exegesis of Scripture as such. Auerbach speaks in general of the 'figurative apprehension of the event in the Middle Ages',[6] and indeed not only did religious art, poetry, and spiritual drama live on the figurative understanding of salvation-history but it reached deeply into real life, into every day, into practical politics. When, say, Charlemagne understood himself to be the new David, he did not use an image, but he was looking at reality; he proclaimed his David-like election by God and built claims upon it.

It must be clear that already with this method of exposition and understanding, at any rate in its mediaeval form, the actualization of the history reported in the Bible was guided into a direction which one may describe as its process of mythologization (*Mythisierung*). It was not the 'Sometimes' (*Jeweils*) which was sought but the 'Everytime' (*Jederzeit*) of history; in place of the concrete claim the significance meant by God entered and, as God's plan became comprehensible to one, one could take possession of God Himself. These consequences were drawn in *the symbolic interpretation of history* which was found among German theologians of the twelfth century, like Rupert of Deutz and Gerhoh of Reichersberg, and which came to its peak shortly before 1200 in the historical perspective of Joachim of Fiore, with its considerable developments in the late Middle Ages. It is rather like a branch of figurative interpretation. Here as in scholasticism the theological tradition of Antiquity was organized, harmonized and brought together; the historical material, known from the Bible, was ordered and given shape. Since it was God who guided history, history must also reflect, they thought, the structure of the divine essence and God's way of acting in the world, both of which one knew from theology. So they thought to understand world history from its beginnings to the present, first as a chain of periods of influence corresponding to the seven gifts of the Holy Spirit, then as a series of ages belonging to the three Persons of the Trinity (Joachim). By summoning up great sagacity and learned fantasy, finely-worked systems of parallels and connections between ages were designed; perfect harmony, the 'unison' (*concordantia*) of the periods of history was proved. The eternal meaning of events alone was still of value, and historical reality was 'tamed . . ., domesticated, and almost brought to heel'.[7] In the background there always stood the need to understand their own present. It belonged in every case to the last age, and the end of history was in every case reckoned to be imminent. The exegete anticipated God's future.

The typological and symbolical methods were not the only way that the Middle Ages used for laying bare Scripture. That is easily explained—there was indeed a gap at a critical point. If it really was God Himself who spoke to man in Holy Scripture, one could not be content with the explanation of specific parts of the book of holy truth. Rather it had to be defended as authoritative in its entirety and in every detail. The Holy Spirit could not have said anything false, superfluous or insignificant, and so, where such seemed to be the case, the exegesis must provide a remedy.

The allegorical method, which performed this service, had a long

tradition; indeed it was not, in contrast with figurative interpretation, a specially Christian procedure. The Alexandrian
Church Fathers, who made it firm in the Church, had prototypes in the profane exegesis of Homer and Virgil, and in the
philosophical hellenistic exposition of the Old Testament. There
such texts, found everywhere, raising contradictions of some
kind if they were to be taken literally, were questioned for their
hidden meaning, and exegetes were successful in bringing out
of the writings of the Old Testament, as if it were their true
deeper meaning, doctrines from contemporary philosophy and
moral teaching. Augustine also approved and richly employed
the allegorical method in a sober, theologically trained form,
and reading him, but reading Origen too, the Middle Ages
received at once the authority and the measure for its use.
Mostly, one made use of it according to the manageable teaching of the so-called four-fold understanding of Scripture, of
which the monk John Cassian had first formulated the rules at
the beginning of the fifth century.

In pre-Christian usage, the allegorical method in the exposition of mythical texts had had something like a demythologizing function. Now, since it was a matter of historical report, the
picture changed. It belonged to the premises for the teaching
of the four-fold interpretation of Scripture, fixed by Augustine,
that beside the general attributes of holiness and thorough-going
spirituality, the aim of the Bible was to teach future Christians
directly in every single place. One could read in the *Glossa
Ordinaria*, the standard exegetical handbook of the Middle Ages,
composed in the twelfth century, the completely Augustinian
sentence '*Nihil est in divina scriptura, quod non pertineat ad eccle-
siam*'.[8] From that it was thought that there was a complete
system of other meanings beyond the grammatical-historical
sense of a Biblical text which referred to the Church as a whole
or to individual Christians either in the course of history or at
the end of the ages—an allegorical, tropological or anagogical
sense, as it was called. The allegoric and anagogical interpretation of Scripture consisted predominantly in communicating;
the tropological in instruction and exhortation. All four senses
were not found in every single place. The scheme was reduced
in essence to differentiating between a direct and a hidden sense.
In some ways this method of exposition was different from the

ones treated earlier, in that the starting-point was not a desire
to understand history and thereby contemporary existence, but
to clarify the meaning of the ancient texts. Therefore it seems
sound, like Auerbach, to consider the two procedures separately,
even if they are not always clearly distinguished in the hermeneutical practice of the Middle Ages.

III

Behind this differentiation really were concealed different ways
of understanding the ancient texts and their meaning for contemporary life. In searching for the four-fold meaning of
Scripture one could manage to equate completely the historical
perspective of the ancient book with the present, and thereby
also completely lose sight of the historical depth of one's own
existence. That could happen if one considered the relationships between the four meanings of Scripture to be static, and
the totality of the holy writings as a well-made mosaic of pronouncements about truth. Definitions like, say, the one of Petrus
Comestor in the twelfth century point in this direction: 'Holy
Scripture is God's dining-room, in which the guests are made
drunk in a respectable way: . . . the *historia* is the foundation,
the *allegoria* the wall, the *tropologia* the roof.'[9] Or Bonaventura's
definition in the thirteenth century: '*Tota scriptura est quasi una
cithara, et inferior chorda per se non facit harmoniam, sed cum aliis.*'[10]
  Certainly, this understanding of the Bible did not reign alone.
Especially the Dominican School at the height of Scholasticism
(*Hochscholastik*) insisted on looking at the historical-grammatical
sense of the Biblical text before the mystical sense: only with the
help of the *sensus litteralis* should theological proofs be carried
out, taught Stephen Langton, and then pre-eminently Thomas
of Aquinas; and the allegorical exposition should only have
power of proof when it agreed with the literal sense of another
text. But even with these principles the strictly static view of
the Bible was not really penetrated. For the aim continued to
be, to understand the Bible as a whole as the work of God, and
like Augustine, to ascribe a present meaning to every *factum* and
every saying in it. They drew the conclusion that they could
track down, with its discrepancies and syntheses, the literal
sense of the Biblical text with the help of the dialectical method,

and could look upon and treat separate sections of the Bible as material for Scholastic '*Quaestiones*'. Moreover, the search for hidden meaning was in no way suspended and, as to whether one must accept that one and the same place in the Bible had at one and the same time several senses, Thomas could say 'yes': since God is the Author of the Scriptures and since at the same time He holds everything in His mind, it is not unfitting to accept multiple meanings of any one place in His holy book and also to ascertain several parallel meanings in its exposition. This multiplicity of meaning is apparent as such only to us, not to God; nevertheless a human exegete will never succeed in comprehending the complete fullness which the Holy Spirit has put into even one single letter in the Scriptures.[11] The literal sense, therefore, had priority over the mystical meaning of Scripture only because it could be more definitely ascertained and more easily controlled, not because of its higher degree of truth. The teacher of Thomas, Albert the Great, interprets the *nudaverunt tectum* of Mark 2:4 as follows: *cum autem domus sit scriptura, tectum domus est historia, et nudatio (tecti) est historiae detectione usque ad Christum per mysterium attingere.*[12]

So in the end even the high evaluation of the verbal meaning of Scripture, and the efforts, which they made on occasion in the late Middle Ages to clarify it linguistically and historically, did not lead to the historical understanding of the Bible and salvation-history. Beryl Smalley expresses strongly and pointedly this incongruity when she affirms that the mediaeval exegete of the Old Testament, who went to the Jews in the town for advice on Hebrew, considered this 'as a kind of telephone to the Old Testament'.[13]

Our results up to now have, therefore, given a certain harmonious conclusion: the mediaeval exposition of Scripture, i.e. the presentation of God's historical act in Christ, was executed in its entirety—if one is allowed to speak so generally—with a disregard for history. Whether or not salvation-history was regarded as a miraculous, but still planned and sensible channel, which was always intended, and whether or not the Bible was understood as a manual of all kinds of pronouncements about truth, it was sometimes supposed that God's world reared up tangibly in the world of men, and it was at bottom nothing other than this which made men interested in the holy writings.

The speculation of Scotus Eriugena is similarly vague and characteristic: *Divina . . . scriptura mundus quidam est intelligibilis, suis quatuor partibus veluti quatuor elementis constitutus.*[14] The Bible and the history reported in it therefore fitted into the large picture of the mediaeval view of the world and of God, and as a consequence the unity of all being was connected within itself into a powerful, many-limbed Cosmos, whose peak was God and through which He wonderfully worked. The contribution of Christianity to this view of the world was the conviction that God's sphere of existence was directly and permanently present in man's sphere of existence, giving direction, elevating, saving. The Bible gave the ground for this conviction, confirmed and illustrated it, and in this lay its great significance for faith and life.

IV

There was certainly one place in which the presence of God's sphere of existence in man's sphere of existence was more directly, more physically and 'more daily' apprehended than in the Bible . . . that was the divine means of grace, the *Sacraments of the Church*, and particularly the most complete and at the same time 'most daily' of them, *the Eucharist*, in which God was present not merely with His gracious power but in Person. 'Christianity stands on two things, reading the Mass and receiving the holy Sacraments', says the Strasbourg Dominican Magister Ingold in the fifteenth century.[15] What the Bible only reported, happened daily in the Mass. God came to men, and the sacrifice on the Cross at Golgotha, from which the reconciliation of the divine and the human spheres first took their origin, was repeated without bloodshed in the daily sacrifice of the Mass. And it needed this repetition: for this past event was here actualized and thus far completed and finished. So the stress shifted: it was the Eucharist which counted as the *mysterium tremendum* for the Middle Ages. It represented not simply the *mysterium* of the Lord's acts but also for those people alive then, it actually replaced it. So after the Middle Ages, following on from the later part of Antiquity, had—so to say— lost the thread to the history of primitive Christianity, the living contemplation of the Church and her possession of divine things, in fact, for faith, took the place of retrospective consideration of the past saving act.

It is after all no accident that the most significant contribution of mediaeval and scholastic theology to the history of Christian doctrine was the fixing and theological formulation of teaching on the Sacraments, and that the Middle Ages produced new doctrines almost only in connection with teaching on the Sacraments. Scholasticism, doing so, was carried forward by the deeds and claims of ecclesiastical piety, and, seen as a whole, supported its tendencies. If, moreover, Augustine had seen grace as efficacious more in the conduct of the sacrament instead of in the elements and liturgical formulae, and had therefore asserted that God's Spirit works when the Sacrament is celebrated—'*noli ergo de baptismate gloriari, quasi ex ipso salus tibi sufficiat*'[16]—in Scholasticism the reticence here expressed was to a large extent given up. Formulae like 'There is salvation in the Sacraments' (*in quibus salus constare probatur*—Hugo of St Victor); or 'They give salvation' (*dant salutem*—Peter Lombard),[17] or 'They contain grace' (*continent gratiam*—Decretum pro Armenis, at the Council of Florence, 1439) now became quite usual. The Sacraments worked their gracious effect through their performance (*ex opere operato*), and without them there was no salvation. The most complete form of Scholastic teaching on the Sacraments, that of Thomas, kept free, it is true, of portraying the efficacy of the Sacrament to be in the substance of the Sacrament as such—the Sacrament is a vessel of grace, an instrument of the gracious will of God. But as such an instrument it was expected to bring about grace and salvation, *causa instrumentalis gratiae*,[18] and this efficacy did not refer to every new endowment by God.

If after that they scarcely avoided the fine division already present in theology, which separated the Sacrament and therefore the reception of salvation from the historical revelation of God, in the practice of eucharistic piety there were even fewer scruples. The celebration of the Eucharist, the present God, consecrated the high moments of life, birth, entry into orders, accolade, coronation; it sanctified legal acts like duels, ordeals and the performance of oaths. Priests went round the fields in the parish with a 'little sack' (*säcklin*) or 'golden coffin' (*vergults särglin*) round the neck which contained the consecrated Host to bless the harvest,[19] or at the head of a military levy in a town. 'God has become a citizen of Berne; who can fight against God?' commented one chronicler on such a procession going to war.[20]

With the wafers of the Host, amazing miracles happened everywhere. They trickled with blood or were changed into small boys, and they accomplished the most glorious mighty deeds. There were girls who lived, simply by receiving the Host; fires were put out by the Host; heretics were unmasked—like the Albigenses, who could walk on water, but who had to drown miserably when a priest under the curse of the devil threw a monstrance containing the consecrated Host into the river—or converted, like the penitents in Liège to whom in 1374 the Host was shown without covering and laid upon their heads.[21] And when the Albigensian heretics in the thirteenth century laid siege to Avignon, they had to withdraw again, when the defenders displayed wafers on the wall.[22] The more the Middle Ages progressed, and the more wonders of this kind happened, the more the desire spread to see with one's own eyes God's appearing. Therefore many kinds of institution were founded to show lay-folk the consecrated Host—covered or uncovered—the elevation at the transformation, Corpus Christi with its procession, and the celebration of other eucharistic (or, as the Catholic liturgical technical term says, theophoric) processions, and, finally, since the fifteenth century, to show laymen occasionally, or even constantly, the Host in a monstrance, in a glass container for everyone. Of these opportunities of seeing God lively, often even moving, use was made—in 1507 Heilbronn Council even complained that 'women, young girls and others stood right up at the altar so that they ended up nearly hindering the priest at the divine office',[23] and it is said of St Dorothea of Montau, who died in 1394, that she was not even satisfied if she had seen the Sacrament a hundred times in the day.[24] But on the other hand, it must be significant that the frequency of communion was increasingly reduced; besides other reasons for it a contributing factor must have been the horror felt in the presence of the God who had become so very tangible.

V

The loss, or perhaps better, the absence of history in the Middle Ages, is nowhere, I think, more clearly recognizable, it seems to me, than in the eucharistic piety of the people, seldom importuned, but for the most part confirmed by ecclesiastical pressures. In it the origin of Christianity as a historical event had almost been lost; the belief in salvation through the strange God who came into real history, had virtually disappeared; and in consequence of that, Christian hope, in so far as it is directed to the free and therefore comforting advent of God, had almost disappeared too. There are many witnesses to show how mediaeval contemplation of a present God brought about a cyclical understanding of history, for which time lost its linear character, and was not movement but only repetition and continuation.

That did not change fundamentally until the end of the Middle Ages and the eve of the Reformation. On the other hand, the spread and the intensity of the eucharistic cult seem to have gone on and on, and the articulation of teaching on the Sacrament in theology obviously furthered this development. Also the gradual transformation of the Middle Ages from a peasant age to a city life changed nothing; the historical self-understanding, as Hermann Heimpel affirms for the fifteenth century in Germany, was 'in every change of relationships, not dynamic, but static, not historical, but mythical'.[25] Important writing of history ceased almost completely in the late Middle Ages, and the figurative interpretation of salvation-history was held without discussion, as the verse from a Shrove-Tuesday play by Hans Volz, which originated about 1500, will show:

> . . . so merk dir und verstee
> Dass alle Geschicht der alten Ee
> Und aller Propheten Red gemein
> Ein Figur der neuen Ee ist allein.[26]

Even the historical and philological interests and hobbies of the Humanists did not bring the Middle Ages to an end. Before and after the humanist chronicles looked the history of the world in the eye, and arranged it according to the old pattern of *aetates*, they did something new, in the context which we are discussing here, only in so far as the date of the end of the world, which had been calculated, was moved away farther from the present—in Pico della Mirandola even till the year 1994. Still a not inconsiderable change in the understanding of history was being prepared. Even if the frame of the picture remained, the 'painting technique of single figures' was changed.[27] There was no longer only a figurative relationship with Antiquity; the present was no longer significant only as a function of the remote past. Rather, there grew, especially in Italian writing of history, e.g. in Leonardo Bruni, the sense of the individuality and conditionality of the past event, and therefore of its unrepeatability. The extent of time and also historical continuity with Antiquity began to be seen; the ancient books and relationships were now called *Fontes*, which it was again important to uncover, and therefore they stopped being prototypes (*Urbilder*).

Humanist biblical exegesis makes it clear that indeed the limitations of the older form of putting the question had not been basically overcome. The great Erasmus, in spite of his philological interests and output, in exegesis laid stress on the spiritual sense, and therefore he only appealed to the Church Fathers instead of to the 'moderns', and he held fast to the complete infallibility of the Bible.[28] And if the French humanist Faber Stapulensis rejected the teaching of the four-fold interpretation of Scripture, the only result was to lay out, instead of its real structure, a double meaning of the words, a carnal and a spiritual; also according to his understanding, probably normatively determined by Augustine, the Bible contained *mysteria, oracula, abscondita,* and if spiritual exegesis discovered Christ everywhere as the hidden meaning, this principle was still rather like the key to a miracle book.

Finally, it was a rather important fact, which was significant for the future, that many humanists and especially Erasmus, who was guided by the motives of Platonism as much as by the *devotio moderna,* had only contempt for the massive sacramental cult of the time. But still there were men who were disposed to humanism who later kept out of the Reformation just because of the Protestant struggle against the Roman Mass—e.g. in Basel, Bonifacius Amerbach—and Erasmus himself returned in his old age to the Catholic belief in the real presence, if not in transubstantiation also, and in 1530 he could exclaim: 'What purity, what reverence, what holy terror this ever-to-be-worshipped mystery demands! . . . Who can worthily express it in words?'[29]

In short: the absence of history, which we have noted for the Middle Ages, had (speaking generally) not come to an end even for the most modern, most enlightened men on the eve of the Reformation; at any rate, when looking at belief in Christ, taken as a whole, the spiritual-religious world in which Luther grew up and from which he emerged was none other than the same static, mythical world of the Middle Ages.

VI

Luther's relationship to this, in the main, closed world of the Middle Ages, had its own peculiar characteristics. He grew out of it—and indeed not as a humanist timorously emancipating himself, but as a monk who was intimately familiar with it. So his thought was in the long run in tune with the tenor of the age. He kept in use many of its motifs and thought forms, and one has no reason for flatly maintaining that in every respect Luther opened a new period by the way he understood the Bible and history. Luther was not a phoenix, and he had not to be one. Still on the other hand his gradual withdrawal from the Middle Ages, his 'conversion' from it, caused him to reject it especially curtly and clear-sightedly, and to take up an especially accentuated counter-position; whilst theology and faith got a new centre, historical self-understanding was also changed in its very essence, and therefore understanding of Scripture and tradition reached another, new level.

Luther studies are today probably agreed, especially after the work of G. Ebeling, that Luther's theological breakthrough to the Reformation came about in direct connection with *the exposition of Scripture*, as a fruit of his calling as a Professor of Biblical Exegesis. That is: it came about in a thoroughly orthodox way. That the Bible is the source and measure of everything Christian, was a conviction common to all the Middle Ages. According to Thomas, it is a fundamental rule for theology: *Successoribus . . . apostolorum et prophetarum non credimus nisi in quantum nobis ea annuntiant quae illi in scriptis reliquerunt.*[30] 'The formula *sola scriptura* was in common use in catholicism (*vulgär-katholisch*)'.[31] One cannot say either that there were new exegetical or hermeneutical principles, which Luther used and which brought him out of the Middle Ages. Taking the literal sense seriously was, as we saw, at any rate the basic principle of a large number of mediaeval exegetes. And that such historical exegesis of the Bible, undertaken theologically, had to be concentrated on Christ had similarly been insisted upon, at least in the first place, by Faber Stapulensis. The new thing in Luther's exegesis was the concentration with which he took in hand the theologically executed exposition of the literal sense of the Bible—and that means now, above all, his readiness to find something new in the ancient text. And the result of his effort was new—that, as Ebeling has formally expressed it, 'in coming to grips with the text he ended by being gripped'.[32]

The earliest extensive document of Luther's theology which we possess, his first lectures on the Psalms (1513–15), already show remarkable advances and irruptions in the new direction. It was, it is true, still a completely mediaeval work in its arrangement; the four-fold meaning of Scripture was tracked down just as was the figure of Christ in the Old Testament; the very energy and, we may say, disregard with which the Psalms, in spite of all historical intelligence, were explained in terms of Christ, exceeded even the Middle Ages. Still even here there was already something new; in contrast even with the Christocentric exegesis of the past, man appeared in Luther's exposition no longer simply as a neutral person, but as one who by his nature stands before God and is exposed to God's judgement. And Christ corresponds to man not simply as the holy shape from the past who overshadows all, but as the *Deus et homo*, who as such is the Saviour. And finally there was the relationship between the Old and the New Testaments, salvation-history, as a coherent event, a logical consequence of promise and fulfilment, in which basic differences were bridged and in which the Christian was interested not to track down mysterious connections but to seek factual history. Therefore the object of exposition, the content of the Bible, had something like a new quality; the exegete himself was directly involved in it. Even in the earliest exposition by Luther known to us, the Bible was no longer the first amongst the wisdom and miracle books.

In the years following the lectures on the Psalms, until 1519, the break with past exegesis of the Scriptures was completed in Luther, together with the great break with theology as a whole. What began in 1513–15 was now given clear expression. In this connection the so-called Reformed principle *sola scriptura*, which was not expressed in its full form until 1520, appears as the slightest of innovations. What was more significant was the elucidation of *exegetical method*, if less in its technical than in its theological aspects. Indeed the search for the four-fold meaning of Scripture was given up in 1517. The figurative meaning came back here and there, however; it still occasionally appears until well on into the lectures on Genesis, and a general allegorical-spiritual meaning on a historical foundation defended itself for many years against the weakened residue of the old *quadriga*— it contradicted reformed principles at the very least. Luther on the other hand laid great stress on inquiry into the literal sense, the *sensus litteralis* of the Bible. He pursued language study and took great pains to understand the meaning of Biblical words, the grammatical context, and the peculiarity of linguistic usage of the Bible as a whole; and he used his lively historical imagination.

But all this did not happen merely for the sake of *historia* but with a theological end in view. The spiritual meaning of Scripture should be found by this means, for the literal sense of the Bible rightly understood is, according to Luther, also its spiritual sense. In the application of this principle, which sounds as if it could come from Augustine, is to be found the real novelty of Luther's understanding of the Bible. Namely, the spiritual sense is always, thinks Luther, only the offering of one and the same simple fact: the justification of the sinner through Christ alone. This 'general aim' (*Generalscopus*)[33] was found in a treatment of the Bible as a whole—which was often forced in detail —whereby the Old Testament in later years was brought into the context of theology for the most part on condition that it remained within its own time. Luther had a theologically impressive and striking argument for all this: the Holy Scriptures mean, as we possess them, the justification of the sinner, the Saviourhood of Christ; this is their centre. So I do not understand them wrongly if I explain the Holy Scriptures with this 'general aim' in mind. But that means: At the moment when I explain them in this sense, historically and keeping to the letter (*buchstabengerecht*), they stop being a merely historical document; for the gospel is about Christ, who does constantly what He once did; who claims to be the Saviour of all men, and therefore the purely historical aim of exposition, which leaves in the past the thing reported, in this case misses the truth. It is not the *quid* but the *quare* of the history of Christ which must be perceived; not how Christ looks to us, but how He sees us.[34] So we will understand the Bible as it wants to be understood—as the Word of God, and it brings out belief in us.

VII

With these premises there was reason for radical renewal of the relationship between the Bible and tradition. The Bible was no longer significant as a mosaic of wisdom sayings, but as a document in which the history of Jesus Christ is comprehensible for us. And this history on its part was not present through the Bible simply as an historical fact, but in its meaning for Christians. If it becomes clear in exposition that what is reported there happened 'for me'—and that means also according to Luther: if the Bible is explained according to its literal sense— then Christ, the Holy Spirit Himself is in His Word which brings grace and leads me to faith and salvation. Thus the authority of the Bible grew for Luther and acquired another quality, which tradition cannot reach, and in seeing tradition rival the authority of Scripture, Luther rejected it.

One may say that, to a certain extent, for Luther the Bible took the place which the Sacraments previously had; the customary teaching, which saw the reception of grace and salvation as tied to the Sacraments, was excluded for him. Anyway, Luther did draw the practical consequences of it, gradually at first, not without external influences and not completely, and he was content to leave himself plenty of room without being too specific. He did not consider the 'mythical', mediaeval interpretation of the Sacrament as such to be his real opponent, however crassly it could be portrayed just on the eve of the Reformation, but the teaching concerning salvation connected with it; and, if there was a demythologizing, it fell away, as it were, as a by-product. But Luther's positive understanding of the Sacrament was early made clear: the administration of the Sacrament cannot have a qualitative advantage over the proclamation of the word of God; the Sacrament is in itself nothing else than a special way of proclaiming the Word, and it has a share in mediating salvation, when it is this. The Sacrament does not meet me on a special plane of existence, and it does not put me on one. It goes back, so to speak, like preaching, to appointment by Christ; its content is the promise of salvation, not its delivery, and it affects my faith—fundamentally like preaching, even if it is by way of being a visual revelation allotted to me in particular.[35] It wants to meet me, like the Bible, as God's Word, and it is also similar in that it comes to me in the form of a sign in which the matter is contained and hidden— as the spiritual meaning of the Bible is contained and hidden in the historical-literal sense. And as in the exposition of the Bible, it all consisted in not leaving aside the literal sense, the literal and spiritual senses not being separated, so likewise Luther laid everything on the reality (*Realität*) of the Sacramental sign— that became clear in the struggle with Zwingli. Disregarding the literal sense of the Bible and disregarding the Real Presence of Christ in the Supper, both alike have the same effect according to Luther: contempt for the real Incarnation of God, on which salvation, however, rests.

Therefore the importance of Luther in the spiritual-religious (*geistesgeschichtlich*) context, which we have been discussing today, consists in the fact that he rediscovered the theological relevance of the history of Jesus Christ. The whole Christ, Christ as the Saviour and Redeemer, according to Luther, is none other than having found Him in His history. Every figurative overheightening or sacramental and allegorical elimination of history does not concern Him because it does not seize Him. Finding Christ in His history on the other hand means that something improper and alien happens, which as such is consoling; God breaks through the promise by fulfilling it; He reveals Himself by veiling Himself in flesh; He shows Himself as the Lord of the world, by becoming man, and my brother. In one word: only when Christ is found in His history, does it remain true that He is there 'for me'.

These historico-theological (*geschichtstheologisch*) principles of Luther may appear so profound and, in comparison with the

Middle Ages, so foundation-shaking that one may not be able to see their limitations. But in truth the conclusions of this insight *were* limited. He scarcely noticed that the result was that the Bible and the history reported in it were two. The additions to theological Biblical criticism were modest, and on occasion he would argue like a complete Biblicist. Likewise he was scarcely conscious of the historical distance of his own time from primitive Christianity, nor was he conscious of the historicity of the present manifestation of the history of Jesus Christ. And such was his conviction that he could make contact directly with primitive Christianity—less restrained, he was harsher in his condemnation of the intervening historical development of the Church, and he was more abstract in his understanding of the continuity of the Church than is perhaps suitable.

Nevertheless, we should notice that by his theological knowledge Luther was led, in understanding history in general too, beyond the Middle Ages. Even in this respect he certainly did not simply found modern history, and indeed he was inferior to many an historian of the Italian Renaissance with regard to the observation of the inner causality of the historical event. Still in at least two spheres he had significant new insights. In him the knowledge of the hiddenness of revelation led to a desanctifying of his understanding of history. Certainly God is also for Luther the One who really acts in history—history is in truth God's struggle with Satan who seeks to suppress the Gospel, but who is going to his final defeat: 'Historians describe nothing other than the work of God which is grace and wrath.'[36] But that cannot be read in history. God conceals His deeds, as in Christ, contrary to His intention, He covers Himself with masks. Whoever thinks he can ascertain God's plan in history is deluded and he offends God. Also the history of the Church, as it takes its course, remains for the observer thoroughly ambiguous—Christians do not get fatter by eating than do other people.[37] And faith cannot have more than the certainty that the God of history is the God of Jesus Christ and cannot afford more than a confident insistence on historical claims.

But for Luther not only these negative insights followed from weighing the history of Jesus Christ. To him came the realization that all historical appearances are unique. From that he could clearly perceive historical reality; he recognized the irreplaceability and unchangeableness of historical events; he had an eye for the concrete form and the worth of individual things given—the law, peoples, great men. But above all the unself-consciousness with which he experienced and worked out his own history is impressive. He was certain that *new* things could and did happen, and the consciousness with which he henceforth saw tasks for what they were and sought to master them, had, I think, no parallels in the Middle Ages.

In consequence of our statements one can perhaps go as far as saying that Luther was—as a result of his theological discovery—the first person after the Middle Ages for whose thoughts about history and his own self-understanding the border-line between Antiquity and the Middle Ages no longer had a formative significance. He was certainly alone with his historical insights for a long time to come and when, in the eighteenth century, they began methodically to come to grips with history in its factuality and its conditionality, it happened in the main without stimulation and influence from his side. So as a rule the new thoughts about history remained foreign to the source to which Luther owed his historical understanding—his insight into the majesty and the significance of the concrete history of Jesus Christ.

NOTES

[1] H. Heimpel, *Der Mensch in seiner Gegenwart* (Göttingen, 1954), 57.

[2] Cf. A. Dove, *Hist. Zs.*, 116 (1916), 213.

[3] E. R. Curtius, *Europäische Literatur und lateinisches Mittelalter* (Bern, 1948), 28.

[4] F. Kern, *Hist. Zs.*, 120 (1919), 15.

[5] W. Freund, *Modernus und andere Zeitbegriffe des Mittelalters* (Köln, 1957), 83. The interpretation of this word given there seems to me unsatisfactory.

[6] E. Auerbach, *Figura* (Istanbuler Schriften, 5 [1944], 11–71), 54.

[7] E. Meuthen in *Geschichtsdenken und Geschichtsbild im Mittelalter* (ed. W. Lammers [Darmstadt, 1961], 212).

[8] *MSL* 113, 844.

[9] Quoted: B. Smalley, *The Study of the Bible in the Middle Ages* (Oxford, 1952), 242.

[10] Quoted: C. Spicq, *Esquisse d'une histoire de l'exégèse latine au Moyen-âge* (Paris, 1944), 269. The idea is Augustine's. Cf. H. de Lubac, *Exégèse médiévale*, 2/2 (Paris, 1964), 97 ff.

[11] 'Auctor principalis sacrae scripturae est Spiritus sanctus, qui in uno

verbo sacrae scripturae intellexit multo plura quam per expositores sacrae scripturae exponantur vel discernantur' (quoted: Spicq, op. cit., 284).

[12] Quoted: de Lubac, op. cit., 306.

[13] Smalley, op. cit., 362.

[14] Quoted: de Lubac, op. cit., 1/1 (Paris, 1959), 75, n. 1.

[15] Quoted: L. Pfleger, *Hist. polit. Blätter*, 140 (1907), 425.

[16] Quoted: W. Jetter, *Die Taufe beim jungen Luther* (Tübingen, 1954), 8.

[17] Quoted: W. Jetter, op. cit., 44, 51.

[18] Jetter, op. cit., 60.

[19] L. A. Veit, *Volksfrommes Brauchtum und Kirche im Mittelalter* (Freiburg, 1936), 106 f.

[20] H. Schmidt, *Die deutschen Städtechroniken als Spiegel des bürgerlichen Selbstverständnisses im Spätmittelalter* (Göttingen, 1958), 86 f.

[21] These and many other examples in P. Browe, *Die eucharistischen Wunder des Mittelalters* (Breslau, 1938), *passim*.

[22] P. Browe, *Die Verehrung der Eucharistie im Mittelalter* (München, 1933), 91.

[23] Quoted: H. B. Meyer, *Zs. f. kath. Theologie* 85 (1963), 194.

[24] Browe, *Die Verehrung*, op. cit., 57.

[25] H. Heimpel, *Vorträge und Forschungen* 9 (1965), 26.

[26] Quoted: Auerbach, *Figura*, op. cit., 36.

[27] W. Kaegi, *Historische Meditationen* 1 (Zürich, 1942), 227.

[28] 'Haud scio inter omnia Scriptorum genera sit ullus liber absque naevo erroris, praeter Scripturam Canonicam, quae tam nescit fallere quam ipse Spiritus diuinus, cuius afflatu prodita est.' Quoted: L. W. Spitz, *The Religious Renaissance of the German Humanists* (Cambridge, Mass. 1963), 339.

[29] Quoted: K. H. Oelrich, *Der späte Erasmus und die Reformation* (Münster, 1961), 154.

[30] Quoted: B. Decker, *Universitas, Festschrift für A. Stohr* 1 (Mainz, 1960), 120.

[31] F. Kropatschek, *Das Schriftprinzip der lutherischen Kirche* 1 (Leipzig, 1904), 439 f.

[32] Cf. G. Ebeling, *Z. Th. K.* 48 (1951), 175.

[33] G. Ebeling, *Evangelische Evangelienauslegung* (Darmstadt,² 1962), 197.

[34] Following Ebeling, *Evangelienauslegung*, 232 ('nicht nur wie Christus aussieht, sondern wie er uns ansieht').

[35] E. Roth, *Sakrament nach Luther* (Berlin, 1952).

[36] Quoted: M. Schmidt, *Luther-Jahrbuch* 30 (1963), 51.

[37] Cf. H. W. Krumwiede, *Glaube und Geschichte in der Theologie Luthers* (Göttingen, 1952), 42.

VIII

Scripture and Tradition
in Modern British Church Relations

B. DREWERY

I

There is a passage in Karl Barth's *Church Dogmatics* (Vol. I, Part 2, pp. 829 f. in the English translation, pp. 927 f. in the original German) in which, after 'marking off' the Evangelical Church as the Church of Jesus Christ from the three 'heresies' of Neoprotestantism, Roman Catholicism and Eastern Orthodoxy, he goes on to distinguish 'at least three great forms' within the Evangelical Church itself—the Lutheran, the Reformed and the Anglican 'branches of the Evangelical Church'. Now an Englishman at once wonders what a large part of the Church of England would feel if it woke up to find itself 'a branch of the Evangelical Church'—or even *eine Gestalt* thereof, the word 'branch' rather unfortunately suggesting, as the German word does not, the highly suspect 'branch theory' of the Church as a whole. But an English Free Churchman would wonder still more whether the Free Churches of his country are not worthy in the mind of Barth of the honourable designation of 'Evangelical', or whether he had for the moment forgotten them. In either case let him be my excuse for a brief sketch of the denominational pattern of British church life, in which our theme of Scripture and Tradition will gradually take form.

The Church of England claims to have preserved its identity in a continuous history from the beginnings of Christianity in this country. British bishops were present at the Council of Arles in A.D. 314. The mission of St Augustine from Rome, at the instance of Pope Gregory I in 597, ensured the preponderance of the Roman over the indigenous Celtic traditions of the Church, the question being resolved, after some decades of conflict, by the Synod of Whitby in 664. The English Reformation has always been in Anglican eyes the reform of an existing body, not the creation of a new one. Financially, administratively, judicially, the suzerainty of Rome was repudiated; the 'Great Bible', in the vernacular, was set up in all the churches; shrines were destroyed and monasteries dissolved. But the three-fold Ministry, with the historic episcopate in apostolic succession, was maintained; and Henry VIII, who as a lay-theologian had dared to strike at the towering crest of Martin Luther, would countenance no doctrinal changes. His death in 1547 made possible the appearance, with successive revisions, of Prayer Book, Ordinal and the Articles and Homilies, which mark the high-level of Continental Protestant influence on the English Reformation, through the mediation of Archbishop Cranmer. The Catholic reaction under Mary (1553–8) was followed by the consolidation of the English Reformation under Elizabeth I (1558–1603), and her own cautious and mediating nature, never conceding until concession was inevitable, and then conceding graciously and regally, may be said to have stamped itself on the Elizabethan settlement—Catholic and conservative, yet where necessary Reformed and even Protestant, and sincerely so.

Such a settlement was peculiarly suited to the English temperament in perhaps the majority of its manifestations; the Preface to the Prayer Book (1662) is very English in its opening words:

It hath been the wisdom of the Church of England, ever since the first compiling of her publick Liturgy, to keep the mean between the two extremes, of too much stiffness in refusing, and of too much easiness in admitting any variation from it.

A contemporary divine put it more drastically, when he defined the 'extremes' as the 'meretricious gaudiness of the Church of Rome and the squalid sluttery of fanatick conventicles'. From the first, the settlement pleased neither. The excommunications of Henry and Elizabeth confirmed a body of continuing Roman Catholics in their allegiance to the Pope, and this was especially true of segments of the country such as Lancashire where the English Reformation had made little appeal to the old Catholic families. This body remained faithful through disabilities and persecutions until the progressive achievement of Catholic emancipation from 1778 to 1829, and has since grown, helped in the present century by waves of Irish immigration, to the

K

formidable total of over 4 million baptized members, or one-twelfth of the population.

On the other side of the Elizabethan settlement stood the more thoroughgoing Protestants, known collectively but rather vaguely as 'Puritans', who took their theology from the Calvinist tradition and stood for a far more radical reforming (or 'purifying') of the Church under the express and literal warrant of Holy Scripture. There was never a Puritan *Church*; most of the Puritanically-minded (if one may so express it) remained in the Church of England, which to this day includes in its many-coloured texture of thought and worship a strong streak of Calvinism. Others, however, taking to the limit the doctrine of the priesthood of all believers, began by the mid-sixteenth century to meet in separatist groups, which were fed by disappointment over the Elizabethan settlement; these groups, bound by God's covenant, free from state-control, flourishing under the banner of 'gathered Churches', through persecution and exile, developed into the so-called 'Independents' who helped to overthrow Charles I and formed the core of Oliver Cromwell's Roundheads. The Savoy Conference of 1658 set forth their polity and principles, and through the centuries the 'Congregationalists' (as we know them) have maintained a sturdily independent Protestantism, with a fine record in education and a distinguished succession of biblical scholars and theologians—but with a limited popular appeal, their membership today being some 200,000 with under 2,000 Ministers. It is perhaps fair to say that the right of each individual congregation to independence of all the others does not now seem to them as conclusively Scriptural as it once did; in practice it has become a source of weakness; and only this year the Congregational Union of England and Wales took the momentous step of recognizing the corporate existence, covenant-bound, of the congregations as 'the Congregational Church'.

Into the long and bitter story of the Reformation in Scotland I cannot now enter. The Calvinist party under John Knox ensured the victory of a more radical Protestantism than in England, and this was consolidated by the exacerbating folly of Archbishop Laud and the Stuart kings in seeking to force episcopacy on the Kirk—a folly which bred counteracting folly, and ensured that the non-theological factor of national animosity would darken and harden ecclesiastical counsel. The Revolution which banished James II finally restored the Presbyterian polity and doctrine (1690). There are some 1⅓ million members of the Church of Scotland today, with 70,000 in the Presbyterian Church of England.

The first Baptist Church in England is dated 1612, and was formed by some members of John Smyth's Church in Amsterdam who had returned to London from exile. The Baptist Churches in England today number over 300,000 members; they stand traditionally on the left wing politically, socially and ecclesiastically. Their doctrines and practices of Believers' Baptism by immersion, of the gathered Church and of a congregational polity are well known. But a Baptist would be emphatic that behind all this is what matters most: that the basis of his whole position is the sole supremacy of Scripture. The various divisions in the past and at the present within the Baptist movement are perhaps a warning that agreement on the sole supremacy of Scripture is not sufficient to present every problem of Church life and faith with a clear and indisputable solution.

The Church of England, then, failed from the beginning to embrace the continuing Roman Catholics on the right and Independents on the left. More important still is its own un-exampled comprehensiveness. Its classical claim to be the *mean*—the Via Media—as between Rome and the Reformers, was classically set forth by Hooker. As against the Puritan insistence not only on positive fulfilment of Scriptural precept but also on the exclusion of everything not expressly commanded therein, Hooker elaborated the doctrine of natural law, founded in the external reason of God, in the light of which everything, including Scripture, must be interpreted. The threefold appeal to Scripture, Reason and Tradition, so characteristic of Anglicanism, is prescribed by Hooker in magisterial terms:

What Scripture doth plainly deliver, to that the first place both of credit and obedience is due; the next whereunto, is whatsoever any man can necessarily conclude by force of reason; after these, the voice of the Church succeedeth.

But when a Church seeks to hold to a Via Media, looking not to one but to a blending of three types of authority, it will of

necessity—theological and historical—embrace and even en-
courage every variety of emphasis and interpretation; and the
Church of England has always combined trends or even parties
verging on the right towards Rome and on the left towards
radical Protestantism. From Archbishop Laud, through the
High Church Caroline divines and the Nonjurors (who refused
on grounds of conscience to take the oath of allegiance to
William and Mary in 1688), then by way of the Oxford Movement of the nineteenth century and the Anglo-Catholic revival
of Bishop Gore and his friends and successors in our own
twentieth century, there has been a continuing witness in
Anglicanism to historic Catholic tradition, the Reformation
being at best a necessary but peripheral and temporary
remedial operation, and at worst a hateful excrescence on the
body politic of the Church. It was, curiously and most en-
lighteningly, in part at least from this High Church background
that there sprang the last of the great secessions in English
Church history.

The Evangelical Revival and the Methodist movement of
the eighteenth century aimed at renewal, not disruption, of the
Church of England, of which the brothers Wesley were ordained
priests. The Holy Club at Oxford and John Wesley's mission
to Georgia show how strong was the strain of High Churchmanship in his family inheritance. Among the many-coloured
influences that subsequently stained the white radiance of
John's High Churchmanship must be included Martin Luther,
the Moravians, and the evangelicalism, both Anglican and
Independent, with which the Methodists found themselves
in increasing relation, although one main pillar of Methodism has always been its instinctive and violent opposition to
Calvinist or neo-Calvinist predestinationism. The nineteenth
century, however, saw from 1833 the second great reform
within the Church of England—the Oxford Movement of
Keble, Pusey, Newman—which sought to recover and deepen
the Catholic consciousness of the Church by renewed emphasis
on just those elements in the pre-Reformation Catholic heritage
which Wesley had found increasingly unworkable and dis-
tasteful. Hence the Methodists, by now seceded from their
mother-Church, were looked on by the Tractarians with a
contempt which was in line with their hatred of the Continental

Reformers themselves; and this the Methodists repaid with interest. Inevitably these children of the Church of England were thrust by reaction more and more into the community of the Free Churches; and thus Methodism, by birth Anglican, by adoption Free Church, stands in a unique position in English church life. It is perhaps not too much to say that those who have most heartily supported the current proposals for Anglican-Methodist union are more conscious of their eighteenth-century Anglican birth, while the dissentients are more aware of their nineteenth-century Free Church adoption. Methodism in Britain today has almost 750,000 members and 4,500 Ministers, and is thus larger than all the other Free Church communions together.

Let me add, to complete the statistical sketch, that the Church of England today, with 11,000 parishes and over 20,000 clergy, has baptized 27 million, or over half of the population, and claims 10 million communicants. Into the mysterious question of what constitutes 'membership' in the Church of England I do not presume to enter.

II

The relative evaluation of Scripture and Tradition will already have shown itself as one vital motif in the whole tangled story of the evolution of the denominations in this country. Let me at this point try to show why the resolution of the problem has been found so perplexing, even within a single denomination.

All parties would agree that ultimately there is but one supreme authority in the Church, and that is GOD. The question is, how has God spoken? Where can I hear and how can I understand His authoritative Word? Now Christianity is bound up with the conviction that God has spoken, once and for all, in certain events that took place in Palestine between 1000 B.C. and A.D. 100—that this segment of history constitutes, so to speak, the *test-case* for the revelation of God's being and purpose. This self-revelation culminates in the personal entry of God into human history in Jesus Christ.

How is this revelation mediated to us? By the Bible, which is our abiding witness to those mighty acts of God in history; by the Creeds, which summarize the biblical witness and by selective emphasis give the key to the correct understanding of the otherwise baffling complexities of the biblical records; by the traditions of the Christian Church, in which the calling of Israel has been perpetuated; by personal experience in the inner life of the believer.

But it is immediately clear that whereas the single voice of God, could we hear it, would constitute an unassailable authority, this mediation in so many different forms blunts its divine edge and opens up wide areas of possible dispute. The original biblical witnesses were by no means infallible; their distance from us in time and idiom allows us to mishear and misunderstand; the Creeds, albeit the best available summaries of the Kerygma, are human productions and not above criticism; the Church throughout its history has followed many a lead that had nothing to do with its divine calling, and often in accents that cannot be harmonized; the personal 'experience' of the believer is notoriously subjective. Where then in all this medley of discordant witness is the unimpeachable authority of the Word of God?

All the parties would, I think, agree in referring us at this point to the one factor that the preceding analysis has forgotten —the guidance of the Holy Spirit, given to and accepted by faith. The Holy Spirit has been potent throughout the history of the Old and the New Israel, in the Word, spoken and written, as it was committed to Holy Scripture, in the forging of the Creeds, in the long ages of Church Tradition, in the secret places of the human heart. The appropriation of God's self-revelation in one and all of these realms is the work of the Spirit, who is active alike in event and understanding, in the act or the word which reveals and the faith which grasps the revelation.

But all this leaves the vital question unanswered. *If* God reveals Himself in Scripture, Tradition, Experience, and *if* the Holy Spirit is at work in all three, how are we to conceive of their relative authority? In all three, as we have emphasized, the Holy Spirit is wrestling with human ignorance and sin. It is not as if the Bible, for example, gave the Holy Spirit a clear field to set forth uncontaminated divine truth, whereas Tradition and Experience can only give it in a relative form, a compound of God's word and man's evil. Yet there is general agreement that the Bible stands pre-eminent, and that in some sense

Tradition and Experience must be tested by it. How can this be, if *all three* are the work of the Holy Spirit on fallible human material?

The question is sharpened when we recall that there is no clear antithesis, in point of form or content, between the three. The Bible is notoriously a 'traditional book'—the record of the traditions of a worshipping community, the blending of traditional documents and of traditions handed down by word of mouth—whose very compilation and canonization were themselves the products of church tradition. Yet church tradition and individual experience are themselves shaped and fed by Biblical mode and content. You cannot set the three alongside as wholly distinct and rival candidates for favour in this matter of authority. Each, as it were, invades the others. The *primacy* of the Bible thus becomes difficult to define or even conceive, and the resolution of any problem in which Bible and Tradition, for example, may appear to conflict, becomes an affair of infinite complexity. What is worse, the defence of any position we wish to uphold which we really inherit from Tradition can always claim a plausible or specious Scriptural buttressing because of the interrelationships of the two.

Here are four examples of this problem in action, so to speak, from the field of modern British church relations.

(1) *Infant or Believer's Baptism*

This difficulty is the *scandalon* on which all moves for union between the Baptist communion and any other have stumbled and fallen. The Baptists, who (as I have said) emphasize perhaps more than any others the sole supremacy of Scripture, point to the New Testament practice and doctrine with unwavering confidence. Infant baptism, they claim, is due wholly to Tradition. The others, however, not satisfied with this admitted preponderance of Tradition in favour of infant baptism, go on to claim that it is an inevitable implication of New Testament doctrine itself—so inevitable that traces of it begin to appear in later New Testament practice; and that the reason why it was not practised universally from Pentecost onwards was simply historical, namely that the first generation of converts to any new movement cannot be other than 'grown up'. Hence the resolution of a difficulty as concrete and clear-cut as this does not, in practice, follow from simple reference to the admittedly primary authority of Scripture.

(2) *The Nature of the Church*

Should it be a 'gathered' church or a universal society? Whenever an exclusive answer in the former sense is given, the result is a sect: witness some of the more recent American importations on British soil, or the 'Particular Baptists'. The major denominations differ in emphasis, and each tends to contain varieties of emphasis among its own members and traditions; on the whole, Congregationalists, Baptists and Presbyterians incline to the former view, Methodists and Anglicans to the latter. But the point is that so deep-reaching a problem, which has perplexed and divided the church since the early centuries, can only be grappled with by a theology which takes in the Biblical witness *as a whole*; and this is an entity the interpretation of which is impossible without recourse to Tradition and even Experience. No swift and certain answer lies to hand.

(3) *Women in the Ministry*

This question has only latterly grown acute in our field. There are already women in the Free Church ministries—although in very limited number. Anglicanism sets its official face sternly against the practice. Methodism, as usual, lies betwixt and between; but the feeling in favour of the practice has grown steadily since the War. The 1948 Methodist Conference turned it down by a majority vote; the 1966 Conference would have accepted it but for the certain knowledge that it would thereby torpedo the Anglican-Methodist negotiations. Tradition—not only Catholic—is against it; and so until the present generation was Methodist sentiment and habit. But the sociological revolution has forced reconsideration of the whole question, and inevitably the alleged Scriptural warrant for the exclusion of women from the ministry has been more and more searchingly scrutinized, with a scepticism which has been richly fed by Scriptural 'vindications' of the Anglican position from men like Dr Mascall and the late N. P. Williams. There is a growing party even in Anglicanism that looks to Methodist reinforcement for removal of the ban. They would maintain that this is a case where tradition has blinded us to the real guidance of Scripture, which we are on our way to discovering. The conservative view would hold that Tradition and Scripture are here at one. The debate continues.

(4) *Episcopacy*

This is the gravest and most long-standing problem of all, and agreement between the denominations is hardly even in prospect. Scripture and Tradition here stand at the very centre of the whole issue, and there is no unanimity either as to how their witness should be related or as to what their witness is.

I think however that one may point to two developments in the current discussion, at least as between Anglican and Free Church in this country:

(*a*) The traditional Anglican appeal to both Scripture and Tradition is here being modified. The old confidence in the plain witness of the New Testament to the threefold ministry and the grounding of the Historic Episcopate in the Apostolic Succession has given place to a search, by the methods of modern biblical theology, for the true foundations of *episcopē* and priesthood in the biblical revelation as a whole. Likewise the old naïve confidence in the unbroken succession of the Historic Episcopate from the Apostles to the corporate episcopate of the church today—any awkward gaps being made good by 'faith'—has given way, before both historical and theological criticism, to a search for the real values that the Historic Episcopate enshrines and a demonstration of their necessary place in the Coming Great Church of the future.

(*b*) The ecumenical encounter of the Free Churches with Anglicanism has forced the former to look with a more searching and theological eye at their own systems of polity, and to seek—not by compromise but by digging more deeply—for a possible common foundation. A Presbyterian will try (not always successfully) to persuade an Anglican that government by presbytery is government by his own treasured *episcopē*—'in commission'. A Methodist will seek to commend the 'diffused' *episcopē* of his own church system. And many of the old harsh but superficial differences are seen to be based on Tradition at its most non-Scriptural—on those non-theological factors which history has planted like an alien yoke on the necks of present-day Christians.

III

On the modern British scene conversations are in varying progress between the following denominations:

(1) *(English) Presbyterians and Congregationalists*

There is perhaps least of all division in principle between these two bodies, between which there is already a so-called 'Covenant' relationship which encourages, for example, interchange of ministers. The problem of Scripture and Tradition hardly arises.

(2) *The Church of Scotland and the Church of England*

These conversations were initiated in 1932, and in 1934 a Report set out the large degree of doctrinal unity between the two, and suggested things that might be undertaken in common. In 1951 a further Report called for a long-term policy of re-integration by modification of the two Church systems, and in 1957 a further Report appeared with its famous (or notorious) suggestion of the new category of 'Bishop-in-presbytery' as the key to the problem. This suggestion was rejected, amid an astonishing outburst of popular indignation in Scotland, by the General Assembly of the Kirk in 1959, as 'clearly unacceptable in that (it) implies a denial of the Catholicity of the Church of Scotland and of the validity and regularity of its Ministry within the Church Catholic'. The intention of the Church to continue to seek closer relations with the Church of England was, however, reaffirmed, in view of the underlying doctrinal agreement; and on this basis further conversations began in 1960, charged to look at certain central issues, the common exploration of which might ease the pathway to future unity. These were the meaning of unity itself, as contrasted with uniformity; validity; the Apostolic Succession; the doctrine of Holy Communion. To these were added, in 1963, the Church as a Royal Priesthood and the place of the Laity in the Church.

Specific proposals for reunion have not been aimed at in the 1966 Report which has just been published; indeed, further areas for future exploration, such as Intercommunion as a possible preliminary step towards reunion, have been uncovered as the talks proceeded. Each issue has been set out in a careful study that seeks to be loyal to the supremacy of Scripture as the rule and ultimate standard of faith, to the Apostles' Creed as the Baptismal Symbol and the Nicene Creed as the sufficient statement of the Christian faith (expressions taken from the Lambeth Quadrilateral of 1888 and acceptable to both parties), and also constantly mindful of the deep and genuine historical divergence between the two Churches— divergences which we may put down to 'Tradition', but concerning which each Church claims Scriptural authority. We are however reminded that 'differences in our understanding of the authority of Scripture in particular, and to a lesser extent of the Creeds, are to be found within as much as between the . . . Churches'. Tradition, and even Experience, might well be added to the word 'Creeds' at this point.

(3) *Anglicans and Methodists*

Finally, the Anglicans and Methodists. In 1946 Archbishop Fisher preached a sermon at Cambridge in which he invited the Free Churches to consider 'taking episcopacy into their system' as a means to make possible Intercommunion with the Church of England. This led to conversations between the Churches and a Report (1950) which invited the individual Free Churches to consider definite negotiations with the Church of England. To this invitation only the Methodist Church responded. This was perhaps natural, because (as we have seen) the origin of Methodism—the rebellious child of the Church of England—was quite different from that of the other Free Churches, which had arisen at least two centuries before and more or less alongside it. The Anglican/Methodist negotiations thus began, and issued in a theological Interim Statement (1958) and the 1963 Report, which set out a procedure for reunion in two stages: stage I to commence with 'Services of Reconciliation' at the main centres throughout the country with mutual 'reception' of priests and ministers, which would inaugurate an unspecified period of 'growing together', culminating in stage II—reunion. Four of the twelve Methodist representatives signed a minority dissentient report; the Anglicans were unanimously in favour. The Methodist Conference and the Anglican Convocations of 1965 accepted these proposals as marking in general the way forward, with reservations (especially on the Methodist side) which necessitated a further consideration of the specific recommendations by revised panels for a period of three years. 1968 will see the die finally cast.

Now the 1963 Report begins with a theological assessment of Scripture and Tradition; and it is of crucial interest—not, indeed, as an academic exercise in abstract theology. The panel was not working in a vacuum, nor was it commissioned (in this matter at least) to think ahead of or even to systematize the standpoints of the two Churches. This was especially true of Tradition, where there is little in the title-deeds of Anglicanism and nothing in those of Methodism to give a lead. Nor must one forget the extreme difficulty of drawing up these 'agreed statements' between different communions. It is perhaps, however, permissible to suggest that here, even more than elsewhere in the Report, is evidence of dual (or multiple) authorship; the connection of thought is not always easy to follow through, and the parts seem more satisfying than the whole.

The chapter begins with an emphatic assertion of the supremacy of Scripture.

The Holy Scriptures . . . constitute the supreme rule of faith: [this is] . . . common ground between our two Churches. . . . The Bible is unique because that to which it bears witness is unique . . ., the divine revelation in Jesus Christ . . . The Church has not made up its Gospel from its own experience, but . . . received it from witnesses, and the Holy Spirit assures us that their witness is true. . . . From, in and out of, this testimony the Church continues to live, for its faith in the eternal God is evoked by response to the divine acts of redemption once accomplished in history. That sacred history . . . constitutes the terms of reference for the whole life and action of the Church until the end of time.

Two points are added which help to define or qualify the sense in which the supremacy of Scripture is to be understood. First: a distinction is drawn (on the lines of the XXXIX Articles) between (a) things necessary to eternal salvation, and (b) things 'expedient or even needful for the proper conduct of life and the ordering of the Church'. Scripture contains the whole of (a) but *not* the whole of (b), and it is in the non-Scriptural segment of (b) that 'reason', 'custom', 'Christian liberty', 'human authority' have their freedom to determine;

and this freedom appertains to the Church, not the individual, with the provisos that nothing is done which is 'repugnant' to Holy Scripture, and that the whole is subject to the lordship of Christ. It was just this non-Scriptural segment that the radical Reformers, the Anabaptists and some of the Puritans refused to recognize. They affirmed that the Church may only do what is explicitly commanded in Scripture.

Second: there is due note of the 'inevitable field of debate' about the varying levels of authority within Scripture itself—e.g. the relevance of the Mosaic Law, the extent to which Scripture contains a blue-print for Church order. There is room for differing estimates of the light which history, tradition and learning may throw on the meaning of God's Word.

So far, so good; it would probably be agreed not only that the intention of the Report to safeguard the supreme norm of Holy Scripture is fully achieved, but that the implicit repudiation of extreme fundamentalism, and the vindication of the historic stand of Hooker against the extreme Reformers in the matter of things not commanded in but not repugnant to Holy Scripture, receive a true and timely emphasis. Certainly there is here a faithful reflection of the mind of the Churches; nor is it easy to believe that even the wildest Anabaptist ever *really* confined his whole practice in living and in Churchmanship to what he found in black and white in the Bible. It is perhaps a minor cavil that the Christian liberty to determine is confined to the Church and refused to the individual in a way that seems to leave no room for an *Athanasius contra mundum* or even for a Luther or a Calvin—although the Report goes on to repudiate the antithesis between Church and individual conscience, affirming that they are parts of one whole. Yet the expression 'the Church *and not* the individual' seems antithetical enough. It is surprising that the point is missed by the Dissentients.

The Report proceeds to deal with Tradition, which is declared to be inevitable from the fact that we live later in history than the salvation-events of the Bible, and defined as the 'handing down of the faith from generation to another'. It is then subdivided into (*a*) the apostolic testimony of Scripture, to be handed down *untouched*, and (*b*) all later teaching, custom, institution; (*a*) should in every case be the 'norm' of (*b*). When the Reformers attacked Tradition, their real target was (*b*) when it was cut loose from or repugnant to (*a*); for they could appeal confidently to the 'great creeds and doctrine of the Church'.

Now we are coming to see, the Report continues, that Scripture and Tradition ought not to be put over against one another (presumably by 'now' the Report means in contrast to, or at least in development from, the Reformers). Both are gifts and instruments of the Holy Spirit within the Church. Tradition was defined at the Edinburgh Conference of 1937 as 'the living stream of the Church's life'; in so far as it consists of human life hallowed by God and of divine gifts to the Church it is indeed a 'holy tradition'. Yet in this wide sense (of the continuing flow of Christian existence from one generation to another) tradition by itself exercises no authority, and cannot diagnose, cure or prevent virus or poison in the bloodstream of the Church's life.

At this point the connection of thought becomes a little clouded; the Report assures us that no simple answer can be given to this problem of the 'poison in the bloodstream', and proceeds to give instead a most valuable list of the elements of Tradition, *headed by Scripture itself*. The elements are: Holy Scripture; primitive Christianity with the great Creeds and Councils; the continuous theological conversation of the Church; liturgies, hymns and writings; and the rise of historical criticism and the historical sense in European thought. It would be hard to find as full and true an analysis of Tradition as this in any Church declaration. Far too often 'Tradition' is used, even by reputable theologians, as an understood entity which on analysis turns out to mean different things for different men or for the same man at different times. But the list of elements in the Report has a more positive value, specifically in its first and last items. The pinpointing of historical criticism and the rediscovery of the historical sense in European thought as a valid element in 'Tradition' is both new and courageous; still more the recognition that the Bible stands at the head of the list of elements *within Tradition itself*. This, combined with the emphatic insistence earlier in the chapter that the Bible also stands *over against Tradition*, suggests an awareness of the real problem which the Churches are facing; and the further hint that there is a distinction between the Word of Scripture and the once-

for-all revelation of God in Christ suggests another fundamental presupposition of its solution.

The difficulty one feels over the connection of thought here
is whether the problem of the 'poison in the bloodstream' has
been shelved, or whether the analysis of Tradition is meant as
at least a partial solution. Scripture (within this analysis) is
described as a 'saving salt' in Church thought and worship; the
faith and practice of the early centuries gives 'guidance to the
Church in its fight against error'; though church order (treated
apparently as a subdivision of the appeal to primitive Christianity) is not a complete safeguard against error and heresy, the
exercise of the authority of the Church is an important element
in Tradition; 'another important element in the safeguarding of
the Church' is its continuous theological conversation; 'of
weight also' are liturgies, etc.

Now it would be quite unfair to expect the Report to answer
questions which may not have been its concern; but one would
have welcomed a recognition that the 'poison in the bloodstream' is also part of 'Tradition', not so much a sixth element
as an infection of all the five, including Holy Scripture. The
Report allows that, while often Tradition is good and holy,
sometimes also it is that which gives us problems (p. 19—'our
problems about Tradition'); but *problems* of course have arisen
from the good, even the divine elements in Tradition. Another
point where clarification is needed is the relation of the authority
of Scripture to that of Tradition *when Scripture is recognized as part
of Tradition itself.* Over against Tradition, Scripture is the 'norm';
within it, it is the 'saving salt'. Is the difference of metaphor
deliberate, and if so what is its significance?

The one terse paragraph in which the Dissentient Methodists
set out their reaction to these pages is a severe disappointment.
One wonders, indeed, whether they had even read them. They
complain that there is no adequate recognition of the pre-
eminent and normative place of Scripture; yet language could
not be plainer than the emphatic assertion of this very point.
They claim that Tradition, while inevitable, contains both good
and evil—something that the Signatories imply throughout,
without expressly stating. 'It is true' (the Dissentients proceed)
'that Scripture interprets (and not infrequently condemns)
tradition rather than that tradition interprets Scripture'. Yet

the Dissentients would presumably accept the Apostles' and Nicene Creeds and interpret Scripture by them; and what are Creeds but crystallized Tradition? 'In a word, tradition represents the worldliness of the Church, scripture points to its supernatural origin and basis.' The Dissentients thus triumphantly conclude with an implied denial of the work of the Holy Spirit in the whole 1900 years of Christian history. The whole problem of Scripture and Tradition, so subtle and intractable as we have found it, is by-passed; the Signatories at least recognize it and offer valuable steps towards its solution.

IV

What, then, is the true relation of Scripture and Tradition? They are both functions of the living Word of God in Christ, and their authority is at every point derivative from and dependent on Him. The authority of Christ is divine, perfect and absolute; theirs is weakened by human ignorance and sin. Yet the authority of Scripture is higher than that of Tradition not only in degree but in kind, because it witnesses to a unique and seminal intervention of God in human affairs, culminating in the Incarnation of Jesus Christ, while Tradition is the re-enactment of that once-for-all revelation throughout the ages. Tradition, like Scripture, is vitiated by the limitations and self-seeking of humanity, while the same Holy Spirit is at work in both. Yet the pre-eminence remains with Scripture, of which Tradition unfolds the unexhausted significance and which it seeks to bring to life for each new generation.

We may illuminate this relationship by the analogy of a great work of music—let us say the Seventh Symphony of Beethoven. The real, the ultimate Seventh Symphony was the musical 'vision' or 'revelation' in the mind of the composer; the musical score is our abiding witness to it, and the integrity of this witness is not impaired by the 'traditions'—of Haydn and Mozart, of dawning romanticism—which can be traced in its texture. Every subsequent performance is an attempt, through the medium of the printed score, to capture again Beethoven's primal 'vision' by the performers for the audience. Both composer and performers were and are 'inspired'; the latter are seeking to bring to life the original 'revelation', and when they are successful a fresh word is spoken to the living audience—fresh, though an unfolding of the significance of the original, which it does not seek to replace. Incompetence or self-regard in the performers can and does vitiate every performance; the whole musical spirit of the age can obscure or destroy the authentic message of the composer. Yet the score remains as the permanent source and corrective of musical tradition. And finally, even Beethoven was not exempt from human limitations; as R. G. Collingwood used to say, his music sometimes mutters and screams instead of *speaking*. No musical score is at all points a perfect witness to its 'vision'. Yet this does not nullify his claim to supremacy over his interpreters.

Vision: score: performers—Revelation: Scripture: Tradition. My analogy is not designed to show more than the possibility of a relationship between three terms, the two latter being functions of the first, and each of the two a blend of the higher— the inspired, the divine—and of the lower—the defective, the human; yet they stand in such a relationship that the second, while under the absolute authority of the first, can nevertheless exercise a relative authority—even a supremacy—over the third. The absolute authority remains with Jesus Christ, the living Word of God. Scripture, His immediate witness, is 'fallible'—it varies in its levels of 'inspiration', it has its dry and barren tracts, it is but an earthen vessel; yet none of these things nullifies its claim to supremacy over the Church of the ages. From Scripture alone the Word can speak anew; and to the divine truths that may break forth in the living, re-creating Tradition of the life of the Church in every generation there can be neither measure nor end.

IX

Present-day Frontiers
in the Discussion about Tradition

ELLEN FLESSEMAN-VAN LEER

I. INTRODUCTION

For a long time it seemed as if in the controversy about scripture and tradition discussion between the Roman Catholic Church and the Protestant churches had come to a deadlock. Both sides had their fixed positions, which were summarized in the respective catch-words 'scripture and traditions' and '*sola scriptura*': the one pointed to two sources in which, with assistance of the Holy Spirit, revelation had been preserved in the Church, the other could see in traditions nothing but human customs and regulations, which were sometimes venerable, but too often unimportant or even detrimental to true faith. The same stock arguments were used by both parties. The Roman Catholics pointed out that there had been a time when the New Testament was not yet written and the Church lived only by oral tradition; that it was the Church which by her tradition fixed the canon of scripture; and that scripture in itself is ambiguous and has to be interpreted by the Church. Against these arguments the Protestants maintained that the Church stands under the Word of God and has no authority over scripture; that the canon was fixed for the sake of safeguarding revelation against all possible distortions and increments of traditions; and that scripture as a whole is perspicuous and sufficient.

In the last couple of years a shift and development in these entrenched positions has taken place. Without attempting to analyse the factors which have caused the change, a few may be mentioned. (1) Studies in the history of the early Church have shown that the original concept of tradition was neither identical with the one which was common in the later Catholic Church nor with the one the Protestants rejected. (2) The renewed interest in biblical scholarship both among Protestants and Catholics directed attention to the importance of scripture and the difficulties attached to its exegesis. (3) The closer contact of the churches in the ecumenical movement has brought about a change in their attitude so that they stand against each other no longer in a primarily apologetic and polemical way. So, through these various causes working together, the problem is approached in a new way: Protestant theologians have come to see that it is a much too superficial view of tradition to equate it with human customs; that scripture itself contains various strands of tradition and that it does not function in the void; and that therefore *sola scriptura*, understood in the traditional way, is an over-simplification. Among Catholics, on the other hand, the importance of scripture is now being stressed, not in such a way as to minimize the rôle tradition plays, but so as to put a question-mark against the idea of the so-called two sources of revelation. Here discussion has centred around the interpretation of the well-known decree of Trent,[1] which said that the truth and discipline of the Gospel is contained 'in libris scriptis et sine scripto traditionibus'. In the textbooks this clause was commonly explained as pointing to scripture and apostolic traditions as two materially complementary sources. However, in 1952 Bakhuizen van den Brink drew attention to the fact that, while the previous draft of this Tridentine decree read that revelation was contained partly in scripture and partly in the traditions, this *partim . . . partim* of the original text was changed to a simple and much more ambiguous *et* in the final edition. This observation has been taken up first by Geiselmann and then by many others as an argument that Trent did not want to teach the material insufficiency of scripture.[2] Today Roman Catholic theologians like Rahner, Küng, Congar, etc., emphasize the normative importance of scripture in words which are hardly distinguishable from Protestant utterances.[3]

To what extent can we speak of a real rapprochement of the two positions? To answer this question the dogmatic constitution *De divina revelatione* of the second Vatican Council, promulgated on 18 November 1965, and the report of the second section of the Fourth World Conference on Faith and Order, Montreal 1963, entitled *Scripture, Tradition and traditions*, will be compared. Both statements deal with identical or similar

problems; both are official statements and can therefore be considered as giving a general overall picture of the respective
positions. One cannot expect bold and new theological insights in documents of this kind, but exactly for that reason
they are a gauge for present-day thinking. There are, however,
certain factors, limiting the importance and partly even the
possibility of this comparison, which should be kept in mind:

(1) Any statement which is drawn up by a commission for
approval by a large body will show traces of a certain give and
take, of theological compromise and even occasionally of in-
tentional ambiguities.

(2) The constitution is a dogmatic declaration of one church;
whatever internal tensions there may have been at the Vatican
Council, there was a large body of doctrinal consensus underlying all differences. The Montreal report, on the other hand,
cannot be considered as expressing the Protestant, let alone the
Reformation point of view; it is the outcome of a confrontation
of many very different churches and mirrors the tension between them. If, for instance, the report had been drawn up
without the Eastern Orthodox Churches, it would have been
less ambiguous on certain points. Even so, to a certain degree
Protestant thinking can be read from the report; for though
every attempt was made at Montreal to represent a fair mirror
of the heterogeneous thinking that went on, the entire framework of the report is alien to Orthodoxy and peculiar to Protestantism. The very title of the report proves this.

(3) The constitution and the report are widely different in
scope. Though the Vatican Council did not promulgate any
new formal doctrines, its pronouncements have binding
authority and will mark theological thinking in the Roman
Catholic Church for a long time to come. A statement of the
World Council, on the other hand, does not bind any church
and has only so much authority as the churches are willing to
afford it in view of its inherent quality; moreover, it can be
superseded any time at a subsequent conference by another
statement. It is significant that the Council worked for three
years on its constitution and that the Montreal report was
drawn up in less than a fortnight.

(4) Both statements should primarily be read and judged in
view of their own theological background. The fact that the

theological situation to which the Montreal Conference and the Vatican Council spoke was here and there widely different, makes a comparison of their documents often difficult and on some points even impossible.

II. TRADITION

Agreement

The following points of agreement between the two statements can be listed:

(1) Both attach great theological weight to the concept of Tradition. That the constitution would do that is not surprising, but the unequivocal admission of the Montreal report, that Tradition is an essential theological concept,[4] can be considered to be its most important single aspect. There is also agreement in the way both statements argue the necessity of this concept: that divine revelation happened at a particular time and place and has to be transmitted through all ages and to all places.[5] Whereas in the first half of this century the main stress— certainly in continental Protestantism—was placed on the vertical line from God to man, in our time the horizontal line receives greater attention in accordance with the general interest in the historical dimension of human existence.

(2) In both documents Tradition is closely bound to revelation. Actually, it is revelation in its course through history. To understand what is meant by Tradition the conception of revelation is therefore of paramount importance. On this point there is agreement too: neither side considers revelation a manifestation or communication of certain conceptual truths or doctrines, but divine self-revelation. In Montreal this was the generally accepted and presupposed view, and it is therefore only in passing expressed in the report.[6] In the Roman Catholic Church, however, this insight was not at all common; on this point the final text of the constitution marks a real break-through in theological thinking. The first schema which was laid before the Council, *De fontibus revelationis*, assumed as a matter of course an intellectualistic and conceptualistic under-standing of revelation. Objections were raised and it was deemed necessary to deal explicitly with the concept of revelation. And the Council was not satisfied to relegate it to the *Prooemium*,

as was done in the second schema, but in the final text the entire first chapter of the constitution is given to it. This more personalistic understanding of revelation[7] implies that, besides the words of God, also his acts are stressed as revelatory;[8] another consequence is a strong christocentric emphasis, in which, as several Council Fathers had said, Christ is not primarily an argument to believe, but rather He himself, in his sayings and his life, his cross and his resurrection, is the content of revelation.

As the introduction of the concept of Tradition is in the Montreal report, so this new orientation regarding revelation is probably the most outstanding feature of the Vatican constitution, which, if really thought through, must have far-reaching consequences for the whole of Roman Catholic theology. In the constitution it has not yet consistently been kept in mind.

(3) Because revelation is essentially one, Tradition, being this revelation as it is transmitted, is one too. Both documents use the word Tradition in its fundamental sense only in the singular. On this point the constitution marks a real advance beyond Trent. Then it was an important step forward that a distinction was drawn between apostolic and ecclesiastical traditions, only the former being on the same level with scripture. Now in the Vatican constitution the plural is superseded by the singular, so that the request made at Trent—and providentially never complied with—to list the apostolic traditions, has now become meaningless.

(4) Real Tradition is transmitted only by the Holy Spirit. It cannot be otherwise; for if Tradition is the gospel as handed on and brought alive, or, in the words of the Montreal report, 'Christ himself present in the life of the Church' (39), it is ultimately not in man's power that this comes to pass. Thus both statements point equally to the guidance of the Spirit, though it must be conceded that, emphatically as this is done, it sounds somewhat traditional and flat.[9]

(5) The report is just as explicit as the constitution in asserting the close and indissoluble tie between Tradition and the Church as the place where the gospel is transmitted. Both also affirm that this transmission is done not merely by means of words, but equally by sacraments, liturgy and action. In other words: the

Church in her whole life, in all that she does, can testify to the gospel, i.e. transmit the Tradition.[10] In this perspective the rather ambiguous words of the constitution should be understood: 'Ecclesia . . . transmittit omne quod ipsa est, omne quod credit' (8). These words, which from the Protestant side have been severely criticized as proving that nothing really has changed in Roman Catholicism, are not particularly fortunate, but can be accepted in what I hold their intention to be: that the Church in her whole being as Church transmits Tradition.[11]

(6) Both documents point to the importance of the apostles: Tradition is 'traditio ab apostolis' (8). The idea of apostolicity is correlated to the insight that revelation is closed and that no new revelation is to be expected before the final consummation. Tradition goes back to the apostles because only by way of them has the once-for-all Christ been made known to later times. In this way the historicity of revelation and the material identity of Tradition is safeguarded against the enthusiasm of direct, personal revelation.

(7) Being anchored in the past by its apostolicity, Tradition has also a forward looking, dynamic aspect.[12] For it has always again to be actualized anew, or rather, it is the always anew actualized apostolic kerygma. The third chapter of the Montreal report, entitled 'The Christian Tradition and cultural diversity', deals with the question how Tradition can be translated into new languages and cultures; the dynamic aspect is developed in view of the actual situation in a non-theoretical way. The Vatican constitution, in speaking of the growth of Tradition, deals with the thought of development in a more formal way.[13] To judge its importance it should be seen in the light of the discussion which goes on, where theologians like Rahner and Küng maintain the temporal conditioning of the formulations of all church statements and doctrines, and others repudiate this notion as a reviving of modernism. The constitution, understandably, does not take sides in this controversy, but it certainly does no longer hold to the static view of Tradition.

Agreeing in this forward-looking element whereby the Church grows to the fullness of divine truth,[14] the two statements show a real difference on this point, which is the result of a still more fundamental difference in ecclesiology (see below,

p. 167). Whereas the constitution knows only about growth and a richer unfolding of Tradition, the report recognizes that there is also the possibility of its deterioration and even its distortion (48).

(8) Tradition precedes scripture. For most theologians this is just a historical statement of fact which has certain theological implications; it is, however, not yet superfluous to point it out in view of some Protestant groupings. Therefore the Montreal report emphasizes it by drawing attention to the fact that it changes the traditional order and speaks of Tradition and scripture instead of *vice versa*; the same change of order is also found in the constitution.

Disagreement

The concept of Tradition will receive its real distinctness only when it is correlated with that of scripture; the conclusion we can draw at this point can only be a preliminary one.

There is, as shown above, in the World Council and in the Roman Catholic Church considerable agreement which should not be minimized. But their respective statements show also a real difference in their understanding of Tradition, mainly due to a different ecclesiology.

According to the constitution, the Church which is the bearer of Tradition, whose very life *is* the living Tradition, is the Roman Catholic Church as a whole, all the faithful together.[15] This Church culminates in, gets its real concreteness in, the magisterium. Just so with Tradition. As expressed in the life of the whole Church it is still something diffuse, non-juridical and not well defined; by tying it to the magisterium it becomes a manageable reality. The assertion of the constitution that only the magisterium can authentically interpret the Tradition[16] implies that, in the final resort, the Tradition is identical with the teaching of this magisterium. The close tie of Tradition and magisterium also makes understandable the optimistic view, that there is only growth and development of Tradition and no deterioration. The Holy Spirit is here the necessary link, for he guarantees that the magisterium cannot go astray in its official teaching; through his guidance the magisterium will teach nothing but the real, true, living Tradition.[17]

The Montreal report has repeatedly been criticized for

having no expressed ecclesiology. The observation is correct, but as criticism it is unfair. The report being drawn up by the representatives of a great many different churches, it is in the nature of the matter that a unanimous pronouncement on ecclesiology was impossible, this being the very point on which the churches are divided. But in one respect at least there is ecclesiological agreement: that the interpretation of Tradition is not exclusively entrusted to a magisterium; thereby the Tradition is not a determinable, empirical entity which can be pointed to. In the report Tradition is not something which is 'available',[18] but it is the ultimate criterion by which all church-realities are judged. And besides this concept of the ultimate, only and undivided Tradition, that of traditions is introduced. Thereby are meant not the human traditions which were so violently rejected by the Reformation, nor the apostolic traditions about which Trent spoke, but they are understood as 'the expressions and manifestations in diverse historical forms of the one truth and reality which is Christ' (47). The real problem with which Montreal wrestled was not so much that of Tradition *per se*, but that we know this Tradition only in its embodiment in various, partly contradictory, traditions; and that each tradition might be a manifestation of the genuine Tradition, but that it might also to a greater or lesser degree be an impoverishment or distortion. Thus the necessity arises to judge these traditions upon their real Tradition-content.

Here the non-Orthodox framework of the report which already has been pointed out (see p. 156) becomes manifest. In Orthodoxy there is no need to search for the Tradition, for the life of the one (Orthodox) Church *is* holy Tradition, perhaps not yet manifested in its fullness but certainly without distortion. To speak of various, partly incompatible traditions as all more or less valid expressions of the one Tradition sounds actually sacrilegious.[19] By questioning and implicitly denying the identity of the Tradition with any of the existing traditions, the whole trend of the Montreal report is typically 'Protestant'. In setting up the Tradition over against all traditions as its critical norm, the report may make this norm so indistinct as to be of no applicable use.[20]

III. SCRIPTURE

In this paper our concern is primarily with the concept of Tradition; the view of scripture of the Montreal report and the constitution will be compared in less detail, and only in so far as it is relevant to the main subject.

Agreement

(1) Holy scripture is the written-down testimony of revelation. According to both documents it is a way in which the original apostolic message has been preserved in order that it may be transmitted to later generations. That is to say, scripture is the embodiment in writing of the Tradition. The Montreal report calls the Bible explicitly 'the Tradition in its written form' (50) and though the constitution does not employ the term Tradition for it, it expresses the same thought in other words (7).

(2) Neither Montreal nor the Vatican Council answered explicitly the question whether the entire apostolic preaching is transmitted in scripture, though neither precludes the possibility. In Montreal the question was not really considered, but its report certainly suggests, without saying it in so many words, that it should be answered in the affirmative. The constitution, on the other side, is intentionally silent about the *sufficientia materialis* of scripture, because on this point there was a very real cleavage among the Council Fathers; the conclusion of the debate was that it is a theologically still open question in which the constitution should take no sides. I am, however, of the opinion that actually the question is already decided by the way in which in Caput I revelation is viewed. That new orientation, if followed through, would make it impossible to speak of Tradition any longer in quantitative terms. Thereby the problem itself has become obsolete.[21]

(3) Both documents stress the particular importance of scripture which expresses divine revelation in a special way. Particularly the constitution is very outspoken in this respect, undoubtedly because scripture has up till now not functioned very well in the Roman Catholic Church. Caput VI: 'De sacra scriptura in vita ecclesiae',[22] which is the most pastoral and probably best written part of the constitution, leaves no doubt

of the high value which is attributed to it. So it is for instance said that by scripture the Christian religion 'nutriatur et regatur oportet' (21).[23]

For Protestantism the absolute primacy of scripture is the foundation-stone of its faith. However, the thought is not clearly expressed in the Montreal report, probably because of the Orthodox churches, where scripture is only one, be it an important, moment in the total life of the Church. Nevertheless, by suggesting that the criterion by which to judge the traditions may be found in scripture, the report certainly implies its priority.

(4) The necessity of scripture to be interpreted has been a main argument of Roman Catholicism against the *sola scriptura* doctrine of Protestantism. But this polemical 'either-or' should be a thing of the past. The Montreal report asserts that 'a mere reiteration of the words of Holy Scripture would be a betrayal of the Gospel' (50), and the report, if analysed, boils down to the question what the right interpretation of scripture is. Both documents agree that this interpretation takes place in and by the Church, but here again their ecclesiological differences play a rôle. In its search for a hermeneutical principle by which the Church can rightly interpret, the report states the problem but does not succeed in finding a solution. In the constitution there is none of this uncertainty: the magisterium has the power and the task of authentic, authoritative interpretation.[24]

(5) It was under the guidance of the Spirit that scripture was written, just as it can only be understood by his assistance. Because the Vatican Council wished to stress the importance of the Bible, the constitution repeats time after time that it was written by inspiration, a thought which is only in passing mentioned in the Montreal report (42). It is also typical for the more searching and critical attitude of Montreal, that whereas the constitution states that the Spirit guides the Church and particularly the magisterium in its interpretation, the report adds that appeal to the Spirit does not solve the hermeneutical problem (52).

Disagreement

In general it is held that in regard to the formal doctrine of scripture there is no real difference between Roman Catholicism and Protestantism, that they only part company when the question of interpreting it is raised. Comparing these two documents, I am not sure that the view is correct; there seems to be a subtle though significant divergence. The constitution has basically a fundamentalistic view; it does not really express it in so many words, but to that conclusion one must come when inspiration of scripture in all its parts is maintained so massively as it is done here; also, when it is said that the holy writers wrote nothing but what God wanted. And while one can speak of scripture as *verbum Dei* (*scriptum*), to say that the *Dei verba* are expressed in human tongues (13) gives a wrong connotation.[25]

The Montreal report is not explicit either; the question of fundamentalism seems not to be intentionally avoided, but is not raised. It is remarkable how reserved the report is in speaking of 'inspiration', and in using the rather ambiguous term 'Word of God' in a theologically significant way. The central pronouncement that 'we live as Christians by the *paradosis* of the *kerygma* testified in Scripture' (45) precludes by implication a simple and immediate identification of the Bible and revelation. The report certainly tends towards a non-fundamentalistic view.

IV. TRADITION AND SCRIPTURE

Besides points of agreement those of disagreement have also been found. When, however, the attempt is made to give Tradition its final clarity and precision by setting it alongside scripture, the report and the constitution can no longer be compared. In ultimate resort they are too different.

In the Montreal report Tradition is a fundamental reality beyond scripture and traditions. That is to say that Tradition has the absolute prerogative, in such a way that it is not an entity comparable to scripture; consequently, the report does not place them side by side, except when stating the problem. The real question in the report is not the relation of Tradition and scripture, but rather of scripture and traditions, both embodiments and manifestations of Tradition. The report implies, without stating it explicitly, that of the two, scripture has unquestionably the supremacy, because it is the primary vehicle in which the Tradition is preserved. That is not to say that it *is* Tradition; rather, Tradition is the kerygma in scripture, to be found by right exegesis—and so the quest for Tradition becomes the quest for a right hermeneutical principle.

If this is kept in mind, the intricate relation of scripture and traditions can be defined in the following way:

(1) the traditions stand under the norm of, are judged by, Tradition, i.e. scripture, rightly interpreted;

(2) traditions are embodiments and manifestations of Tradition, i.e. they are the outcome of interpretations of scripture;[26]

(3) the interpretation of scripture is inevitably conditioned by Tradition; the report speaks of 'loyalty to our confessional understanding of Holy Scripture' (54).

Stated in the terse way as done here the tension between these points is more manifest than it is in the report; however, if the report is analysed, the conclusion must actually be that this final, unsolved tension lies at the bottom of it.

The Vatican constitution does not give ultimate clarification either, in that it fails to be fully consistent. At first glance Tradition seems to be an all-inclusive concept, more or less identical with the one of the Montreal report: the revelation as it is transmitted. When, however, all instances where the term Tradition is used are listed and analysed, it appears that a great number of them make that understanding impossible; in many places Tradition is used exclusively for oral Tradition alongside scripture. Actually, the word Tradition nowhere unequivocally denotes the ultimate reality beyond scripture; to designate that the term *praedicatio apostolica* is employed. This could seem a merely terminological observation, but in reality it points to the fundamental ambiguity of the constitution; on the one side Tradition seems to be conceived in a quite new way, whereas on the other side the 'traditional' tradition-concept of Trent still plays its rôle. In the main line of the constitution Tradition and scripture are two parallel streams which both transmit the apostolic kerygma; again and again both are mentioned side by side. In an attempt to answer the question of their relation and respective authority the following observations can be made:

(1) Both in their own way are without error.

(2) The last chapter of the constitution seems to suggest the pre-eminence of scripture. When one compares the schemata it

appears that repeatedly, on request of Council members, additions in the text were made emphasizing Tradition; it was feared—as the '*relationes*' testify—that the value attached to scripture was so stressed that it would detract from Tradition.

(3) But it could also be maintained that both streams of Tradition and scripture, flowing out of one source, are so much intertwined that the question which has the primacy is meaningless; the one cannot exist without the other.[27] The term 'mutual inherence' coined by G. H. Tavard[28] seems applicable here. And indeed, whatever importance scripture has it is never without Tradition, for only Tradition makes these writings recognizable as scripture, and again, Tradition interprets it and actualizes it always anew.[29] In this perspective the remark seems to be unexceptionable that the Church draws her certainty about revelation 'non per solam Sacram Scripturam' (9), though the actual wording is not particularly fortunate and sounds unnecessarily polemical.

Considering the above it seems at first glance strange that the dependence of Tradition on scripture is, on the other hand, not expressed. There is a curious silence in this respect; scripture apparently needs Tradition in order to function, but Tradition seems to be an independent stream.[30] It may be objected that this cannot really have been the intention of the Council, that it is at its utmost an oversight. This interpretation, however, cannot be maintained. At this point the refusal to state whether Tradition contains certain truths which are not in scripture takes its revenge. As long as that possibility has to be kept open, the Tridentine concept of Tradition and its quantitative thinking is not really overcome; no more is it possible to bind Tradition in a strict way to scripture, let alone allow it to stand under its judgment. Consequently, the assertion that the ultimate source of faith is the Word of God, deposited in the togetherness of Tradition and scripture (10), does not sound convincing; for ultimately scripture is dispensable.

V. CONCLUSION

The continuing difference in the concept of Tradition can perhaps best be grasped if seen from the standpoint of the ultimate norm in the Church. In the Montreal report the final authority is the Tradition, a reality which we do not possess, which is not available, and which judges all empirical realities: traditions, scripture, churches. The Vatican constitution seems in no way in need of such critical norm, not because Tradition and scripture are its empirical, inerrant authorities—for both have to be interpreted—but because of the living magisterium. It is perhaps unjust to maintain that in this way the magisterium in its interpretative function is the ultimate norm, for the constitution tries to guard against that misconception by stating that the magisterium stands under the Word of God and ministers to it, and that it is only thanks to the Holy Spirit that it teaches nothing but what has been divinely revealed.[31] But notwithstanding all these cautions, the final inference can only be that the magisterium *has* this assistance and can base upon it its nearly juridical claim (*credenda!*).

At this point we again come upon the fact that the ecclesiological difference is the basic one. Both documents hold that only the Spirit is the real Interpreter of revelation, or—in other words—can show forth the one true Tradition. But in the constitution the Spirit is bound to the Church as it is summed up in the magisterium. Montreal too believes that the Church in its interpretation is guided by the Spirit, but this guidance does not get a well-defined visible form; it is something to be believed, not something to be pointed to and seen.

Is then this difference the last word that should be said, and should our conclusion be that, if systematically analysed, nothing has really changed between Roman Catholicism and Protestantism? It can indeed be argued that the Montreal report, by stating that the Tradition is to be found by the right interpretation of scripture, did only reformulate the former *sola scriptura*. And the Vatican constitution can well be understood as implying two vehicles of Christian truth (even in the sense of a traditional *partim . . . partim*) with the magisterium as *norma proxima* above them.

But I believe that this judgment would be premature. There definitely is a change in climate; on both sides there is a certain openness and mobility; the attempt is made to speak in a common language and to listen to what the other says. Neither party has fully succeeded; it is true that the Montreal report shies away from the final question of ecclesiology and rather defines the problems in a new way than that it solves them; and that the constitution time and again forgets its new understanding of revelation and that it can no longer hold the Tridentine concept of Tradition. But in spite of these shortcomings the changed climate of which both bear witness may be an indication of a real breakthrough and a real rapprochement. Whether it is, only the future can tell, for everything depends here on the influence the Montreal report will have in the Protestant churches and especially on the interpretation which the constitution will receive. For the time being it may be best to look forward to future developments, realistically and not uncritically, but with expectant hopefulness.

NOTES

[1] H. Denzinger, *Enchiridion Symbolorum*, denuo ed. C. Rahner (Herder, 1960), 783.

[2] J. N. Bakhuizen van den Brink, *Traditio in de Reformatie en het Katholicisme in de 16e eeuw*, in *Mededelingen der Kon. Ned. Akademie van Wetenschappen*, afd. Letterkunde, Nieuwe Reeks 15/2 (Amsterdam, 1952); J. R. Geiselmann, *Das Konzil von Trient über das Verhältnis der H. Schrift und der nichtgeschriebenen Traditionen*, in *Die mündliche Überlieferung*, hrg. M. Schmaus (München, 1957). Against the latter H. Lennerz, *Scriptura sola?* in *Gregorianum* 40 (1959) argued that the change of 'partim . . . partim' into 'et' was done for purely stylistic reasons, and that therefore the latter has to be understood according to the former.

[3] K. Rahner, *Was ist eine dogmatische Aussage?*, in *Catholica*, 15 (1961), p. 180, speaks about the 'einmalige Stellung' of scripture as 'die bleibende und unüberholbare norma normata für alle späteren dogmatischen Aussagen'; Y. Congar, *La tradition et les traditions II* (Paris, 1963), p. 177: 'L'Écriture est absolument souveraine.'

[4] 'We exist as Christians by the Tradition of the Gospel' (45). The bracketed number points to the paragraph of the report as printed in *The Fourth World Conference on Faith and Order*, ed. P. C. Rodger and L. Vischer (SCM Press, 1964).

[5] '. . . we have received the revealed truth, the Gospel, through its being transmitted from one generation to another' (45); '. . . Deus disposuit, ut in aevum integra permanerent omnibusque generationibus transmittentur' (7).

[6] Christian faith is 'not only a sum of tenets, but a living reality' (46); 'God's self-giving in Christ' (ibid.); 'God has revealed himself' (42).

[7] 'Placuit Deum . . . se ipsum revelare et notum facere sacramentum voluntatis suae' (2).

[8] '. . . fit gestis verbisque intrinsece inter se connexis' (2).

[9] Cf. N. A. Nissiotis, *Report on the Second Vatican Council*, in *Ecumenical*

Review, 18/2, p. 193: 'The mention of the third person of the Trinity in the Decree on Revelation seems to be merely nominal rather than truly Trinitarian, nor is it adequately expounded ecclesiologically.' I suspect that Nissiotis might give the same judgment of the Montreal report.

[10] 'Tradition . . . is actualised in the preaching of the Word, in the administration of the Sacraments and worship, in Christian teaching and theology, in mission and witness to Christ in the lives of the members of the Church,' as the Montreal report expresses it (45).

[11] Cf. Relatio de n. 8 G, July 1964: 'affirmatur per Traditionem perpetuari non tantum doctrinam, sed integram Ecclesiae vitam', as opposed to a purely conceptualistic word-transmission.

In the final text the words 'omne quod habet' of a former schema are rightly excised; thereby the impression as if that what is transmitted is the possession of the Church, is toned down.

[12] 'All are agreed that there is this dynamic element in the Tradition' (64). Relatio de n. 8 H, July 1964, mentions the 'aspectus dynamicus'.

[13] 'Traditio sub assistentia Spiritus Sancti in Ecclesia proficit' (8). In a note the constitution refers to Conc. Vat. I, *Const. Dogm. de fide catholica*, c. 4: Denz. 1800. The difference in scope is interesting; in Vaticanum I the emphasis lies on the immutability, in Vaticanum II on the development of the doctrines.

[14] 'Ecclesia scilicet, volventibus saeculis, ad plenitudinem divinae veritatis iugiter tendit, donec in ipsa consummantur verba Dei' (8). '. . . the dynamic element in the Tradition . . . which looks to the consummation of the victory of the Lord at the end of time' (64).

[15] One has only to compare the 2nd and 3rd schema of Caput 10 to be aware how much importance is attached to this thought of the entire Church 'quae simplices fideles simul ac hierarchiam complectitur' (relatio de N.10 C, July 1964). Cf. also Const. *De Ecclesia*.

[16] 'Munus autem authentice interpretandi verbum Dei scriptum vel traditum soli vivo Ecclesiae Magisterio concreditum est, cuius auctoritas in nomine Jesu Christi exercetur' (10).

[17] 'docens nonnisi quod traditum est, quatenus illud, ex divino mandato et Spiritu Sancto assistente, pie audit, sancte custodit et fideliter exponit' (10).

[18] It 'is not an object which we possess, but a reality by which we are possessed' (56).

[19] The problem of Tradition and traditions exists also in Orthodoxy, but there traditions are human customs and rites which have no absolute and eternal validity, but create 'a normal diversity inside the one Church' and are a check against authoritarian uniformity. (Cf. J. Meyendorff, *The Meaning of Tradition*, in *Scripture and Ecumenism*, ed. L. J. Swidler, Duquesne Univ. Press [Pittsburg, 1965], pp. 51 ff.)

[20] A. C. Outler, *Scripture, Tradition and Ecumenism*, in *Scripture and Ecumenism*, describes it nearly as a kind of Platonic idea: 'the reality of a singular, transcendental Tradition identifiable and active in all the various epochs and segments of Christian history' (p. 19).

[21] The beautiful image of Tradition and scripture as 'speculum in quo Ecclesia . . . contemplatur Deum' (7) points in the same direction.

M

²² The proposal to change the title so as also to include Tradition has not been taken up (Relatio ad Cap. VI A, last version).

²³ In the former schema scripture was called 'norma et auctoritas' for preaching and faith, but several of the Council members judged that to be too absolute (cf. Relatio ad n. 21 E, final schema).

²⁴ 'Munus autem authentice interpretandi verbum Dei scriptum vel traditum soli vivo Ecclesiae Magisterio concreditum est' (10).

²⁵ The successive redactions of (11) point in the same fundamentalistic direction. Schema 3 read: the books of scripture in all their parts teach 'veritatem sine ullo errore'. Because the wish was expressed to describe the 'objectum inerrantiae' the next schema added 'veritatem salutarem'. In the promulgated text this is changed into 'veritatem, quam Deus nostrae salutis causa Litteris sacris consignari voluit'. Because 'nostrae salutis causa' can just as well or perhaps even better be taken with 'consignari' than 'quam' the reading has become more ambiguous and the impression is avoided that the truth of scripture is limited to what is relevant to salvation.

²⁶ 'The Tradition in its written form, as Holy Scripture . . . has to be interpreted by the Church in ever new situations. Such interpretation of the Tradition is to be found in the crystallization of tradition [i.e. here the traditional process], in the creeds, thel iturgical forms of the sacraments and other forms of worship, and also in the preaching of the Word and in theological expositions of the Church's doctrine' (50).

²⁷ 'Sacra Traditio ergo et Sacra Scriptura arcte inter se connectuntur atque communicant' (9). Cf. also the last clause of (10).

²⁸ See his comment in his translation of the constitution in the edition of the Paulist Press (Glen Rock, N.J.), p. 30.

²⁹ 'Per eandem Traditionem integer Sacrorum Librorum canon Ecclesiae innotescit, ipsaeque Sacrae Litterae in ea penitius intelliguntur et indesinenter actuosae reddantur' (8).

³⁰ Cf. Relatio ad Caput II, De titulo, July 1964: '. . . (Traditio) quippe quae immediate cum ipsa revelatione transmittenda coniungatur, ac etiam post sacrorum librorum scriptionem perseverat.' By this 'commentary' to the text the impression that Tradition flows on as an independent stream, in the same way as before the writing of the holy books, is confirmed.

³¹ 'Magisterium non supra verbum Dei est, sed eidem ministrat, docens nonnisi quod traditum est, quatenus illud, ex divino mandato et Spiritu Sancto assistente, . . . fideliter exponit, ac ea omnia ex hoc uno fidei deposito haurit quae tamquam divinitus revelata credenda proponit' (10).

X

Scripture and Tradition in Catholic Theology

MAURICE BÉVENOT

I

It is generally agreed that Vatican II has presented the question of Scripture and Tradition in a very different way from what was ordinarily thought to be the way the Catholic Church understood it. One might, then, fairly ask whether in doing so the Council was merely correcting misapprehensions about the Church's real understanding of the question, or whether in fact the Church was correcting itself, abandoning its previous positions and adopting a line which would be more up-to-date, at least ecumenically. Only a few of the main topics which bear on this question can be outlined here and even these would each call for a fuller treatment; but enough may be said to throw some light on what, of its nature, is a very complicated subject.

The chief problem lies in the meaning of the term Tradition, ambivalent and elusive as it is. Does it mean some doctrine or doctrines which have been handed on to us from the past, or does it mean the process of handing them on? If it means the doctrines, have they Christ as their author, or are they the inventions of man? We also speak of *traditions*, in the sense of practices, customs, Church regulations, religious rites and sacraments, and again we can ask, what is their authority? Some of these are already found in Scripture and persist today; on the other hand, a few, though found in Scripture, have been long-since dropped, as was recognized in the Council of Trent itself; and, of course, there are also traditions of this kind that seem to have no basis in Scripture at all.

As such confusion surrounds one term of our comparison, it may be wiser to look first at the other term, which seems to offer more consistency: I mean, Scripture. Even here there is some ambiguity, in face of the 'Apocrypha' or, as we call them, the deutero-canonical books. But, apart from that, we all recognize what the Bible is: *that* is our Holy Book, that is the 'Scripture' alongside of which we place Tradition, in a sense not as yet clearly determined. But by starting from the Holy Book we may perhaps be able to narrow down and consolidate what we mean by Tradition. For in the case of any religion that has a Holy Book, the crucial and most interesting point is what those who profess that religion think of the relation between their religion and the Book: how they explain that relationship and what place that explanation holds in their religion. Perhaps, at least in the case of the Catholic religion, we shall find in its relation to and its attitude to and use of the Bible, just what it is that it understands by Tradition.

From the earliest days of Christianity, the Bible was accepted as the word of God, inspired by the Holy Spirit, and the human author was (originally, at least)[1] described as being only an instrument whom God used, a lyre on which He played, to convey His message to mankind. A Holy Book it was, revealing the inner mysteries of God, and also what He had done for men, what He purposed for them, what He expected from them in return. Much in it was, in the nature of the case, beyond full human comprehension, and this encouraged readers and preachers to find new deeper meanings in it, to find allusions and hints in every phrase and word to aspects of divine actions or of man's corresponding responsibilities. These were perhaps already well known, but they received fresh life and meaning from such accommodations of the sacred text. In this way, meditation on the *sacra pagina* created a net-work of religious thought drawn together from every part of Scripture, usually regardless of differences of time, of author, or of literary genre. Some, no doubt, of the great exegetes, like St Jerome, had paid some attention to these factors, and their findings were respected: but what did such things really matter? It was the same Holy Spirit who had inspired the authors of all the different books: it was all alike the word of God. And so, in the Middle Ages, many could sincerely say that they found all their religion in the Bible. No doubt a St Basil or a St Augustine had recognized that many Christian ceremonies and practices were not expressly vouched for in the Bible, and believed them to be apostolic simply because they were in universal use. But in time, through the lavish use of allegorical interpretation, these very things were 'found' in the Scriptures too—or else they were not looked for, as being merely incidental in comparison with the massive presentation of God's revelation to be found there.

As an integral part of that revelation was the Church itself, not only as it appeared in the New Testament, destined to be the beneficiary and the herald of God's mighty deeds in Christ, but as it had existed *in concreto* through the centuries since his coming. Well enough aware of the unworthiness and unfaithfulness that existed within the Church, the commentators of the Scriptures never lost sight of the promises that Christ had made to his disciples and to those who would believe through their preaching: the Church was his Body, his Spouse, supported and guided by His Spirit till the end of the world, the pillar and bulwark of the truth. The Church was there; they were of it, conscious of the faith which they owed to it, and of the help of the Spirit which they experienced from its ministrations. They saw, in the hierarchical structure of the Church, the realization of Christ's intentions and promises, 'for God is faithful'; they saw, in the charges he had laid on the apostles—to go and make disciples from all the nations, to feed his lambs and his sheep, so that 'he that heareth you heareth Me'—the justification not only of the priestly order, but of a specifically teaching authority in the Church, vested in the bishops and in the Pope. And as they readily applied the denunciations of the prophets to the wicked of their own day, so too they found, not only in the New Testament, but in the Old as well, types and parables applicable to that authority, the exercise of which they were conscious of, in one way or another, from day to day.

II

Then Luther came. Stirred to his inmost depths by the simplicity of the Gospel as he understood it, he revolted against the *consuetudines ecclesiae*, those multifarious rules and regulations emanating from Church authority, and the abuses which they represented or gave rise to. In this he was only carrying on the demand for 'reform in head and members' which had been repeatedly voiced especially in the preceding hundred years. That a *moral* reform was called for had been recognized by all the spiritually-minded, not least in the handling of the Church's finances. But Luther, unexpectedly, went further, and initiated a *doctrinal* reform too. All these rules and regulations were so many human ordinances, a reinstatement of the Law on which men had come to rely, instead of looking to the incoercible grace of God. Faith in Christ had come to be replaced by these man-made *traditions*, and the word of God by the abuses which the Church authorities had created.

The definition of the Church in the Confession of Augsburg is here very significant: 'congregatio sanctorum, in qua evangelium pure docetur, et recte administrantur sacramenta.' It has two of the elements of a Catholic definition—*fides* and *communio*—it omits the third, *auctoritas*. The application of the Word of God to the life of the Church had been in the hands of the officials of the Church: henceforth all office in the Church must be judged by the Word of God. This was a further, dogmatic, reason for the rejection of Tradition; for once all authoritative interpretation of the Word of God was denied to the Church's official ministers, the 'Word' was reduced to a self-explanatory Scripture, which could not tolerate alongside itself any such independent factor as 'Tradition'. It meant the canonization of 'Sola Scriptura'.

The nature of the attack predetermined the lines of defence. And the trouble thereafter was that, as with so much else laid down by the Council of Trent, what was merely emergency legislation calculated to secure Catholic doctrine against these precise attacks, came in the following centuries to be taken as an adequate and complete presentation of that doctrine. Trent reasserted the Catholic Church's devotion to both Scripture and Tradition, and repudiated, in general, all interpretation of the Scriptures which went counter to that which the Church had always held. Trent then proceeded to a more detailed exposition of particular doctrines, and at the same time to the correction of the real abuses which the revolt had so strongly underscored. But the Council never troubled to define what it meant by *traditiones*, and it probably could not have done so had it tried. What it was clear about was that the Church lived by something more than the written word of Scripture, however sacred that might be, and that 'something more' was vaguely referred to as deriving from Christ and the Apostles, even though not written down in Scripture. Thereafter, especially when Protestantism itself had crystallized its 'Sola Scriptura' into a far narrower and more rigid meaning, the Catholic Church simply opposed to this the conception of two sources for her teaching, 'Scriptura et Traditio', and, no doubt as a result of the Enlightenment, over-emphasized the intellectual character of that teaching: where Trent had said 'the Gospel', Vatican I said 'the supernatural revelation'. Once again the what and the how of Tradition were left undefined, and the relationship between Scripture and Tradition was left in the vague.

III

But thought both inside and outside the Church had been moving. The new appreciation of historical studies, the critical approach to ancient documents and in particular to the Holy Book itself, the application of the notion of evolution and progress to every sphere of life, all combined to create a crisis at the beginning of this century. The Church at the time could only meet this Modernism, as it called it, by a freeze, which indeed saved the situation for the moment, but only to the distress of many of its most devoted sons. Yet already an important step had been taken when Newman published his *Essay on the Development of Christian Doctrine* as early as 1845. That, and other contributions of his which were rather frowned on at the time, are now coming into their own. So too are those of Scheeben on the nature of the Church. In the heat of the crisis, the writings of Maurice Blondel were pointing to a solution, especially his treatment of Tradition. Père Lagrange, too, was breaking new ground in the Biblical field. Such pioneers have inspired an immense output of work by Catholic scholars who, loyal to the Church, have faced up to the problems which modern research and discoveries have raised, welcoming and adopting all that sound scholarship could contribute, whatever its source. It is all this intense work, especially in the last thirty years, which has made possible the treatment of Scripture and Tradition which we find in the documents of Vatican II. But it is worth noting here, if the Catholic position is to be understood, that the old *concept* of Tradition, which had been defended as vigorously as it was attacked, was a very narrow and abstract one, and did not include [though it did not exclude] many elements essential to Tradition *in its living reality*. The 'new look' which Tradition now has (and which admittedly still needs to be filled in) does not deny the truth of the old outlook, but recognizes that it was only 'a first approximation' (in the mathematical sense of the term).[2]

That new look is to be found chiefly in the Constitution on *Divine Revelation*, with some important additional insights from that on the *Church* and that on *Liturgy*. All revelation comes from God, and is revelation of Himself and of the mystery (or hidden purpose) of His will for mankind, shown by His deeds and words of old, and culminating, once for all, in the person of Christ—the eternal Word made man—and all He did and said and initiated. The record of these divine deeds and words is contained in the scriptures, but these are only a *record* of revelation, and are not the revelation itself. God, the object of revelation, cannot be confined in words, not even in the words which He Himself addresses to man. Therefore, man's response to the words he hears or reads is not simply agreement with them: in the words of the Council, it is:

the obedience of faith (Romans 16:26, cf. Romans 1:5; 2 Corinthians 10:5–6), by which a man freely yields himself completely to God, paying him the full homage of his mind and will, and heartily making his own whatever God has revealed. But to be able to do this man needs the prompting and the help of God's grace, for the Holy Spirit alone can move his heart and turn it Godwards, open the eyes of his mind, and 'grant him the relish to be found in accepting and believing the truth' (Arausic. II, can. 7). Moreover, the Holy Spirit, through His gifts, is constantly developing that faith still more, leading man on to an ever deeper understanding of the revelation [Revelation 5].

This gives us several points that bear on tradition. The first is that revelation is to be appropriated by *all* the faithful: it is not a preserve of any privileged section of the Church. The second is the indispensable part played by the Holy Spirit. And the third, that there is possibility of a development in the faith, which development consists in a deeper understanding of the mysteries of God's revelation.

Some description of this development is given a little later. After speaking of the divine intention that the revelation should endure for the salvation of all men, of Christ's charge to His Apostles in this sense, the Council briefly recounts both their preaching of the Gospel by word and example, and the writing of the New Testament, dependent on that preaching. The living Gospel was committed in its entirety by the Apostles to their successors, the bishops, to be proclaimed and taught by them, so that the whole Church, during its pilgrimage towards the final face-to-face with God, to whom it owes everything, might already contemplate Him in the mirror, as it were, of this sacred Tradition and of the sacred Scriptures, Old and New together. In what the Apostles thus handed on ('quod ab Apostolis *traditum* est'), is included everything conducive to holy living and to the growth in faith of the People of God, and so the Church, in its teaching, its life, and its worship preserves and passes on to each new generation all that makes it what it is, all that it believes. The next paragraph must be given in full. It presents several difficulties to the translator, but from the context it is clear that the opening words 'Haec quae est ab Apostolis Traditio' mean everything that has come from the Apostles, so that it includes not only their oral preaching, but its special expression in the inspired writings, as well as those practices and institutions they were led to establish:

What has thus been inherited from the apostles develops in the Church under the assistance of the Holy Spirit, for there is a growth of insight into all that they handed down whether in actions or in words. It grows both from contemplation and study by those who believe as they ponder these things in their hearts (Luke 12:19, 51), and from the interior enlightenment which they experience of spiritual realities, as also from the preaching of those who with the apostolic succession have received the sure gift of truth (*charisma veritatis certum*—Iren.). In other words the Church, as the centuries follow one another, is ever stretching after the fullness of God's truth, until such time as the words of God are completely realized in it [Revelation 8].

Here we have an outline of the development of dogma such as has never before been given in any document of the Church. It indicates, too, some of the chief factors in this development, naturally presupposing what the Council had already said: that God's revelation had culminated in Christ and that no further public revelation was to be expected before the final manifestation of our Lord Jesus Christ in glory (I Timothy 6:14; Titus 2:13) [Revelation 4]. But what Christ had left with the Apostles to broadcast and to pass on was inexhaustible in depth: its first formulations and practical realizations pointed to a mystery behind them, and all who, through their influence and the enlightenment of the Spirit, came to believe, could ponder them in their hearts and, living by them, pierce through them to a better understanding of the mystery to which they pointed. The Scriptures, the sacraments, the preaching of the authorized teachers developed the faith of the Christians, who were stimulated, no doubt, too, by their own questionings and the scornful criticisms of the world about them. And it was a true development of what was already there, not a change caused by the addition of something new. Vincent of Lérins' description of the contrast cannot be bettered: 'Ad profectum pertinet ut in semetipsum unaquaeque res amplificetur; ad permutationem vero ut aliquid ex alio in aliud transvertatur' (*Commonitorium*, 23). [The essence of *development* is that a thing grows more fully into itself; *change* occurs where something is turned from one thing into another.]

The part played in this development by the faithful is more fully described in the Constitution on the Church, where they are said to share in the *prophetic* rôle of Christ as well as in His priestly and royal rôles. All the faithful share in the supernatural sense of faith: as a body they are true to the faith once delivered to the saints (Jude 3), penetrate deeper into it with true insight and keep applying it more fully in their lives [On the Church 12]. It is thus that not only the hierarchy, but the laity too share in Christ's prophetic office as His witnesses, by the understanding He has given them of the faith, so that the power of the gospel may shine forth in their daily social and family life [On the Church 35].

IV

It was important to stress the part played by the body of the faithful in this development, so that the bearers of the Tradition are not the hierarchy alone, but the whole body of the faithful—lest the part played by the hierarchy in the Church, with its special importance, should seem to blot out all other witnesses.

But before we deal with this, a more general criticism must be considered which touches on fundamental aspects of our problem. Revelation is something from God *which faces* mankind: it is God speaking to men, and men (or more specifically, the Church) hearing, accepting, believing. And so it always is. But, it is objected, in *our* presentation of the development of dogma within the Church, we have no longer a dialogue between God and man, but a monologue—the Church talking to itself, and as a result there is a proliferation of newly thought-up dogmas, a mass of weeds growing in the garden of the Church, so that God's clear paths laid down in the Scriptures have become cluttered up and obscured. These new dogmas, it is said, are invested with the same authority as the Scriptures; moreover, Pope and bishops set themselves up as judges of the Scriptures—above the Word of God instead of being subject to it.

No doubt, that is the image of the Roman Catholic Church in the eyes of some today, and it may be partly its own fault. If many of its official statements suggest it, and some even in Vatican II, when isolated from their context, can be quoted in this sense, it is a construction which is already belied by some of the facts which have been quoted above. Indeed, this image should go out of currency, if the total evidence in Vatican II is taken into account.

In the first place, the development in the Church's doctrines is not the result of the Church's talking to herself, creating a spider's web out of her own vitals, on her own. For the Catholic, the Holy Book is the starting-point of the whole process: it is as much a creation of God as is the Church itself; indeed, as Karl Rahner has so ably argued, it is a constitutive part of the Church which Christ founded, the Book through which God speaks to us.[3] Others may read it and not hear God's voice: only within the context of the Church can that voice be heard. And as the Book is the product of the Holy Spirit, so is it the Holy Spirit who enlightens the mind of each to grasp its meaning, and by the grace of faith to welcome the Revelation. And as the Holy Spirit produced the Book through the free agency of its human writers, and as Christ initiated his Church through the agency of men too, whom he charged with this same Holy Spirit, it is only within the Church that the meaning of the Book—the fullness of God's revelation, now complete in Christ—is preserved.

This is something objective, given from the first, dominating the thought of all Christians; and all development, whatever part speculation may play, is continuously being checked by that norm: the dialogue with God goes on.

By this revelation the invisible God, out of the abundance of His love, speaks to men as His friends, and lives with them [Revelation 2].

Through what was bequeathed to it by the Apostles[4] the Church has come to know the complete Canon of the Sacred Books, and in the Church the Scriptures themselves are ever more fully understood and exert their influence; and in this way God who spoke of old, is in continuous colloquy with the Spouse of His divine Son, and the Holy Spirit, through whom the living voice of the Gospel resounds in the Church and thereby in the world, guides the believers into all truth, and makes the word of Christ dwell richly in them (Colossians 3:16) [Revelation 8].

Is this perhaps mere verbiage? Is there not evidence of independent excogitations and wild, if pious, speculations in the Catholic Church? If so, there is anxiety also within the Church about such movements and at least the wildest get pruned before they go too far. In any case, the Council puts before us the Church's ideal in the matter, and the over-all evidence of the centuries, not to mention contemporary experience, provides us, along with deplorable periods, repeated examples of extraordinary recovery and renewal.

V

But the chief gravamen is the claim of the Church's authorities —Popes or Councils—to make infallible definitions. Propositions are laid down, which are claimed to be part of God's revelation, and are to be believed absolutely, as irreformable, binding for all time. You are expected to commit intellectual suicide. Further, they are not in Scripture, or if some scriptural basis is given them, this is so tenuous as to be more ingenious than convincing. The teaching authority—the Magisterium as it is called—sets itself up as the interpreter of Scripture, above it and not subject to it.[5]

This is no place to make an apologia, but some reflections from the inside may help to make the position a little more tolerable. First of all, what is an *interpretation* of Scripture? It can be of many different kinds. It can be the meaning which the author meant to convey, and to find this out the literary form which he was using must first be recognized. The language, time, place, circumstances, the author's character and style, etc., must be reckoned with, before we can be sure of what he meant to say. But if pure scholarship could, ideally, give us this answer, there may be a further question. Did the author himself realize the full meaning of what he was writing (or collecting and editing)? If we believe in the sacred character of the Scriptures, and if the history of the Israelites is one of divine guidance and pedagogy, might there not be, at times, in some written word a further meaning of which the author was only dimly aware, if at all, but which was intended by God to be conveyed by that word—at least to a later generation? If then, all interpretation must begin with the author's conscious intention, it need not end there; indeed, sometimes we *must* go further, if we are to be true to the way later sacred authors, not to mention Christ himself, have explained what their predecessors wrote down. Here the pure scholar must be supplemented by the man of faith: it is a delicate task, but clearly his is interpretation at a different level. Finally, the allegorical 'interpretations' of the Fathers are obviously of a different kind again, which need not detain us: those of the type of St Gregory's explanation of the seven sons of Job, who besides representing the seven chief virtues, also represented the twelve apostles, for if $3 + 4 = 7$, $3 \times 4 = 12$.

But very few indeed are the Scripture texts of which the Church authorities have defined the meaning,[6] and even there, their intervention has generally been to say what Scripture does *not* mean, otherwise leaving open what it does. Such oversight of the interpretation of Scripture does not imply that they regard Scripture as their property, over which they are masters, and with which they can deal as they like, any more than a Court of Appeal, which determines the meaning of a law—i.e. 'interprets' it—is set over the law. On the contrary it serves the law and respects it, explaining what it meant to say. In fact any real interpretation accepts and respects what it is interpreting.

So Pope and Councils, when they claim to be teaching the faith, are claiming to teach and explain only what was committed to the apostles by Christ and his Holy Spirit, as this was enshrined in the Scriptures and understood in the apostolic Church. That this understanding of God's revelation should have developed under the guidance of the Holy Spirit through the centuries, as we have seen, certainly makes it *appear* that new dogmas are being defined: at the same time it underlines the boundaries that limit the Magisterium, for if it defines, it is in doing so *subject* to both Scripture and Tradition.

But the great bugbear is infallibility: witnessing to the Christian faith and preaching it is one thing; defining it infallibly is another. I admit that 'infallibility' is extremely difficult to define, as are other such words as *validity*, and *atonement*, and *tradition* itself. But let us see whether the exercise of infallibility is as deleterious as was suggested. Consider the great christological disputes of the first centuries, settled substantially at Chalcedon. Did the acceptance of that definition cause the cessation of all intellectual activity about the person of Christ? Throughout the Middle Ages, in all the Scholastics, during the Reformation and beyond, even to this day, whole libraries have been written on the basis of that definition. Systematic theology, Mystical theology, Moral and Pastoral theology have all profited by it: one would like to know what kind of intellectual suicide all these writers, thinkers and saints had committed in accepting such a definition as infallible. The mathematician and the astronomer are glad to be able to rely on their tables. In fact the definition of a dogma is not so much an end as a beginning.

The reason for this is that the formulation of a dogma, like the words of Scripture, does no more than *point* to a divine fact or truth without covering it adequately. The formulation is true in the sense that it excludes its contradictory because this does not correctly express the divine truth in question. But since it does not itself profess to express that truth adequately, it does not exclude the possibility of better, fuller formulations as the result of further study, discussions, and the comparison with the formulations of other relevant parts of the Revelation. And just as this Constitution encourages the biblical scholars to work towards a deeper understanding and clearer presentation of the meaning and unity of the sacred Scriptures, so as to help the Church in forming its mind [Revelation 12], so too Paul VI, only a few weeks ago, said that theological scholars in general had a two-fold task vis-à-vis the Magisterium: first the study of Christ's revelation as expressed in Scripture and Tradition, in preparation for its better presentation by the Magisterium, but secondly (and this is important here) the elaboration and explanation, in language 'understanded of the people', of whatever formulations of doctrine the Magisterium itself may have made. Incidentally, this will include the evaluation of those pronouncements which do not pretend to be infallible, but which yet deserve respect and cannot be ignored as irrelevant [On the Church 25].

With regard to the interpretation of Scripture by the Magisterium, there are, as was said above, very few passages of which the interpretation can be regarded as defined. But there is one point where Scripture and Tradition meet, and where the ruling of the Magisterium has been generally *de facto* accepted, even by those who do not accept its *de iure* authority. This is the Canon itself of Scripture. It presents a certain problem to Catholic theology, though Karl Rahner's handling of it, if not definitive, seems to be pointing in the right direction. But for those who reject Tradition altogether, or who, accepting the inevitability of tradition, deny it any permanently binding character through an authoritative Magisterium, the problems it presents are enormous. Did the Canon impose itself of itself? Or must one today recognize that there is a Canon within the Canon? Might not some books be excluded, or others added? Various positions have been taken up—and disputed. To one outside that controversy, the confusion suggests that the problem has no issue. Even Professor Cullmann, who sees in the establishment of the principle of a Canon (about A.D. 150), an act of humility and renunciation on the part of the early Church, needs to tell us whether this was merely an historic fact (in which case it might some day be modified or even reversed), or was it part of the *Heilsgeschichte*, as his stress on it as a turning-point would suggest (in which case we can ask how he comes to know it as such). But he, too, is, it would seem, guarding against the Catholic idea of an authoritative magisterium, which would be enabled, by the action of the Holy Spirit within the Church, to recognize what belongs to the revelation of Christ, and so, in this case, to determine the Canon as a norm for all time.[7]

VI

These rather disparate considerations, the bearing of which on our main theme may not always have been clear, will perhaps help to bring out the meaning of two short paragraphs from the Constitution on God's Revelation, which can form the long-awaited conclusion to this paper. After declaring that Pastors and faithful alike find in Scripture and Tradition (as together forming a sacred deposit in the Church's keeping), the source of their common faith, worship and witness, the text proceeds:

But the authentic interpretation of the word of God, written and/or transmitted, is a function that has been entrusted to the Church's living Magisterium alone, which exercises authority in the name of Jesus Christ. However, this Magisterium is not above the word of God, but is there to serve it, teaching only what has thus been handed down. For by Christ's command and with the aid of the Holy Spirit, it is the word of God which the Magisterium listens to prayerfully, preserves reverently, and faithfully expounds, and it is from this deposit of faith alone that it draws whatever it proposes for belief as revealed by God.

It is therefore clear that holy Tradition, the sacred Scriptures, and the Church's Magisterium are, in the wisdom of God's plan, so interconnected and interdependent that none can stand without the other two, but all three, each in its own way, under the action of the same Holy Spirit, together contribute powerfully to the salvation of souls [Revelation 10].

NOTES

[1] This over-simplification, which aimed at emphasizing the uniquely sacred character of the Bible, has long been recognized to be inadequate. The freedom and individuality of the human authors is fully allowed for in any modern treatment. Cf. p. 179.

[2] Thus in the Constitution the two-source theory (as understood in the old outlook) was neither endorsed nor rejected. All were agreed that Tradition had an essential function, whether or not it contributed material that was not somehow already contained in Scripture. The text deliberately avoids the issue, which in any case seems to be of secondary importance; cf. K. Rahner and J. Ratzinger, *Offenbarung und Überlieferung* (*Quaest. Disp.*, 25 [1965], pp. 30–3—Eng. ed., *Revelation and Tradition* [1966], pp. 32–5).

[3] Karl Rahner, *Über die Schriftinspiration* (*Quaestiones Disputatae* I, 1959²); Eng. ed., *Studies in Modern Theology* (1965): 'Inspiration in the Bible', pp. 7–86.

⁴ 'Per eandem Traditionem'—in the sense already explained.

⁵ Cf. the questions which Catholics and Protestants are putting to each other, as Fr. Ratzinger sees them (op. cit., p. 29; Eng. ed., p. 31): Can the word be given over to the Church without fear that it will forfeit its own power and vitality under the shears of the magisterium or in the rank growth of the *sensus fidelium*? That is the Protestant's question to the Catholic. Can the word be posited as independent without thereby delivering it up to the caprice of exegetes, evacuating it of meaning in the controversies of historians and so robbing it entirely of binding force? That is the counter-question which the Catholic will immediately put.

⁶ Cf. Pius XII's encyclical *Divino afflante Spiritu* (1943).

⁷ Cf. P. Lengsfeld, *Tradition, Écriture et Église* (Paris, 1964), pp. 99–106.

N

XI

Scripture and Tradition in Orthodox Theology

H. CUNLIFFE-JONES

It is not because I am an authority on the subject on which I am to speak that I have chosen it. The reason is simply that there seemed to be an obvious gap in the programme at this point, and that somebody, even if he could only speak at second-hand, ought to fill it.

There is a great need for more detailed research into the History of Orthodox Theology, but there is also a great need to make the results of research already done part of the common outlook. I am very conscious of the Western provincialism of too much study in the History of Christian Theology, and of the need to overcome it. It is as a Westerner standing in a mixed Reformed and Anabaptist tradition that I seek to come to some understanding of the meaning of *Tradition* in the Orthodox Churches. This, I believe, is abundantly worthwhile doing, though it is no substitute for an exposition by a master of the subject.

I believe that we should begin by picturing to ourselves the very different story of Church History in East and West. In spite of the fact that the Orthodox Church cherishes the unity between East and West in what it has called[1] 'the divine and apostolic traditions of the first nine centuries of Christianity', there seem to be, for practical purposes, *two* Church Histories not *one*. Western Christians need to alter their teaching perspectives, and make a new effort of thought and imagination to enter into that other mainly unfamiliar and certainly strange Church History from which they have no right to dissociate themselves.

Brother George Every in what to me is the most illuminating of all his studies of the Orthodox Church, *Misunderstanding between East and West* (Lutterworth Press, 1965), has three sentences that show us the way (pp. 10, 68):

The division of Christendom is a disjointed process extending through the whole history of the Church from the fourth century to the nineteenth, fluctuating rather than continuous, and only now beginning to show distinct signs of movement in a reverse direction . . .

The Byzantine East was able to continue the tradition of Hellenistic culture in the Roman Empire. To Western eyes this continuity, like Chinese history, looks immobile and ossified, but the ossification took place mainly, if not entirely, in the Turkish period, when Roman culture in the East suffered the same kind of disaster that the West had encountered a millennium before.

Let us try to picture this.

Western Church History is familiar to Catholics, Anglicans and Protestants alike, even if some patches are vague, and we avert our attention from others. East and West march together in the first centuries, but whether we date the beginning of the Dark Ages with the Fall of Rome (410), or the death of Theodoric (526), after the fourth century, the Western Church began to have its own destiny, which for some centuries was a tragic one. Then there began what we call *The Middle Ages*, meaning the *Western* Middle Ages, which reaches its climax in the thirteenth century, and reveals decay and the seeds of new life in the fourteenth and fifteenth. This led to the Renaissance, the Reformation, and the Catholic Reformation of the sixteenth century, the new development of science and the transition from old to new ways of thinking in the seventeenth century, the Enlightenment of the eighteenth century, the widening of horizons and revolutionary changes of the nineteenth century, and the increasing scepticism and the possibility of new unity in the twentieth.

Eastern Church History is quite different from this. The Fall of Rome, while a pity, is only an incident for the Empire and the Church, which have their capital in Constantinople. The Age of the Councils lasted through much of the Western Dark Ages; and a distinctive Byzantine civilization flourished from 680 to 1453, though towards the end of the period the decay is palpable. The Dark Ages for the Eastern Church lay in the domination of Islam against which it had earlier battled on behalf of both East and West. These lasted from 1453 up to the nineteenth century. The Dark Ages were lifted earlier in the century for the Greek Church, and later for the Russian Church. This emancipation has meant the beginning of new life in the midst of revolution.

True, the two Church Histories are not wholly separate. There are desultory contacts at many places, but these are not always happy ones. The relations between East and West are bedevilled, partly by misunderstanding, and by the wrong kind of political relationship; and partly by hurtful attempts at proselytism by both Catholic and Protestant; in these relations the exploratory contacts of Anglicans with Orthodox in the eighteenth and nineteenth centuries is a hopeful sign for the generally better relations of the twentieth.

This is a very rough picture that I have painted but I believe it to be helpful to draw it. Karl Barth in his early period spoke of 'the strange new world of the Bible'. We need to think of the 'strange new world' of the Orthodox Church in the history of its life and thought as well as in its present reality, in order to make the effort of imagination, study and readiness to learn in a new way from a great Christian Communion.

·I. TRADITION

To begin with, the formulation of the subject as *Scripture and Tradition in Orthodox Theology* is not Orthodox. It is a Western formulation. It would be better to say: *The Meaning of Tradition in Orthodox Theology*. This would not exclude Scripture. Scripture is a very precious element in Tradition for the Orthodox, as we shall see, but it is understood from within Tradition, and as a living part of it. 'To separate and contrast the two is to impoverish the idea of both alike.'[2] So we must start from the understanding of the meaning of Tradition to the Orthodox.

Tradition is the living sense of continuity in the Orthodox Church. It rests on the conviction that the Holy Spirit abides in the Church, and will guide it as he has guided it, into all truth. So tradition is at once an attitude of preservation and of creative innovation. Tradition is both more rigid and more flexible than it is in the West. The determination of what is tradition is the sense of what the Orthodox Church thinks.

Here we learn the right approach from Fr Emmanuel Amand de Mendieta's study of the controversial twenty-seventh and twenty-ninth chapters of St Basil of Caesarea's treatise *On the Holy Spirit*,[3] in which St Basil did not make a clear distinction between traditions recently established, and traditions of apostolic origin, and this has given rise to misunderstanding.

Fr de Mendieta says of the beginning of chapter 29 (op. cit., p. 27n):

If, at the first glance, one gets the impression that St Basil introduces here a double authority, a double standard, a real double source, Scripture *and* Tradition, he is in fact very far from doing so. The 'apostolic' Tradition (or, more generally, the Church liturgical and doctrinal tradition) is for him the 'unwritten' rule of Catholic faith, without which it is impossible to grasp the true intention and the global doctrine or teaching of the inspired Scripture (θεόπνευστος Γραφή). This 'unwritten' Tradition is enshrined in the sacred and secret rites of the sacraments of the Christian initiation, and also in the doctrines implied in these liturgical prayers. In Basil's appreciation, this Tradition is an indispensable guide and companion in the study, and for the right appreciation of the Holy Writ. On the other hand, Scripture must be primarily read, expounded and preached in the Churches, in the liturgical assemblies, in the context of the administration of the sacraments.

This is the characteristic Orthodox approach to Scripture as a part of, and to be understood in the context of, Tradition (cf. George Every, op. cit., pp. 67–8).

In the Tradition not everything has the same importance. Some things are absolute and not capable of revision: such as the Bible, and the doctrinal definitions of the Ecumenical Councils. Lesser things, however, can be altered within the one life of the Orthodox Church. If we should ask why the unalterable elements are unalterable, I suspect that the answer is that it is un-Orthodox to think of changing them, and un-Orthodox even to ask the question.

Yet the attitude of the Orthodox Church is in some ways more flexible than the West, for example, over *synodical* decision. This is true not only of lesser synods, such as those of 907 and 920, but also of the dogmatic decisions of Nicaea and Chalcedon. 'In the West when these were once received, any attempt to contravene them was regarded as treason. The East was more prepared to consider amendment, modification, amplification,' (see George Every, op. cit., p. 55). If we then ask why the

Orthodox found the addition of the *filioque* clause to the Nicene-Constantinopolitan Creed so objectionable, the answer does not lie mainly in the difference of theological approach, but mainly in the fact that it was an insertion into THE Creed of the Whole Church, without the authority of a decision of what the Orthodox could regard as an Ecumenical Council.

There have been times when the tradition of the Orthodox Church has been purely conservative and defensive. Both Friedrich Schleiermacher and John Henry Newman in the nineteenth century dismissed the Orthodox Church from serious consideration. Periods of defensiveness have come about largely through political oppression and the attacks on Orthodoxy by other Christian traditions. But there has been a creative movement within the Orthodox Church since the nineteenth century; and there is a real recognition at the present that it is necessary to discriminate between abiding and temporary elements in the Tradition.

This discriminating attitude has been fostered by the pressure of contemporary scepticism, new opportunities of discussion with Western Christians, and new endeavours of scholarship. Among other things, it involves a readiness to see some truth in the literary and historical criticism of the Bible. But for the Orthodox, the acceptance of new critical standards must be done, not in what seems to them a rationalistic Western way, but only in so far as it can be assimilated within the living continuity of the Orthodox outlook.

II. SCRIPTURE

What, then, is the understanding of the Bible within the living sense of Tradition in the Orthodox Church?

(1) First, *the Bible is a sacred book addressed primarily to believers*. It was a creation of the community both in Old Testament times and in the life of the Church, selecting, authorizing and authenticating the documents to be accepted. The message is divine—it is the Word of God. But it is the faithful community that acknowledges the Word and testifies to its truth. It was the People of the Covenant to whom the word of God was entrusted under the old dispensation, and it is the Church of the Word Incarnate that keeps the message of the Kingdom.

The total dependence of the Church on the Word of God does not mean that it depended solely on its written account in the New Testament text. The image and teaching of Christ as proclaimed by the apostles were not a truth mastered once and for all; 'the Word of God is quick [i.e. living] and powerful . . .' (Hebrews 4:12), and is constantly proclaimed in the preaching of the bishop. Christians commune with it in the sacraments and are inspired by it in prayer; it is the source of the unanimity that links them. In all the sources we find reference to the words and teachings of Christ which were obviously known to all from the very start.

When records of the apostolic preaching began to appear, since this was evidence of the Word of God, it acquired the same significance as the tradition about Christ in other forms, such as preaching, liturgical prayer, and preparation of new converts for baptism. Since they already possessed the Holy Scriptures of the Old Testament, Christians naturally added these writings to them as their completion, interpretation, and fulfilment.[4]

(2) So far as the text of the Bible is concerned it is natural that the Orthodox Church should hold that the *Greek text* of both the Old as well as the New Testament *is the authoritative one*. Where the text of the Septuagint differs from that of the Hebrew, the belief is that the alterations were made under the inspiration of the Holy Spirit, and are to be considered part of God's continuing revelation. This, however, does not exclude historical criticism within the conviction that the Church is the interpreter of Scripture.

(3) *In the Bible are to be found not only the revelation of God, but also the answering response of man.* The response of man is integrated into the mystery of the Word of God.

Yet man's intimate relation with God in his revelation does not diminish the divine sovereignty and transcendence. God 'dwells in unapproachable light', and 'no man has ever seen' him 'or can see' him (1 Timothy 6:16). Yet this light 'enlightens every man' and came 'into the world' (John 1:9). This is the paradox of God's revelation of himself.

(4) *The Bible is sacred history centred in Christ.* It is history—historic events are the source and basis of all Christian faith and hope. It is sacred history—the mystery of Christ in whom 'the whole fullness of deity dwells bodily' (Colossians 2:9) cannot be understood fully within the earthly plane. Faith lays hold of the historical datum in its full depth but without obliterating

historical boundaries. And the Bible is centred in Christ—who is the *archē* and the *telos*, the beginning and the end. The picture of Christ in the Gospels is not that of a chronicler. The evangelists give us his image—an historic yet a divine image. It is not a portrait but rather an *ikon*, but an historic *ikon*, an image of the incarnate Lord.

[Here we must interrupt the exposition to make clear the meaning of *ikons* in the life of the Orthodox Church. To Western Christians this is often strange or unknown, because of the historic differences of attitude that influence, often unconsciously, present practice. A valuable account of these differences is to be found in Edwyn Bevan's fourth lecture in his book *Holy Images* (George Allen and Unwin, 1940), pp. 113–178. (He points out the influence of the statement in Acts 19:12 that St Paul's handkerchiefs and aprons effected cures; the decisive influence on Western thinking and practice of the pronouncement of Pope Gregory I [about A.D. 600] that it is one thing to offer homage to a picture, and quite another thing to learn by a story in a picture to what homage ought to be offered; and the stress in Protestantism on the direct application of the Second Commandment to the life of the Church.)

His conclusion is (p. 165):

> The question of the veneration of images is by itself, a trivial one; the question of the Invocation of Saints is the important question behind the controversy, between Protestants on the one side and Roman Catholics and Orthodox on the other side, just as the question whether a divine virtue resides in the image or not is the important question on which Protestant and Roman Catholics agree against the Orthodox.

The most vivid testimony to the meaning of *ikons* in the life of the Orthodox Church known to me has been given by Dr Nicholas Zernov:[5]

> There is nothing exactly similar in the experience of Western Christians to the place which ikons occupy in the life of the Christian East. The sacred pictures are not merely suitable decorations for the centres of worship; they are not even regarded as a means of visual instruction. To the Orthodox, they reveal the ultimate purpose of creation: to be the temple of the Holy Spirit; and they manifest the reality of that process of that transfiguration of the cosmos which began on the day of Pentecost and which is gradually extend-

ing to all sides of earthly life. At home, or on a journey, in hours of danger or in happy moments, an Orthodox wishes to see ikons, to gaze through these windows into the world beyond time and space, and be reassured that his earthly pilgrimage is only the beginning of another and fuller life.

Ikons are prayers enshrined in painted wood, they are sanctified by Church blessing and in return assist worshippers in their aspiration to the heavenly realm by actualizing the divine presence. Thus, ikons differ from religious paintings by the symbolic treatment of subjects, by their special technique of design and colouring, and above all by the change in their substance through the love and transforming prayer of those who made them and those who venerate them.]

(5) *The Church is the interpreter of revelation.* This interpretation comes through the permanent assistance of the Spirit given to the Church which is 'the pillar and bulwark of the truth' (1 Timothy 3:15). The Church is the divinely appointed and permanent witness to the truth and meaning of the Biblical message, because the Church is part of the Revelation as the Body of the Incarnate Lord. The witness of the Church is a continuous rediscovery of the message once delivered to the saints and ever since kept by faith. And Christ is ever present in the Church, and continues his life-redeeming office in the Church. The truth of the book is revealed and vindicated by the growth of the body.

(6) The Church has summarized the Scriptural message in creeds, and in many other ways and methods. Both Scripture and systematized statement must be kept side by side—but their relation constitutes a problem. *What is the theological use of the Bible?* In particular, why are not the earlier stages of revelation superseded in Christ?

The easiest solution would have been if we could overlook or overcome the diversity of times—the duration of the process itself. This is what is done in allegory. But allegory, which is a method of exegesis which denies history, must be set aside in favour of typology which is an interpretation of events and an historical method.

The earlier stages of revelation in the Old Testament are not superseded in Christ, because:

(a) The 'mystery' of the Old Testament was Christ not only

in the sense that Moses and the prophets 'spoke' of him, but primarily because the whole stream of sacred history was divinely oriented towards him. In this sense he was the fulfilment of the prophecies.

(b) The only true continuation of the Old Covenant is in the Church of Christ. The Old Testament is not a link holding together the Church and the Synagogue, but is to be interpreted as a book of the Church. It is to the Church that it belongs. This was seen as early as Justin Martyr.

(c) There is a new use of the Old Testament in the Church of Christ. The Law has been abrogated because it has been superseded by the truth, which fulfils it. Further, we must interpret the Old Testament in relation to the life of the Church. We have no right to isolate certain elements of the Old Dispensation from the immediate relation to the life of the Church, and set them up as a Scriptural pattern for the temporal life of nations. Finally, we must distinguish carefully between what was permanent, and what was situation-conditioned in the Old Testament. Situation-conditioned is to be understood not primarily in the sense of a general historical relativity, as in the sense of belonging to a previous stage of revelation. The Lord Jesus Christ created a new redemptive situation. Everything that belongs essentially to the earlier phase keeps its meaning only in a prefigurative sense. The national frame of the provisional Church has been superseded by the universality of salvation.

(7) The Bible is complete, because the Word of God has become incarnate. But the sacred history is not yet completed. *The Bible is still a prophetic book pointing to the Future.* Indeed the whole being of the Church is, in a sense, prophetic. Yet Christ has given a different meaning to the future. For he is not now in the future only, but also in the past, and so in the present. The history of redemption is still going on in the history of the Church. No complete system of Christian faith is possible for the Church is still a pilgrim Church. And the Bible as a book of history continually reminds the Church that God is a living and acting God.[6]

III. THE SEVEN ECUMENICAL COUNCILS

Together with Scripture are to be accepted the doctrinal definitions of the *Seven Ecumenical Councils*. Professor Hans Küng has recently written in his book *Structures of the Church* (Burns and Oates, 1965, p. 52):

> Without trying to belittle or disregard the importance of later councils, it remains a fact that the first four ecumenical councils (and especially Nicaea which occupies a unique position among the four) defend the Catholic faith in a fundamental and decisive fashion. Hence they provide a definite norm for all subsequent Councils, and they vary in importance. This is particularly relevant to the question of reunion with the East.

This is a very Western statement. It is understandable in view of the fact that the Seventh Ecumenical Council was only finally accepted in the West by the great Canonists of the twelfth century.[7] Whatever truth there is in it, its general acceptance among Western Christians has resulted in widespread ignorance of the fifth, sixth and seventh Ecumenical Councils; and this is most unhelpful to an understanding of the Orthodox Church.

There is a sense in which the Seventh Ecumenical Council— The Second Council of Nicaea 787—is the most precious of the Ecumenical Councils to the Orthodox, because it recapitulates the affirmations of the earlier ones, and draws out their implication in the veneration of ikons.

Here is the central declaration:

> So we confess, so we teach, just as the holy and ecumenical six Synods have decreed and ratified. We believe in one God the Father Almighty, maker of all things visible and invisible; and in one Lord Jesus Christ, his only begotten Son and Lord, through whom all things were made, and in the Holy Spirit, the Lord and Giver of life, consubstantial and co-eternal with the same Father and with his Son who has had no beginning. The unbuilt-up, indivisible, incomprehensible, and non-circumscribed Trinity; he, wholly and alone, is to be worshipped and revered with adoration; one Godhead, one Lordship, one dominion, one realm and dynasty, which without division is apportioned to the Persons, and is fitted to the essence severally.
>
> For we confess that one of the same holy and consubstantial

Trinity, our Lord Jesus the true God, in these last days was incarnate and made man for our salvation, and saved our race through his saving incarnation, and passion and resurrection, and ascension into heaven; and delivered us from the error of idols; as also the prophet says: Not an ambassador, nor an angel, but the Lord himself has saved us. Him we also follow, and adopt his voice, and cry aloud. No Synod, no power of kings, no God-hated agreement has delivered the Church from the error of the idols, as the Judaizing so-called Council, which raved against the venerable ikons, madly dreamed; but the Lord of glory himself, the incarnate God, has saved us and snatched us from idolatrous deceit. Therefore to him be glory, thanks, eucharists, praise and splendour.

For his redemption and his salvation alone can perfectly save, and not that of other men who come from the earth. For he himself has fulfilled for us, upon whom the ends of the earth are come through the economy of his incarnation, the words spoken beforehand by his prophets, for he dwelt among us, and went in and out among us, and cast out the names of idols from the earth, as it was written.

But we salute the voices of the Lord and of his apostles through which we have been taught to honour in the first place her who is properly and truly the Mother of God and exalted above all the heavenly powers; also the holy and angelic powers; and the altogether to be praised Apostles, and the glorious Prophets and the triumphant Martyrs which fought for Christ, and the holy and God-bearing Doctors, and all holy men; and to seek for their intercessions, as able to render us at home with the all-royal God of all, so long as we keep his commandments, and strive to live virtuously.

Moreover we salute the image of the honourable and life-giving Cross, and the holy relics of the Saints; and we receive the holy and venerable ikons; and we salute them, and we embrace them, according to the ancient traditions of the holy Catholic Church of God, that is to say of our Holy Fathers, who also received these things and established them in all the most holy Churches of God, and in every place of his dominion.

These honourable and venerable ikons, as has been said, we honour and salute and reverently venerate: that is, the image of the incarnation of our great God and Saviour Jesus Christ and that of our spotless Lady the all-holy Mother of God, for whom he pleased to take flesh, and to save and deliver us from all impious idolatry; also the ikons of the holy and incorporeal Angels, who as men appeared to the just. Likewise also the figures and portraits of the divine and wholly to be praised Apostles, also of the God-declaring Prophets, and of the struggling Martyrs and of the holy men. So that through their representations we may be able to be led back in memory and recollection to the prototype, and have a share in the holiness of some of them.[8]

The Christian meaning attached to the veneration of ikons is further to be seen in the anathemas made at the Council by Basil bishop of Ancyra, who had been influenced by the teaching of the Iconoclasts, but now asked to be received back.[9]

Anathema to the calumniators of the Christians, that is, to the breakers of ikons.

Anathema to those who apply the words of Holy Scripture which were spoken against idols, to the venerable ikons.

Anathema to those who do not salute the holy and venerable ikons.

Anathema to those who say that Christians have recourse to the ikons as to gods.

Anathema to those who call the sacred ikons idols.

Anathema to those who knowingly have communion with those who revile and dishonour the venerable ikons.

Anathema to those who say that another than Christ our Lord has delivered us from idols.

Anathema to those who spurn the teachings of the holy Fathers and the tradition of the Catholic Church, taking as a pretext and making their own arguments of Arius, Nestorius, Eutyches, and Dioscorus, that unless we were evidently taught by the Old and New Testaments, we should not follow the teachings of the holy Fathers and of the holy Ecumenical Synods, and the tradition of the Catholic Church.

Anathema to those who dare to say that the Catholic Church has at any time sanctioned idols.

Anathema to those who say that the making of ikons is a diabolical invention and not a tradition of our holy Fathers.

Here it is quite clear that the veneration of ikons has its place within a Christocentric faith. Its intention is to strengthen and communicate that Christocentrism.

IV. THE CHIEF SECONDARY DOCTRINAL STATEMENTS

Timothy Ware in an admirable chapter on Tradition lists the outward forms of Tradition, and gives as additions to the Bible and the Seven Ecumenical Councils: (1) Later Councils (which may be set aside or corrected); (2) The Fathers (where the judgment of the Church is selective); (3) The Liturgy (in which Orthodox belief is contained on many points rather than in formal dogmatic definitions); (4) Canon Law (which, if inapplicable today illustrates Orthodoxy applied to differing practical situations); and, (5) ikons.

Of special importance is his listing of the chief Orthodox doctrinal statements since 787. These cover the whole of the period since the ninth century, and so, in some sense, are an introduction to the history of Orthodox theology. Most of them are statements to defend Orthodox tradition against attack. The *History of Doctrine* needs urgently both a greater availability of the documents and an interpretation of the history so that a living awareness of the main elements in the history of Orthodox theology may be part of the perspective of every student.

Here are the chief Orthodox doctrinal statements which Dr Ware lists, with my own brief comment:

i. *The Encyclical Letter of Saint Photius* (867). He was the greatest scholar in ninth century Constantinople, though unfortunately he could not read Latin. His name as 'a great Churchman, a learned humanist and a genuine Christian' has been rescued from calumny by the great Catholic scholar Professor Dvornik. His encyclical as Patriarch of Constantinople was not unprovoked, and complained of Latin missionaries in Bulgaria, and expounded Orthodox objections to the addition of the *filioque* clause to the Creed.

ii. *The First Letter of Michael Cerularius to Peter of Antioch* (*1054*). Michael Cerularius was Patriarch of Constantinople from 1043. In the controversy of 1054 he attacked the addition of the *filioque* clause, and the use of unleavened bread in the Eucharist.

iii. *The decisions of the Councils of Constantinople in 1341 and 1351 on the Hesychast Controversy.* The two local Councils signify what proved to be permanent acceptance by the Orthodox Church of the great fourteenth century theologian Saint Gregory Palamas. Hesychasm is the practice of the belief that quiet (*hēsychia*) of mind and body is a preparation for seeing the divine light.

iv. *The Encyclical Letter of Saint Mark of Ephesus* (*1440–1*). Saint Mark was Archbishop of Ephesus. He was the only

Orthodox bishop who refused to sign the declaration of reunion at the Council of Florence in 1439. He attacked especially the addition of the *filioque* clause to the Creed.

v. *The Confession of Faith by Gennadius, Patriarch of Constantinople (1455–6).* Gennadius was George Scholarius, a teacher of philosophy and a civil court judge, who became a monk. He was made patriarch by Sultan Mohammed II after the fall of Constantinople in 1453. He opposed reunion with the West, though he had previously supported the scheme for reunion at the Council of Florence.

vi. *The Replies of Jeremias II to the Lutherans (1573–81).* This is the first authoritative Orthodox judgment on the theology of the Reformation, given in three letters 1576, 1579 and 1581, in answer to the presentation of a Greek translation of the *Augsburg Confession*, and to two replies to his letters. He discussed mainly free-will and grace, Scripture and Tradition, the Sacraments, prayers for the dead, and prayers to the Saints.

vii. *The Confession of Faith by Metrophanes Kritopoulos (1625).*

viii. *The Orthodox Confession of Peter of Moghila* in its revised form (ratified by the Council of Jassy 1642).

ix. *The Confession of Dositheus* (ratified by the Council of Jerusalem 1672).

These three Confessions are all related in some way to the tragic career of Cyril Loukaris who was Patriarch of Alexandria from 1602–38—a most remarkable and gifted man. To facilitate closer relations with protestantism Cyril published in 1629 a confession which is distinctively Calvinist in much of its content.

Metrophanes Kritopoulos was Loukaris' principal chaplain, and sent by him to study at Oxford and at Helmstedt. The Confession that he published in 1625 is influenced by Protestantism but is substantially Orthodox. The Confessions of Peter of Moghila and Dositheus are the most important of the repeated attempts to refute Loukaris. Peter of Moghila, Metropolitan of Kiev, was anti-Catholic in his approach, but based his instruction on Latin Catholic models, and this influenced his presentation. His Confession was only approved after it had been revised by Meletios Syrigos.

Dositheus was Patriarch of Jerusalem from 1669. He also

borrowed from Catholic sources, but he expounded the Orthodox standpoint. He refuted Cyril Loukaris point by point on free-will, grace, predestination, the Church, the sacraments and ikons. His confession is the most important and influential of these three seventeenth-century Confessions.

x. *The Answers of the Orthodox Patriarchs to the Non-Jurors* (*1718, 1723*). The eighteenth century saw this remarkable Anglican approach to the Orthodox Church. It shows how far apart the correspondents were, but it opened the door to later understanding. The Non-Jurors objected to the direct invocation of the saints, the veneration of ikons, the adoration of the Eucharistic elements, and particularly the special devotion given to the Mother of God. In return the Patriarchs warned them to give up their Lutheran-Calvinistic heresy.

xi. *The Reply of the Orthodox Patriarchs to Pope Pius IX (1848)*. This made clear the different conceptions of infallibility held by the Orthodox and Catholic Churches. Infallibility, they said, does not belong to the episcopate in isolation. It belongs to the whole Church.

xii. *The Reply of the Synod of Constantinople to Pope Leo XIII* (*1895*). Leo XIII when he became Pope in 1878 changed the Catholic attitude represented by the establishment of the Latin Patriarchate in 1869. So his encyclicals of 1894 represented a genuine attempt at reconciliation. But the ground had not been prepared—the Orthodox were not ready for it. The reply, of which there is a copy of the Greek text with an English translation in the University of Manchester Library, complains of the innovations of the Papal Church, and says there are essential differences relating to the divinely instituted canonical constitution of the administration of the Churches. They see the Old Catholics as the defenders of the true faith in the West.

xiii. *The Encyclical Letters by the Patriarchate of Constantinople on Christian Unity and on the Ecumenical Movement (1920, 1952)*. These should be familiar. They are to be found in G.K.A. Bell's *Documents on Christian Unity*, First and Fourth Series. The first says that a closer intercourse and a mutual understanding between the several Christian Churches is not prevented by the doctrinal differences existing between them and is highly desirable and necessary. The second considers that the participation and cooperation of the Orthodox Church with the World Council of Churches in the future is both necessary and desirable.

V. SAINT GREGORY PALAMAS

In the remainder of this paper I want to give some account of the theology of the great fourteenth-century Orthodox theologian, Saint Gregory Palamas (1296–1359), whose thinking developed the insight of the Cappadocian Fathers and is so deeply Orthodox; and of the main convictions of Alexei Khomiakov (1804–60), who like Metropolitan Philaret of Moscow (1782–1867) exemplifies that renewal of Orthodox thinking and confidence which began at the beginning of the nineteenth century.

(1) *The thought of Saint Gregory Palamas must be understood in its own right* before it is subjected to criticism—otherwise the result will be confusion and stupidity. In F. L. Cross's indispensable but not entirely flawless *Oxford Dictionary of the Christian Church* (1958), the article on *Hesychasm* (p. 633) says:

The fact that the Hesychast theology, which conceives God as a compound of essence and activity, substance and accident, is radically opposed to Latin doctrine, furthered its success in the East.

This is to force Palamas' thinking into Thomist categories, with an absurd result which belittles his greatness. Such a description goes back to the misunderstanding of Petavius (1583–1652), the Jesuit historian and theologian. As Professor Lossky has said:

Essence and energies are not, for Palamas, two parts of God, as some modern critics still imagine, but two different modes of the existence of God, within His nature; the same God remains totally inaccessible in His essence—and communicates Himself totally by grace. As with the dogma of the Trinity, this dogma of divine energies in no way detracts from the simplicity of God as long as simplicity does not become a philosophical notion which claims to determine the indeterminable.[10]

We must realize that this theology comes out of a quite different intellectual situation and tradition from that of the rationalism of the Western Middle Ages.

(2) The theology of Saint Gregory Palamas was a *Christian humanism*. It was rooted in the centrality of the intervention of God in history through the incarnation of his Son. All discussions of man's knowledge of God must take into account the change which God himself has brought into his relationships with man through this act. Palamas constantly affirms the reality of the Incarnation. It is the ground on which he based his teaching of deification, the sharing by man in the divine life, developing the meaning of the Church as the Body of Christ. Through Christ man is no longer alone in face of God, for God has come to put himself within man's reach, and to accompany him in his ascension to his Creator. 'If', he says, 'the Word of God had not been incarnate, the Father would not in plain fact have manifested himself as Father, nor the Son in plain fact as Son, nor the Holy Spirit as proceeding from the Father; then God would not have revealed himself in his essential and hypostatic existence, but only as an energy contemplated in creatures.' It is on this basis that he insists on the superiority of Christian spirituality over all psychological aspiration or mysticism outside the grace of the Incarnation.

(3) On this basis Palamas' exposition of the theology of Hesychasm is profoundly Christian. Hesychasm owes much to Saint Symeon the New Theologian (949–1022) in the tenth century, the greatest of the Byzantine mystics, but Palamas was the theologian of the movement. Hesychasm in his teaching is essentially a method of responding to divine grace. Man cannot save himself, and his mind needs the grace of God and can find it nowhere but in the Body of Christ united to our bodies by baptism and the Eucharist. The divine life is accessible to man as a gift which is common to all the baptized. Vision and deification is never a way of possessing God and of submitting him to the laws of creatures. Though he really communicates himself, he dwells in mystery all the more. Monasticism must always keep faithful to its evangelical simplicity.

Within its response to the divine grace, the hesychast method of prayer is not a denial of human activity but its true functioning. Hesychasm is that state of inner rest and quiet, which is the result of victory over the passions and enables the one who prays to contemplate and respond to God's revelation of himself. It is, in the literal sense of the word, 'apathy'—this does not mean that the passionate part of the soul has been killed, but that it is set free for its true task of doing good. Prayer is not a passive state, but a conscious activity of the human being, in supplication and thanksgiving. It is above all a communion with a personal God. For Palamas vision, divine union, is equivalent to Saint Paul's conception of faith, and his thought is deeply rooted in his understanding of Biblical truth. Faith is the complete activity of man turned towards God. It is a vision of our heart, which passes beyond all sensation and all understanding. It is a vision of God who is Light and in whom is no darkness at all, of which the natural symbol is the light of the Transfiguration of Jesus on Mount Tabor—a symbol which draws all its reality from God.

'He who participates in divine energy', Palamas says, 'becomes in some way light in himself; he is united to the light and with the light he beholds with all his faculties all that remains hidden to those who do not have this grace; thus he surpasses not only the corporeal senses but also all that can be known by the intellect . . . for the pure in heart see God . . . who as light dwells in them and reveals himself to those who love him, to his well-beloved.' This same uncreated light communicates itself therefore to the whole man, making him live in communion with the Holy Trinity. It is this communion with God, in which the righteous will be finally transfigured by light and will themselves become as resplendent as the sun, which constitutes the beatitude of the age to come—the deified state of creatures, where God will be all in all, not by His essence but by His energy, i.e. by grace or uncreated light, 'the ineffable splendour of the one nature in three hypostases'.[11]

This is an eschatological vision rooted in history, which is akin to the thought of Irenaeus—rather than to the Alexandrian ideal of Clement and Origen.

(4) Behind this lies *an illuminating and articulated doctrine* of God, which develops the thought of the Cappadocian Fathers, and the decisions of the Sixth Ecumenical Council, the Third Council of Constantinople of 680, which affirmed two energies, divine and human, in Christ. This has been expounded in the Christology of Saint Maximus the Confessor (*c.* 580–662). 'We know our God from his energies,' Saint Basil of Caesarea had written, 'but we do not claim that we can draw near to his

essence. For his energies come down to us, but his essence remains unapproachable.'[12]

This distinction Palamas accepted and developed. He formulates his theology in terms of three elements: essence, energy and the Triad of the divine hypostases. The personal nature—tri-hypostatic—of the divine being represents its simplicity; whereas the essence and the energies represent the paradox of the Unknowable making itself known, the One multiplying itself, and the sole Existent making creatures share in its existence. These distinctions are necessary to show how God can really share his authentic life while remaining unassailably God.

Energy is neither essence, nor accident, he says, and if some theologians have used the word 'accident', that was only to show that everything in God is not essence. Nor are energies to be understood as 'qualities'. In a certain sense essence and energy are identical in God, but in another sense they are different. They involve a certain distinction in the divine being, but do not divide it.

Essence, in fact, is not the whole of the divine being in this theology. 'The essence', Palamas says, 'is necessarily being, but being is not necessarily essence.' And he does this, because it is essential to his thinking that he should affirm that God can reveal himself in his very being, and yet that it is impossible to participate in his essence.

The three divine hypostases possess one sole energy, and every divine act is necessarily the act of the Holy Trinity because of their consubstantiality. Consubstantiality establishes 'co-penetration' (*perichōrēsis*) between the hypostases which is in fact their common energy.

(5) This theology *is the outcome of a struggle* between Palamas and Barlaam the Calabrian, a learned Greek from Italy. Barlaam's apophatic theology was directly dependent on Neo-Platonism and understood the transcendence and unknowability of God as a result of the limitations of the created mind. Knowledge of God comes from going beyond oneself, being detached from created things, and becoming unified with oneself.

But Palamas without repudiating the vocabulary of 'the Great Dionysius', who was still revered as the convert of Saint

Paul, modifies it in a Christian sense. For him the knowledge that God is unknowable does not come from abstract reflection but through a religious experience which constitutes a revelation of the living God. Divine transcendence is a property of God which no human discipline can remove. It is the God who is in his essence 'unknowable' who reveals himself, when he so wishes, and upon conditions which he himself fixes.

Those who have been purified by *hesychia* [Palamas says], know that the Divine surpasses these contemplations and these initiations, and so possesses that grace supra-intelligible and super-additional in a way that surpasses us; they possess it not because they do not see after the fashion of those who practise negative theology, but because there is in the very vision which they know something which surpasses vision by undergoing negation and not by conceiving it. Just as the act of undergoing and seeing divine things differs from cataphatic (affirmative) theology and is superior to it, so does the act of undergoing negation in spiritual vision, negation linked to the transcendence of the Object, differ from negative theology and is superior to it.[13]

The theology of Saint Gregory Palamas is clearly *the work of a great theologian,* and Christians in the West must make an effort to understand it against the background of the development of Orthodox thought up to this time. The differences between it and the theology of Saint Thomas Aquinas are not due to incompetence on the part of Palamas. They are due partly to differing tradition—the Western Scholastic development with its roots in Boethius (*c.* 480–*c.* 524) is not paralleled in the Orthodox Church—and partly to an honest difference of judgment over Aristotle. Thomas had a natural liking for and satisfaction in Aristotle's type of thinking; Gregory, on the other hand, was acutely sensitive to what he considered the inadequacy and unsatisfactoriness of Aristotle's way of thinking to express the Christian Mystery.

VI. ALEXEI KHOMIAKOV

(1) Let us jump from the fourteenth to the nineteenth century and consider a very remarkable layman—a landowner, Alexei Khomiakov, who has a prophetic importance, as signalizing the renewal of confidence in Orthodox theology

after centuries of purely defensive thinking, as a foretaste of that flowering of Orthodox theology which has enriched the twentieth century, even if Orthodox theology has not, for understandable reasons, been focused in anything like Vatican Council II.

Nicolas Berdyaev wrote of him:[14]

Khomiakov was a theologian of genius. In him the Orthodox East became conscious of itself, expressed in its original religious way. Khomiakov wanted to formulate the consciousness of the Catholic Church and to express its very essence. Nevertheless, his religious consciousness remained always that of the Orthodox East, not of the whole Ecumenical Church. His consciousness was opposed to the Catholic West. To the Catholic world Khomiakov refused membership. All the sins of the Slavophiles developed from this basis. In that is rooted their narrowness.

He compares Khomiakov with the Catholic layman Joseph de Maistre (1753–1821). 'In Khomiakov and Joseph de Maistre', he says, 'the Orthodox East and the Catholic West became conscious of themselves in their exclusiveness and onesidedness'.

(2) Khomiakov brooded over the state of and prospects for European civilization. He saw it as leading inevitably to disaster, due to the individualism of the whole Western Church. Protestantism, he thought, was nothing more than the logical outcome of Papal individualism. Rome symbolized unity without freedom, and Protestantism freedom at the cost of unity. They both meant the isolation of man and his exclusion from the redeeming influence of true Christian fellowship. This was a rejection of the love on which the life of the Church is based.

Love seemed to Khomiakov the characteristic feature of living in the practice of Orthodox tradition. 'Truth', he said, 'looks as if it were the achievement of the few, but in reality it is the creation and possession of all. The highest knowledge of truth is beyond the reach of an isolated mind; it is possible only to a society of minds bound together in love.'

The Church is the first fruit of the new order to come, in which men will be restored to harmony with the Creator, and recover their fellowship with one another. The Church anticipates the richer and fuller life which God had meant for all men, but which unredeemed men could not attain. Only in the

Church can man find himself and establish right relations with the rest of creation, for, within her, his heart, mind and will are regenerated and purified and his being is made whole by the action of the Holy Spirit.

(3) He used the word *sobornost* (the Slavonic word for *catholic*, derived from the root *sobirat* to bring together) to express that catholicity of love which is to be found in the Orthodox Church, a catholicity which has the power to bring all men into a true unity. In this fellowship each may find the fullest expression of his personality, for it is unity in freedom, as opposed to uniformity and compulsion. This is due to the oneness of Divine grace dwelling in reasonable creatures who freely submit to it. The Church itself is prior to the response to the Holy Spirit. Its love and also its faith and hope are expressed in its worship, in prayers and rites inspired by the spirit of truth and by the grace of Christ.[15]

This is at least one aspect of Orthodox tradition and its confident reaffirmation in the early nineteenth century was life-giving.

I want to end with two quotations.

The first is from John Meyendorff's exposition of Gregory Palamas (op. cit., pp. 179–80) and expresses for me the Orthodox understanding of *the infallibility of the Church*. Note the remarkable combination of an unwavering belief in the infallibility of the Church of God, with a very frank and realistic admission of the fallibility of the empirical Church.

Sin separates us from the Church, and only repentance reconciles us with it; and sin against the truth is the worst sin of all. Bishops themselves, invested with the *magisterium* of truth, are not exempt from this rule; if they are faithful to tradition and act in accord with the whole Church and if they dwell in their dioceses, then they dwell in truth. But if they abandon Orthodoxy, then they lose not only their *magisterium*, but their very status as Christians, and their anathemas have no value. Not bishops only, but whole local Churches may stray from the path of truth. Palamas recalls that in the course of history all churches have so strayed, but only the Latin Church has not yet returned to Orthodoxy, 'although it is the greatest and the first, and includes the more exalted of all the patriarchal thrones'. The Church, pillar and foundation of truth, 'nonetheless stands firm and unshaken, resting solidly on those who maintain the truth; and, as a fact, those who belong to the Church of Christ, dwell in the truth, and those who have once and for all abandoned truth, have also left the Church'. The miracle of ecclesiastical infallibility is thus realized in the whole ecclesiastical body, that is to say that it finally remains the exclusive privilege of Christ, head of the Church, who, while granting to men the charisms of the Spirit—the Apostolic *magisterium* in particular—of which all may prove unworthy, continues to live and to manifest himself in the whole Body. This Church, the Body of Christ, is not just a sociological or geographical entity, of which only the living form part; it equally includes the Angels and the just of all times. This 'recapitulation' of the whole creation is one of the consequences of the Incarnation.

The other quotation is from the Archbishop of Canterbury, Dr Michael Ramsey, quoted in Dr Ware's book (p. 318). In the context of presenting the Anglican comment upon it, he stated his own interpretation of the Orthodox understanding of Tradition. It is not his comment that I wish to quote, but his positive exposition.

The Tradition is for the Orthodox one indivisible whole: the entire life of the Church in its fullness of belief and custom down the ages, including Mariology and the veneration of ikons. . . . The Orthodox appeal to the one indivisible organism of Tradition, to tamper with any part of which is to spoil the whole, in the sort of way that a single splodge on a picture can mar its beauty.

Whatever difficulty this view of tradition presents to other Christians, there is no doubt that those who take it for granted as the basis of their life can show a vitality of thought and life from which other Christians can learn.

NOTES

[1] *Answer of the Great Church of Constantinople to the Papal Encyclical.* Published by the Orthodox Greek Community in Manchester (1896), p. 18.

[2] Timothy Ware, *The Orthodox Church* (Penguin, 1963), p. 205.

[3] *The 'Unwritten' and 'Secret' Apostolic Traditions in the Theological Thought of St. Basil of Caesarea* (Oliver and Boyd, 1965).

[4] Alexander Schmemann, *The Historical Road of Eastern Orthodoxy* (Holt, Rinehart and Winston, New York, 1963), p. 43.

[5] *Eastern Christendom* (Weidenfeld and Nicholson, 1961), pp. 276–7.

[6] This account of the meaning of Scripture in Orthodox Tradition is based on *Revelation and Interpretation*, by Georges Florovsky, in *Biblical Authority for Today*, ed. Alan Richardson and W. Schweitzer (S.C.M., 1951), pp. 163–80.

[7] See F. Dvornik, *The Photian Schism* (Cambridge University Press, 1948), pp. 312, 315, and George Every, op. cit., p. 56.

[8] *The Seven Ecumenical Councils of the Undivided Church*, by H. R. Percival: A Select Library of Nicene and Post-Nicene Fathers of the Christian Church, Second Series, volume XIV (James Parker, Oxford, 1900), p. 541.

[9] Op. cit., p. 534.

[10] V. Lossky, *The Vision of God* (The Faith Press, 1963), p. 127.

[11] Ibid., p. 133.

[12] Quoted T. Ware, op. cit., p. 77.

[13] *Triads* II. 3, 26, quoted by John Meyendorff, *A Study of Gregory Palamas* (The Faith Press, 1964), p. 207. On this book the present exposition is based.

[14] Serge Bolshakoff, *The Doctrine of the Unity of the Church in the Works of Khomiakov and Moehler* (S.P.C.K., 1946), pp. 300–1.

[15] See the exposition of Khomiakov's thought in N. Zernov, *Three Russian Prophets* (S.C.M., 1944).

XII

Holy Book and Holy Tradition in Islam

GEO WIDENGREN

Today Islam is possessed of about 400 million believers, living in the area between the Atlantic in the west and the Pacific Ocean in the east. In our days Islam has begun to gain individual adherents even in Western Europe and in the United States of America. But Islam is still above all an Asiatic and African religion, though with a not insignificant number of Muslims living in the Balkans and within the borders of the U.S.S.R. Islam, as next to Christianity having the greatest number of adherents, claims our special interest.[1] It has been rightly said that Islam is a religion losing to none, but gaining from all other religions. From our western point of view it calls for notice that Islam, being historically associated with the Jewish and Christian religions, to a great extent shares the same doctrines and therefore also the same theological problems. This is quite evident as far as the theme of our colloquium is concerned.

I

In Islam the Holy Book occupies such a central and dominating position that we may well ask whether in Jewish and Christian religion the Scriptures have dominated the whole religious and dogmatic development to the same extent.

The Holy Book, the Qur'ān, as its Arabic name is, above all is a writing sent down from heaven.[2] Modern research tends to emphasize the importance attached by Muḥammad to the conception of the Heavenly Book.[3] We cannot in this short treatment of such a vast complex present a complete survey of the Qur'ānic ideas of the Heavenly Book but we must restrict ourselves to an analysis of the idea of a Divine Scripture as handed

over by God to His Apostle, the bringer of the revelation given
by God to mankind.

The Qur'ān says expressly that the Book is one and is preserved in Heaven. It contains all God's decrees and sums up all
wisdom. This is clear from Sūrah 6:59 where we read of God:[4]

> And with Him are the keys of what is hidden:
> none knoweth them but He.
> He knoweth whatever is in the land and the sea,
> and no leaf falleth, but He knoweth it.
> Neither is there a grain in the darkness of the earth,
> nor a thing, fresh or withered,
> but it is in a Book Manifest.

The same thought recurs with but slight variation in Sūrah
10:62:

> And not the weight of an ant
> in earth and heaven escapeth from thy Lord,
> neither is aught smaller than that, or greater,
> but it is in a Book Manifest.

Instead of quoting more passages of the same character (cf.
11:8, and 34:3 where the same fixed formula as in 10:62 recurs)
we may refer to the more general assertion found in Sūrah
22:69 (cf. 27:77):

> Knowest thou not that God knoweth
> whatever is in heaven and earth?
> Surely that is in a Book,
> surely that is easy for God.

The Qur'ān strongly emphasizes that before anything
happens on earth it is already written down in the Heavenly
Book as Sūrah 57:22 says:

> No affliction befalleth either on earth
> or in your own persons,
> but it is in a Book, before we create it,
> surely that is easy for God.

It calls for notice that not only what thus happens to man is
written down in this Book, but also the deeds of mankind, if
Sūrah 33:6 is to be interpreted in this way:[5]

Those who are relatives
are nearer one to another, according to the Book of God,

than the believers and the emigrants,
except in so far that you commit to your near relatives
a well-known kindness which has been written down in the Book.

This announcement could also be understood as a commandment to 'act towards your friends honourably, that stands inscribed in the Book', as Arberry's translation goes. In that case
the commandment as such is inscribed in the Heavenly Book.

This Heavenly Book has been received prior to Muḥammad
by Mūsā (28:43; 32:23; 37:117; 40:56; 41:45), Yaḥyā (19:13)
and 'Īsā (3:43; 19:31). This is expressly stated, but we must
ask ourselves whether not all such bringers of revelation who
in the Qur'ān receive the name of 'Apostle', *rasūl*, were sent
out with a heavenly message written in the Book *al-kitāb*. The
communities founded by those Apostles are actually called *'ahl
al-kitāb* which means 'people in possession of the (Heavenly)
Book'. It is in accordance with this presumed conception that
Sūrah 13:38 says:

> We have truly sent Apostles before thee . . .
> and it was not for any Apostle to bring a sign
> but by God's permission,
> for every epoch there is a Book.

To each epoch every Apostle thus brings a Book. For the rôle
played in Muḥammad's preaching by Ibrāhīm and for the fact
that Islam is connected with 'the religion of Ibrāhīm', it calls
for notice that Ibrāhīm, though never styled an 'Apostle', nevertheless is said to possess leaves of the Scripture, *ṣuḥuf* (53:37;
87:19).

When it is said in a revelation to Muḥammad in Sūrah 29:46:

> And thus We have sent down to thee the Book,
> and those to whom We have given the Book believe in it,

then it is obvious that the Book communicated to Muḥammad
must be the same as that given to the Apostles before him, for
the Qur'ān is actually this Heavenly Book. The Qur'ān is found
on the so-called 'preserved tablet', *lauḥ maḥfūẓ* (85:21-2) or is
written in 'a treasured Book', *kitāb maknūn* (56:77). The Qur'ān
preached by Muḥammad is accordingly the terrestrial edition
of this heavenly Scripture, for we read in an important passage
(43:1-3):

> By the Book that maketh clear!
> Behold, We have made it an Arabic Qur'ān,
> that perhaps ye may understand,
> and behold, it is in the Mother of the Book, with Us:
> truly lofty and wise.

This conception as found in the message of Muḥammad ex-
plains—as it has been said—'very neatly his insistence that the
content of his own message was in Scriptures of former peoples'.[6]
A very typical passage which may well be called decisive is
found in Sūrah 26:192–7:

> And behold this is a sending down from the Lord of the Worlds,
> with which the faithful Spirit has descended
> upon thy heart, that thou mayest be among the Warners,
> in a clear, Arabic tongue.
> And behold, it is truly in the Writings of the Ancients.
> Was it not a sign for them,
> that the learned among the children of Israel knew it?

In this passage the word used for 'Writings' is *zubur*, the
plural of *zabūr*, a Jewish-Christian term, denoting the Psalter
of David.[7] The use of it in the Qur'ān 'makes it clear that it was
used interchangeably with *kitāb*'.[8] What God told Muḥammad
to be preached 'in a clear Arabic tongue' as 'a sending down
from the Lord of the Worlds' is stated to be found 'in the
Writings of the Ancients', and is also understood by 'the learned
among the children of Israel'. The Qur'ān as presented by
Muḥammad is *au fond* identical with earlier Books of Revelation
and ought to be accepted by those people who acknowledge
these Heavenly Writings previously sent down to them, i.e.
Taurāh and 'Inǧīl (Torah and Gospel 2:115; 5:72).

The followers of Muḥammad are said to 'believe in the
entire Book' (3:115, 9:112, cf. 2:3) and therefore the Muslims
may say to the People of the Book in Sūrah 5:64:

> Say: O People of the Book! Do ye take revenge on us[9]
> for another reason than that we believe in God,
> and what has been sent down to us,
> and what was sent down before.

Sūrah 29:45 states expressly that the Muslims and the
'*ahl al-kitāb* have both the same God and that the Muslims be-

lieve in both the Revelation sent down to themselves and in what has been sent to the People of the Book:

> Dispute not with the People of the Book
> and say: We believe in what has been sent down to us,
> and what has been sent down to you:
> our God and your God is One.

The disciples of Muḥammad accordingly accept both the Old Testament, the New Testament, *and* the Qur'ān.

The possessors of the Book actually possess *only a portion* of the Heavenly Book and for this reason are spoken of as 'those who have received a portion of the Book' (3:22; 4:47, 54). Presumably the same holds true also of Muḥammad who according to Sūrah 35:28 has received 'from the Book', *min al-kitāb*.

Every Revelation sent down serves to *confirm* a Revelation previously sent down. The Taurāh given by the hands of Moses was confirmed by the Gospel given to Jesus.[10] The same holds true of the Qur'ān as is stated in a message to the People of the Book in Sūrah 4:50:

> O ye, who have been given the Book,
> believe in what We have sent down,
> confirming what is with you.

This same idea is expressed in a revelation directed to the Apostle himself, assuring that the Book given to him is the confirmation of what was sent down before as part of the Heavenly Book, Sūrah 35:28:

> And that which We have revealed to thee of the Book
> is the Truth, confirming what was before it.

We have spoken here only of *the* Heavenly Book, assuming the *'umm al-kitāb*, the celestial archetype of the revealed Books brought by the Apostles sent out by God, to be but *one single* Book. Some scholars, however (e.g. Jeffery), assumed that there were several Heavenly Books. This supposition rests on a false conception of the idea of a Heavenly Book. In a rather detailed investigation we have tried to demonstrate that both in Mesopotamian and Israelitic-Jewish religion there already existed a notion of the Heavenly Book exactly corresponding to the ideas expressed in the Qur'ān. Following in the steps of earlier scholars, e.g. Pedersen,[11] we have traced the history of a special pattern, according to which this Heavenly Book was handed over to the Apostle, the bringer of divine revelation, in his meeting with God after his ascending to heaven. We were also able to point out that previous research has established all the different aspects of this Heavenly Book (aspects which led some scholars to the false hypothesis of several Heavenly Books) in Israelitic-Jewish literature too. We were further able to establish the fact that all these different shades of meaning attached to this divine Writing could easily be explained from the very nature of the Babylonian Tablets of Destiny, these tablets being the perfect equivalent of the Islamic Heavenly Book as already Pedersen had ascertained.

Moreover, as the Babylonian Tablets of Destiny were thrown by the High-god Marduk at New Year's Day, so according to Sūrah 44:2; 97:1; 2:181 the Qur'ān was sent down in the month of Ramaḍān in the Night of Power, the *lailat al-qadr*, in which night 'Allāh decrees every term and work and all food till the same day of the next year', Ṭabarī, *Tafsīr*, XXX, p. 143.[12] The *lailat al-qadr* thus is a New Year's night and the Qur'ān corresponds also in this regard to the Mesopotamian Tablets of Destiny.

There is thus only *one* Heavenly Scripture, but there are different conceptions of this Writing in the Qur'ān, and different terms are used to designate this entity, as we already had the opportunity of seeing. Sometimes we hear of a *kitāb*, and this is the most common designation, sometimes of *ṣuḥuf*, once of *zubur*, very often also of a *lauḥ*. What do all these various terms denote?

That *kitāb* corresponds to 'book' is as clear as its Aramaic-Syriac background, the *keṭābā* being the usual name for 'scripture'. The word *zubur* too, is a Jewish-Christian technical term, the singular *zabūr* denoting the Psalter. This word *zabūr* was known in Pre-Islamic times as a designation of the holy Book of Christian hermits, cf. the Dīwān of Imru 'ul-Qais, ed. Ahlwardt, 63:1; 65:2.[13] The term *ṣuḥuf* has as its singular *ṣaḥīfah*, 'sheet, leaf', a South-Arabic word.[14] The word *lauḥ* again, corresponds exactly to Hebrew-Aramaic *lūḥ*, in its turn a perfect equivalent of Acadian *lēʾu*.[15]

There are accordingly two different conceptions of the outward form in which the Heavenly Writing is written: it is *either* written as a sheet, or a scroll, or as a *kitāb*, a real book, or even in a way—at least partly—identical with a special Jewish-Christian Book, the single *zabūr, or* this Heavenly Scripture is not a book, but tablets, or rather one tablet, *lauḥ*.

This difference has its historical explanation for there existed in pre-Islamic times in the Near East the idea that the Divine Scripture handed over to the Apostle in heaven is either a tablet (or tablets) or a book, or a scroll of a book. This difference is connected with the development of writing and writing material as well as with the shift of the method of writing: from the cuneiform script to an alphabet, the tablet being succeeded by the scroll or the book, but nevertheless in religious tradition preserving in some quarters something of its old reputation.

This variation of the concrete image of the Heavenly Scripture has thus passed over into the Qur'ān as a heritage of the past.

II

The Qur'ān as the Message brought to Muḥammad is the Book dictated to him in portions by the angel—identified by him with Gabriel—who is sent down to him. Muḥammad by bringing the Book only part after part differs from the previous bringers of revelation, for the Qur'ān says that Moses was given the whole Torah once for all (2:50, 81; 5:48; 17:2, 4). The same holds true of Jesus who received the Gospel, *'inǧīl* (3:43-4; 5:50; 57:27). The manner in which the Qur'ān is communicated to the Apostle is described in Sūrah 17:107:

> And We have parcelled out the Qur'ān into sections,
> that thou mightest recite it to mankind at intervals,
> and We have sent it down as a successive sending down.

The angel who brought Muḥammad the first revelation according to Sūrah 81:23 was seen by him 'on the clear horizon'. The tradition of their first meeting makes the angel proclaim the following words:

> O Muḥammad, thou art the Apostle of God,
> and I am Gabriel.[16]

The tradition of how Muḥammad met Gabriel further states that he heard a voice from heaven. On looking up to heaven he saw Gabriel in a human shape, standing with his feet parallel on the horizon of heaven. In the Qur'ān there is a close agreement in Sūrah 53:6-10, adding an interesting supplementary detail:

> He stood balanced,
> being in the highest horizon.
> Then he approached and glided down,
> and he was at the distance of two bows, or closer,
> and revealed to his servant what he revealed.

The Angel according to this Sūrah even *descended* to Muḥammad from heaven and came very close to him, whereupon the revelation followed. This revelation according to the tradition quoted above had the form of an introductory formula of an 'I am' type, and a vocation of Muḥammad to be the Apostle of God.

This pattern of address it is possible to trace back to earlier schemes as related in the case of both Zoroaster[17] and Mani.[18] In Iranian religion no Book is handed over, but the Apostle receives his commission from an Angel, descended from heaven. There is, however, another tradition about the vocation found in Ibn Saʿd *Ṭabaqāt* I.1, ed. Mittwoch, p. 131:5-7. Here it is said that when Muḥammad heard the voice from heaven he lifted his head and saw Gabriel sitting on a throne between heaven and earth, pronouncing much the same formula as already quoted. We here meet with another familiar scene— the Apostle before the heavenly throne, being addressed from the Being that is sitting on the throne, and given the commission to be His Apostle and to convey the message from him. This scene is found repeatedly in older religions and religious movements in the Near East. The Mesopotamian king Enmeduranki was introduced into the divine assembly in the temple Ebarra where Šamaš and Adad handed over to him 'the tablets of the gods, the bag with the mystery of heaven and earth'. In Israelite religion Moses receives from God the tablets of law. In the Samaritan liturgies it is said that Moses received from the hand of God 'the great Book that exists from the days of creation'. King David, according to 1 Chronicles 28:19, was instructed from God by means of a writing from Yahweh's own hand. The prophet Ezekiel got his commission in heaven before

P

the throne of God. When God has said to him: 'I am sending thee to the sons of Israel' (2:3), a roll of a book in which were 'lamentations and mourning, and woe' was handed over to him (2:9–3:2). In the book of Daniel 10:21 is proclaimed what is written in the Book of Truth. The same holds true of the Ethiopic Book of Enoch where Enoch has read the Heavenly Tablets and seen the holy Books. Elxai, finally, had received his Holy Book from heaven by an angel.[19]

The Mandaean Saviour too, has read the heavenly books and does not forget what he has read in them, but brings to mankind the primordial revelation contained in these Heavenly Books. We still possess a Mandaean writing that claims to reproduce this revelation and thus to be brought down to their community by the Saviour.[20]

The literary tradition in Arabic language carried on this pattern. Leaving out of consideration the Arabic literature of a Gnostic-Hermetic character where this pattern often is found[21] we may concentrate on Biblical figures. We may then mention that God according to notices preserved in Arabic literature handed over certain books, 'asfār, or leaves of writing, ṣuḥuf, to Adam, Seth and Enoch. These writings were sent down to them in such a way that Adam received thirty-one, Seth twenty-nine and Enoch thirty leaflets. Other relations give other numbers. What calls for notice is the fact that the traditions about Adam, Seth and Enoch, and their secret knowledge find no support in the Qur'ān. But it is also said that Moses received from God ten leaflets, thereby filling out the number of the sacred writings to one hundred.[22] These traditions are certainly of Jewish origin, for in 4 Ezra 14:37–46 it is related how Ezra received the heavenly wisdom and dictated it in ninety-four books, out of which only twenty-four were published, the other seventy being kept secret for the exclusive use of the wise men among his people. Enoch, according to the apocryphal 'Book of John, the Evangelist', had ascended to heaven, received his divine knowledge, contained in books, whereafter he had descended to earth, proclaiming his message. Ezra, on the other hand, never leaves the earth.

There are accordingly two types of the inspired bringer of revelation who receives the heavenly knowledge, contained in mysterious books: one is the divine Messenger, ascending to heaven, there receiving his heavenly knowledge, contained either in one or a great many books which he carries with him when descending again to mankind, in order to proclaim his message. The other is the perfectly human prophet to whom revelation descends in one way or the other, and who here on earth *dictates* this divine knowledge.

Muḥammad who is such a typical representative of this second type shares with the first type the designation of 'Apostle of God' (or 'the Sent One') or 'Messenger'. The term *rasūl Allāh* means 'sent out by Allāh', i.e. the Apostle of God, and corresponds exactly with Syriac-Christian expressions as I tried to demonstrate at some length more than ten years ago.[23] In both types of the Revelation-Bringer found in the Ancient Near East as well as in Gnostic religion it is a most characteristic trait that he is 'sent out' by God and for this reason receives the name 'the Sent One' or 'Messenger' (Syriac: *šelīḥā 'izgaddā*). We saw that Muhammad definitely remains within the human sphere. He does *not* ascend to heaven to receive a Book containing the Revelation. The Qur'ān (Sūrah 17:95) expressly states that the adversaries of the Prophet demand of him two things as his prophetical signs, able to demonstrate his position as a true bringer of revelation: firstly, that he should mount up into heaven, and secondly, that he should bring down to them a Book which they are able to read. The Qur'ān gives the following message in this case:

> Say: Glory be to my Lord!
> Am I but a man, an Apostle?[24]

In spite of the clear statement of the Qur'ān there has grown up a whole literature describing the ascension of the Apostle of God and his receiving in the highest heaven from the hands of God himself the Qur'ān, taken from the treasures of Allāh's throne. But moreover, again in spite of the Qur'ān itself, he is reported to have received an esoteric knowledge from God. This is in flagrant opposition to Sūrah 6:50:

> Say: I say not to you:
> 'I possess the treasures of God.'
> Neither say I: 'I know things secret.'

We are entitled to say that the old pattern of the Ancient Near East has triumphed over the historical truth. In the congregation of the Apostle of God this pattern of the Apostle's ascension to heaven and his receiving the Scripture has proved far stronger than his actual declarations in the Qur'ān![25]

III

For lack of space we do not treat here in detail the process by which a collection of the revelations received by the Apostle of God was brought about. Some stages of this process are still somewhat obscure but the general outline is well known. What should be emphasized in this place is an ever-recurring characteristic feature in every establishment of the text of a Holy Book: at the outset there are to be found a great many recensions exhibiting quite a lot of variant readings. Ultimately a so to speak 'normative' text is established and the endeavour is undertaken to eliminate all variants. The Holy Book being a revelation from God on principle should exhibit a rigidly fixed text, without any variability. In this regard the story of the standard recension, the edition brought about by the Caliph 'Utmān, is typical. The amanuensis of the Prophet, Zaid ibn Ṯābit, played a central rôle in this editorial activity and we have no reason to doubt the traditional notice as given by the traditionist al-Buḫārī (III. 392) that Zaid first made one recension of the Qur'ān under the first Caliph Abu Bakr, when the writing material would seem to have been rather casual.[26] This collection was given to Ḥafṣah, one of the wives of Muḥammad. The second recension was intended to be an official revision of the Book and traditional notices relate that a whole commission was given the task to carry out the collection and revision. When the task was finished the Caliph 'Utmān is said to have destroyed everything else from the Qur'ān in the form of ṣaḥīfah or muṣḥaf. He further, according to these reports, to put his 'official' edition into circulation, sent to every province a copy of what Zaid had written down. The story is repeated under the Umayyad Caliph 'Abd al-Malik who is reported to have sent copies of the Qur'ān to various provinces. If this report is true it shows at any rate that 'Utmān had not succeeded in making his recension the only accepted version. It is generally held that the process of canonization came to an end about the year 86 A.H. (706/7 A.D.). We know, however, that of the four recensions existing at the time of ʿUṭmān and intended to be succeeded by his own official, canonical recension that of Ibn Masʿūd held the field for a long time to come. Actually traces of this recension have been found in manuscript form and carefully collected and analysed by Jeffery whose researches have done so much to elucidate the early history of the Qurʾānic text.[27] The four recensions had a local spread and it is interesting to observe that they differed very much, not only in exhibiting different readings in the text itself but above all in the number and arrangement of the Sūrahs. It calls for notice that the recension of ʿAbdullāh ibn Masʿūd lacks the Sūrahs 1, 113 and 114. That Ibn Masʿūd did not accept these Sūrahs in his recension was obviously due to the fact that he considered them spurious.

IV

Once the Qurʾān was collected and spread in a standard recension the next task was to expound the text of the Scripture. The first expounders were the so-called 'readers' in Medina, Kufa and other centres of Qurʾānic learning, who used to recite the text of the Holy Book and in doing so came across several difficulties in the text as it was handed down. One typical passage is quoted by Goldziher in his masterly exposition of Islamic exegesis.[28] He draws attention to the passage Sūrah 12:110, where the Qurʾān speaks of the earlier prophets whom God sent out before Muḥammad to bring the divine revelation to the various peoples:

> Till, when the Apostles despaired,
> deeming they were liars,
> Our help came to them
> and whomsoever We willed was delivered.
> And Our might will never be turned back from
> the people of the sinners.

The difficulty in this passage is found in the words 'deeming they were liars'. This translation is based upon the reading *kaḍabū*, the active form of the verb *kaḍaba*. But that the former Apostles could have thought that they had been liars was to a pious Muslim an intolerable idea. Help was found in various ways. One of the most usual methods was to read *kuḏibū* instead of *kaḏabū*, thus a passive form instead of an active, thereby gaining the meaning: 'deeming they were counted liars'. Accordingly the earlier prophets would have been of the opinion that they were accused by the pagans of being liars. This is now the *lectio vulgata* and the official Egyptian recension I am actually using when writing this article gives the reading *kuḏibū*. It is moreover accepted in the latest English translation of A. J. Arberry (in The World's Classics, 596), where the passage in question is translated: 'deeming they were counted liars'.

However, as Goldziher has shown, it is easy to demonstrate that the reading *kaḏabū* is the correct one. One of the best exegetes, Zamaḫšarī (of whom more below) has this variant and many exegetes have tried to save it by various exegetical devices. Thus some interpret the passage syntactically by assuming a shift of subject in the sentence, understanding it in the following way: '(the pagans) deeming that they (i.e. the Apostles) were liars'. Other exegetes, however, proceeded the other way round, proposing to understand the same passage in the following way: '(the Apostles) deeming that they (i.e. the pagans) were liars'. It stands to reason that one would never have taken refuge in such desperate explanations had not the reading *kaḏabū* been well established as the sure one.[29]

The older exegetes were mainly concerned with such difficulties which were created by readings that could be eliminated by introducing a slight variant reading. It was explained that the variant causing the difficulty had crept into the sacred text owing to the careless work of the copying writer. The variant proposal by the exegete therefore aimed at restoring the original text. But such difficulties which were due to grammatical harshness, or even incorrectness, were later explained away by the grammarians of Baṣra and Kūfa who exercised their inventiveness to save the traditional readings.

All this belongs to the first period of exposition which is—as Goldziher underlines—characterized most of all by a very latitudinarian, not to say highly individualistic freedom in the establishing of the text of the Holy Book.

It goes without saying that it could not be long before it was felt that some fences had to be put against an unrestricted freedom in this respect. After this loose practice in the beginning, content to accept all such variants for which competent traditional authorities could be invoked, the number of admitted variants was narrowed down to only those variants that belonged to the so-called 'seven *'aḥruf*'. The word *ḥarf*, plur. *'aḥruf* or *ḥurūf*, was in this connection interpreted as a variant reading. The starting point was found in a tradition going back to Muḥammad according to which the word of God had been revealed in seven variant readings, *ʿalā sabʿati 'aḥrufin*, of which every one was to be held to be of divine origin.[30] This saying was ultimately thought to indicate the legitimacy of seven schools, each representing one type of variants, each one supported by a reliable tradition. For this reason it is demanded of every one who is a specialist in the science of Qurʾān-recitation that he should master the holy text in all these seven types of variant readings.[31] However, this principle was not accepted as the only dominating view, but met with strong opposition in some quarters. The theological thinkers, *al-mutakallimūn*, were opposed to the principle that their free interpretation of the sacred text should be restricted in the way indicated. They maintained that they should be allowed to use their subjective opinion, *al-raʾy*, and their independent judgment *al-ʾiğtihād*, if only no objections on the ground of correctness of language could be raised against the conclusions arrived at.[32] Moreover, the theological commentators were not always willing to accept the judgment of philologists as to what was correct language in the Qurʾān and what was not. To the theologians it was not the correct Arabic usage that could master the Qurʾān, but the Qurʾān to which the Arabic usage had to conform.

As time went on, the exegesis, *al-tafsīr*, grew into one of the most cultivated sciences in Islamic civilization. The great authority was ʿAbdullāh ibn ʿAbbās, the cousin of the Prophet. He has left no exegetical work to posterity, but his alleged exegetical statements have been brought together in collections.[33] It is, however, extremely difficult to form an opinion about his exegetical methods and opinions as the most conflicting statements are handed down to us in his name, and with equally good—or bad—authenticity. On the whole it must be said that traditional exegesis did not arrive at any accepted method. Hence the most opposite varieties of exposition, varieties leading the exegete after having presented the various possibilities to exclaim: 'But God, praise be to Him, knows best of all what He wanted to say', *wallāhu subḥānahu ʿaʿlamu bimā ʾarāda.*

We know that from the eighth century A.D. the Islamic theologians used to compile vast commentaries, *tafāsīr*, on the Qurʾān, but nothing is preserved of these early exegetical works. The loss is easy to bear because all the achievements of traditional exegesis were collected and summed up in the monumental *tafsīr* written by the great historian and theologian al-Ṭabarī (born 838, died 923), a work of thirty volumes and about 5,400 pages. Ṭabarī emphasizes that the knowledge, *ʿilm*, concerning the Qurʾān is founded upon tradition, tradition as it has been handed down from the companions of the Prophet and from their successors in an unbroken chain of traditionists. This is the principle of the traditional exegesis, the *tafsīr biʾl-ʿilm*. His commentary actually is a real treasure where all kinds of variant readings and exegetical explanations have been stored. He is not uncritical, but criticizes the authenticity of a tradition when it seems to him suspicious. He underlines further the principle that in the exposition the clear, exterior meaning, *al-ẓāhir*, of the text has to be preferred, unless other passages or necessary arguments motivate another explanation. He further declines to discuss questions of exegetical details where we have no chance of getting a sure answer, e.g. Sūrah 12:20, where it is said that Joseph's brothers 'sold him for a paltry price, a handful of counted dirhams'. The older commentators speculated much on the possible sum: was it 22 dirhams (two for each one of the eleven brothers), or was it perhaps for twenty or forty dirhams and so on. Ṭabarī says expressly that we will never get an answer to such a question. As an excellent expert in philology it is but natural for him to recur to quotations from ancient poetry in order to elucidate a difficult passage or word. For lexicographical investigations his commentary accordingly is an invaluable source. But also his grammatical analysis is of the greatest value to us. At the same time Ṭabarī, in accordance with his principles, is very careful to point out that philology must not be allowed to contradict the exposition of a Qurʾānic passage founded upon the authentic tradition of the companions of the Prophet. In his dogmatic positions he is dominated by the wish to be firmly grounded in the orthodox opinions of his days. His exegesis from time to time passes to dogmatic digressions, e.g. concerning the much discussed question of the anthropomorphic expressions used in the Qur'ān of Allāh.

After Tabarī the great names in Qur'ānic exegesis are Zamaḫšarī (died 1143), a brilliant lexicographer, the greatest exegete of a Muʿtazilite type, and Baiḍāwī (died 1286) whose comparatively concise commentary is much used.[34] One of the last men of science, the many-sided Suyūṭī has in his *Itqān* given a general introduction to the Qur'ānic sciences, of much value to western scholarship.

Islamic exegesis in modern times on principle has not moved far from traditional, mediaeval exegesis. An expert on modern Islam, however, is rather optimistic about the future of a really scientific Qur'ānic exegesis, for he says: 'But there is little doubt that exegesis is on the move and that the Qur'ān is increasingly undergoing, if we should not also say inspiring, an exegetical emancipation, and the end is not yet.'[35] For reasons indicated below (cf. pp. 230 f.) I am not so optimistic.

V

There was already an allusion to the fact that the Qur'ānic sayings about Allāh were the subject of dogmatic debates among Muslim theologians. Even more discussed was the dogmatic position of the Holy Book itself. That the Qur'ān is the Word of God is clear to the Muslim from its own text. But how is it to be understood that God receives the attribute of speaking? This problem is of course closely connected with the development of the dogmatic doctrines about God's attributes, one of the most debated problems in the history of Islam. But the question of how God's speaking in the Qur'ān was to be conceived of was separated from the dogmatic discussion of his other attributes and made the subject of very hard theological thinking.

Orthodoxy had its answer ready at hand: God's speaking is an eternal attribute of God, and His Word as the expression of the activity of this attribute must therefore also be eternal. This means that his revealed Word as contained in the Qur'ān exists from eternity and that the Qur'ān as expressing God's word is *uncreated*. This is orthodox dogma even today, a dogma which has found a striking formula in the saying that what is between the two covers of the Qur'ān—*mā baina'l-daffataini*—that is God's uncreated, eternal Word.

The theological school called the Muʿtazilites opposed, however, this orthodox dogma and with the support of some Caliphs they succeeded in the ninth century to get their doctrine of *the createdness of the Qur'ān* accepted as official dogma. A court of inquisition was instituted and orthodox theologians, among them Aḥmad ibn Hanbal, the head of what later developed to the Hanbalite school, were exposed to prosecutions of all kinds, including torture. With the arrival of the Caliph al-Mutawakkil, however, orthodoxy again got the upper hand, not to lose it any more. Such a dominating figure in dogmatics as al-Ašʿarī had to abandon his earlier, more rationalistic formulas and accept the more rigid orthodox formulas. In the definite fixation of his dogmatic opinions, *Kitāb al-'ibānah ʿan 'uṣūl al-diyānah*, he expresses himself in the orthodox way.

VI

The Qur'ān and its commandments from the outset regulated the life of the Muslim community. The Book was the highest norm, both juridical and religious. But the Book did not answer all questions. During his life-time the Apostle of God had been next to the Qur'ān, the highest instance in juridical and religious matters. He had *inter alia* functioned as supreme judge. Now that Muḥammad was gone a substitute for him had to be found, and this substitute was 'custom', *sunnah*, namely the *sunnah* of Muḥammad in the first place. But where this *sunnah* was non-existent, or deficient, one had to recur to the *custom* of his companions. The problem then, was how to get a clear knowledge of this *sunnah*. This problem was solved thanks to all the collections of so-called traditions which now were established. The tradition-collections did not treat only of juridical and religious questions, but also of a lot of conditions concerning the believer's behaviour in daily life, for this too is regulated by means of commandments and prescripts.

Accordingly we meet there with regulations concerning

washing of head, beard and hands, rinsing of mouth, nostrils and ears, use of sand for prescribed purifications when it is impossible to get water. Further it is prescribed what clothes and personal adornments are allowed. Also the manner in which greetings are exchanged, whether when putting on the daily dress the left or the right shoe is to be taken first, all this is the subject of juridical prescriptions by means of the citation of traditions which echo the *sunnah* of the prophet. In this manner purely juridical commandments, e.g. concerning civil, commercial and capital law, are mixed with prescriptions concerning hygiene and etiquette. The result is that Islam in this way implies not only religion, but also the law of the Islamic society, and even the social behaviour of the individual member of this society. Islam regulates the daily life of a Muslim from birth to burial, and in this way religion has exercised an enormous influence in Muslim society.[36] This all embracing religious-juridical legal system is called *šarī'ah*, which we may translate as 'Religious Law'.

That the *šarī'ah* was founded on *Qur'ān* and *Sunnah* was already stated. Because of the great importance ascribed to *sunnah* it was necessary to have these usages motivated by *tradition* as we also saw. We mentioned the existence of big collections of tradition, in which the *sunnah* of the Prophet was handed down in the form of a short narrative, called *ḥadīṭ*, 'statement'. The *sunnah* is accordingly dependent upon the *ḥadīṭ*, and moreover upon the historical reliability of the *ḥadīṭ*. The Muslim scholars themselves were forced to use some criteria to sort out the reliable from the unreliable *ḥadīṭ*. But it cannot be said that they were successful from the point of view of historical exactness. It was only the great Ignaz Goldziher who in his *Muhammedanische Studien* succeeded in laying the foundations of a critical study of the *ḥadīṭ*.

However, even if the standard collections of *ḥadīṭ* were accepted, as e.g. that of Buḥārī and five other authorities, the Hadith-literature was not sufficient to supply a canon for deciding legal matters. The Qur'ān and the Sunnah had to be supplemented by recurring to the so-called *qiyās*, analogy. This means that a problem was solved by the application of principles underlying an already existing decision of another related problem. The use of *qiyās* was rejected by many strict experts, but after endless debates succeeded in establishing itself as a third legal principle.

Even so, however, there remained a difficult problem to solve. The Muslim community possessed the Qur'ān, the Sunnah, and the *qiyās*, analogy. It stands to reason that the community as far as all these three principles are involved was confronted with a lot of conflicting opinions. The Holy Book itself had variant readings and was expounded in various ways by the commentators and exegetes. The Holy Tradition had to be sorted out from an enormous mass of Hadith collections. The analogy, *qiyās*, could of course be applied in various ways. With all these conflicting interpretations of Book and Tradition it was necessary to find some rule making it possible on the one hand to secure the authority due to Qur'ān and Sunnah, and on the other hand, in a manner as uniform as possible, apply their regulations to the changing problems that arose in different countries in different epochs. This supreme rule of interpretation was found in the so-called *consensus* of the community, *al-'iğmā'*. But the community, *'ummah*, for practical reasons had to exercise its authority by means of the *'ulamā'* (plural of *'alīm*), the theologians who were at the same time jurisconsults.

In this way the religious law, Sharī'ah, the system of faith and jurisdiction, was dependent upon four principles: Qur'ān, Sunnah, Qiyās, and 'Iğmā'. This means again, that the consensus of the community is the highest instance when it comes to deciding problems arising out of the directions given by Book and Tradition.

As time went on, more and more dubious points were decided by the consensus of the doctors. This means that the right of individual interpretation, the so-called *'iğtihād*, 'was in theory (and very largely in practice also) confined to the points on which no general agreement had yet been reached'.[37] It used to be said that 'the gate of *'iğtihād*' was shut once and for all. In this case, however, modern times have brought about a considerable change, as we shall see.

The development sketched here is valid only for the so-called Sunni Muslims, the overwhelming majority, called so because they follow the Sunnah. However the minority, called Shī'ah, 'the Party', the followers of 'Alī, the son-in-law of the Prophet, also follow a Sunnah, but a different Sunnah. Shī'ah rejects the doctrine of consensus and does not recognize the community, but the leader of the community, the Imām, as highest authority, when it comes to deciding the interpretation of Qur'ān and Sunnah. In Shīʿah the Imām is 'in concealment'[38] and for this reason the shīʿitic ʿUlamaʾ decide on behalf of him on all existing problems, exercising unreservedly even al-ʾiǧtihād. To the Imām in Shīʿah is moreover attributed an esoteric knowledge, very often materialized in occult writings of which he is said to be the possessor.[39] The revelation accordingly is *not* restricted to the Qur'ān, but was continually given to the Shīʿitic Imām. Here we meet with a most important difference in the idea of revelation as manifest in Scriptures. Against the static conception of revelation dominating in Sunni circles, we come across in Shīʿah quarters a dynamic idea of revelation, the idea that divine revelation has been communicated after Muḥammad to the Imams.

VII

The difficulty of ascertaining the authenticity of the tradition, *ḥadīṯ*, coupled with the 'puritan' reaction against later accretions, as it found expression in the eighteenth century in the Wahhābī movement in Arabia, led to interesting reform movements as far as Qur'ān and Hadith are concerned. These movements started a campaign for abolishing later traditions and returning to the authentic Prophetic Tradition. These tendencies found an organizable expression in several congregations calling themselves the *ahl-i-ḥadīṯ*, the people following the (true) tradition. This movement accordingly accepts both Book and Tradition, but rejects all the subsequent interpretations which ultimately led up to the established Sunnah.

Much more radical is the trend in a movement whose battle-cry is: 'Back to the Qur'ān!' This movement has adopted the name of *ahl-i-Qur'ān* and its position has been characterized as fundamentalistic, though it is difficult to say whether one needs to be a fundamentalist because one falls back upon the Qur'ān. The so-called modernists in today's Islam undoubtedly have been influenced by this movement because there is a tendency in modernist circles to stress above all the importance and value of the Qur'ān, neglecting or abrogating the Sunnah.

A rather typical approach to the problem in question is that of the editor of the journal *The Islamic Literature*, Shaykh Muhammad Ashraf. In 1948 he published in his journal a series of articles where he tried to take a middle course between the traditional Sunnah and the 'back-to-Qur'ān' movement. Against the *ahl-i-Qur'ān* who reject the whole tradition-literature as an infallible guide in the life of believers he holds the view that 'what the Prophet said or did, provided it has been correctly reported, is of great importance in explaining the real intent of the Qur'ān'.[40] This is, however, the crucial point, because the difficulty lies in stating what traditions are correctly reported as we have seen. Shaykh Muhammad Ashraf actually touches on this problem when observing that Muḥammad's Companions did not write down his sayings. But he uses this observation above all for asserting that this fact shows Qur'ān and Hadith to be of unequal value: the Qur'ān was written down in the first generation, but not so the Tradition. However, he is alive to the real problem, for from the fact that the most authentic *ḥadīt-s* may have been misunderstood and misinterpreted he draws the conclusion that the Hadith never can be anything but secondary to the Qur'ān.

In spite of its shortcomings the author is not prepared to reject the Hadith altogether because he is an adherent of the Sharī'ah, and the Sharī'ah stands and falls with the Hadith. Therefore the Hadith is the basis of law and practice and must occupy the place next to the Qur'ān.

This position may be said to be typical of those people who tackle the problem from a religious point of view. But the attitude taken by the present-day governments in several Muslim states shows that such governments on the whole have abolished the Sharī'ah from the domain of public law while leaving the Qur'ān untouched. Actually, no Muslim government could dream of minimizing the value of the Qur'ān. This again demonstrates the incontestable fact that in our time the position of the Qur'ān *de facto* is infinitely superior to that of Tradition. This fact moreover is considerably stressed if we take into consideration the central rôle played by the Qur'ān in the religious life of the Muslim community, a rôle about which we shall presently have some words to say.

To this still dominant position of the Qur'ān of course the

doctrine of its uncreatedness as God's own word contributes immensely. It is characteristic that Sayyid Amir 'Ali's endeavour in his famous booklet *The Spirit of Islam*, first published in 1891, to look upon the Qur'ān as the work of Muḥammad was not accepted by the majority of the modernists. On the contrary, to an overwhelming extent these people still follow the orthodox view that the Qur'ān is in a literal sense the Word of God. For this reason a long time will certainly pass before we will see produced in believing Muslim circles commentaries on the Qur'ān, showing anything like an historical approach to the problem of its origin.

VIII

Finally a few words must be said of the importance of the Qur'ān as an instrument of mission and propaganda, as a means of religious education, and as the object of prayer, meditation, and mystical exercise.

It is well known that the Qur'ān is one of the most important instruments of spreading the Islamic faith, quite especially when it comes to education and instruction of such adherents of Islam who only possess a superficial knowledge of its doctrines.

The process is well attested from, e.g., Indonesia and Africa. Because Africa is the most important area of Islamic mission in our days we may quote what a competent authority in the field of Comparative Religion has witnessed in an African country, Nigeria. He states that teachers periodically come down from the north to give instruction to the believers. At the festivals 'groups of the faithful may then be seen all over the town, in mosques or streets, in houses or fields, sitting round some long-robed teacher who expounds to them the sacred book or the traditions'.[41]

The other means of spreading and establishing Islam is by the permanent Qur'ān schools which are attached to many mosques. 'Groups of small children can be seen chanting texts in sing-song fashion, while an old teacher leads or corrects them with a rod. The Qur'ān is learnt by heart, in Arabic. First the shorter sūrahs are learnt . . . and then the longer and later ones. The children have no knowledge of most of what they learn, as it is entirely mechanical and alien.'[42] We know from several areas of Africa where Islam is gaining more and more ground that the Qur'ān schools have played a great rôle in the dissemination of Islamic ideas and in giving a more solid education.[43]

But also in old Muslim countries it goes without saying that the special Qur'ān schools are of great importance for the fortifying of religious knowledge. In Egypt, e.g., special schools for the memorization of the Qur'ān 'are sponsored by organizations of Muslims who think that insufficient attention is given to the study of the Qur'ān and the religion of Islam in the public elementary schools'.[44] By the end of the fourth year the pupils are expected to memorize the whole of the Qur'ān.[45]

However, the Primary Schools of Egypt, 1945–6, disposed for the study of Qur'ān and religion not less than 3 periods per week 1st year, 2 periods 2nd year, 2 periods 3rd year, 2 periods 4th year.[46] In Iraq for the same years the periods per week for the 1st to 6th grade in the public Primary Schools for the same subject were 4, 4, 3, 3, 2, 2, thus slightly more than in Egypt. Even in such a country as Tunisia where modern tendencies are very marked 'Islam is an integral part of what is called "religious and civic instruction"'.[47] This implies that in the Primary School the Qur'ān occupies a considerable part of the syllabus. In the first two years the children are taught to memorize both whole sūrahs and groups of single verses, while later on selections from the Qur'ān are chosen to teach morals and religious duties.[48] This example is an appropriate illustration of the central position occupied by the Qur'ān in the new Islamic National States. That this position is still stronger in such a country as Pakistan, which owes its existence to Islam, goes without saying.

In the Muslim prayer-ritual it is the duty of the worshipper to recite the opening Sūrah, *al-fātiḥah*, to which is given the supreme position in Islamic worship. On this sūrah also various devotions are built and on the whole the questions from the Qur'ān very often serve as the basis of the *munāǧāt*, the devotions. This fact emerges clearly from the study on Muslim devotions, recently published by Constance Padwick.[49] She quotes from a popular prayer-manual what is said of the Qur'ān: 'It is recited by tongues, written in volumes, memorized in breasts.' The mystic piety too, is deeply influenced by Qur'ānic reminiscences.

Mystic literature abounds in Qur'ānic quotations and allusions. It would seem that a mystic like al-Ḥallāǧ is quite especially influenced by the Qur'ān which he expounds or alludes to, e.g. in his *Kitāb al-Ṭawāsīn*.[50] The technical language of the Islamic mystics actually is dominated by the Qur'ān which has been— perhaps—their greatest source of inspiration,[51] even if we have to take into account other, non-Islamic influences, above all Christian and Gnostic.[52]

The liturgical practice in the Sufi orders, above all their 'recollection', *ḏikr*, and 'audition', *samā'*, is based on quotations from the Qur'ān.

'It is related that Shibli said, on hearing the verse "And remember thy Lord when thou forgettest",[53] "Remembrance (of God) involves forgetfulness (of self), and all the world has stopped short at the remembrance of Him," then he shrieked and fell senseless. When he came to himself, he said: "I wonder at the sinner who can hear God's word and remain unmoved." '[54]

Many more examples could be chosen to illustrate the rôle played in *samā'* by the Qur'ān but I shall content myself by saying in conclusion some words about the *ḏikr*. This well-known practice has developed into 'a great system of devotion',[55] flowering not only in Sufi circles, but of the greatest importance in the darwish orders. The word *ḏikr* implies in the first place the invocation of God by mentioning, 'recollecting' his name. But ultimately 'the word has come to stand for recitations of certain fixed phrases ... in a given order'.[56] The Qur'ānic texts quoted in support of *ḏikr* are 2:200; 3:41; 7:204; 72:25, and especially 2:152, 'Remember Me, and I will remember you,' *'uḏkurūnī 'aḏkurkum.*

The position of the Holy Book in Islam, as compared with that of Holy Tradition, is infinitely stronger than Tradition as we have had occasion to see more than once in the preceding pages. The purely liturgical rôle of the Qur'ān has, moreover, only been alluded to, but it stands to reason that the place occupied by the Qur'ān in all worship gives it a unique position. At the same time it should be observed that this Holy Book, literally the Word of God in our days too, is still read and interpreted in the light of Tradition. This fact in its turn makes it so difficult to leave out Tradition, concentrating only on the Book. The future will show how Islam is to solve this problem.

Q

NOTES

[1] Hinduism is so split up in various sects that it does not really compare with Islam.

[2] The Arabic word qur'ān goes back to, or is at any rate influenced by, the Syriac word qeryānā, cf. Noeldeke-Schwally, Geschichte des Qorans, 2, ed. I, pp. 31–4 (loanword with adaptation to the fuʿlān-type).

[3] For this section I have drawn heavily on Chapter VI in my work Muḥammad, the Apostle of God, and His Ascension (Uppsala, 1955).

[4] The translations extant in English have been used and checked with the Arabic text of the official text of the Qur'ān. The metrical arrangement of Arberry has been gratefully adopted (though with smaller modifications), but the translations adopted here are rather different.

[5] Cf. Widengren, op. cit., p. 116, where the translation given by Rodwell was accepted. A more correct translation is given above. It takes into account above all the Swedish translation given by Zettersteen.

[6] Jeffery, The Muslim World, xl (1950), p. 53.

[7] Cf. Jeffery, The Foreign Vocabulary of the Qurān, p. 148 f.

[8] Jeffery, The Muslim World, xl (1950), p. 53, n. 14.

[9] Cf. for this translation Noeldeke, ZA, xiii (1898), p. 111 f.

[10] Qur'anic passages are: Sūrah 3:43–4; 5:50; 57:27.

[11] Cf. Pedersen, Der Islam, v (1914), pp. 110–15.

[12] Wensinck, Arabic New-Year and the Feast of Tabernacles, p. 3.

[13] Cf. Ahrens, Muhammed als Religionsstifter, p. 132 with n. 3; Horovitz, Koranische Untersuchungen, p. 69; and already Fraenkel, Die aramäischen Fremdwörter, p. 248.

[14] Cf. Fraenkel, op. cit., p. 248; Jeffery, Vocabulary, p. 192 f.

[15] Cf. Jeffery, op. cit., p. 253 f. and Widengren, The Ascension of the Apostle, p. 25 for the correspondence lūḥ-lēʾu.

[16] Ibn Hišām, Sīrah, ed. Wüstenfeld, p. 150:6.

[17] Cf. Widengren, The Great Vohu Manah and the Apostle of God, p. 61 f.

[18] Cf. Widengren, op. cit., pp. 25 ff. and Muḥammad, the Apostle of God, p. 124.

[19] All necessary references are found in Widengren, The Ascension of the Apostle.

[20] Cf. Widengren, op. cit., pp. 59–76.

[21] Cf. Widengren, op. cit., pp. 77–85 and Muḥammad, p. 24.

[22] Cf. Widengren, Muḥammad, p. 23 f. Another example quoted by Von Grunebaum, Islam. Essays in the Nature and Growth of a Cultural Tradition, p. 93, n. 17, gives one hundred books of which fifty were revealed to Seth, thirty to Enoch, twenty to Ibrāhīm. To these are added: the Torah revealed to Moses, the zabūr to David, the ʾingīl to Jesus, and the furqān (an enigmatic name of the Qur'ān, from Syriac purqānā, salvation) to Muḥammad.

[23] Cf. Widengren, Muḥammad, pp. 7–22.

[24] Not 'Messenger' as Arberry constantly translates rasūl, which corresponds exactly to the Syriac šelīḥā, as already observed.

[25] Cf. for all this Widengren, Muḥammad, pp. 110 ff., 204–8.

[26] He collected the Qur'ān from *riqāʿ*, pieces of paper, *laḥāf*, stones, *ʿasib*, palm, *'aktāf*, shoulder-blades, *'aḍlāʿ*, *qitaʿ* *'adīm*, pieces of leather, according to the various traditions. All these things are known as writing materials from Arabia and Africa. cf. Noeldeke-Schwally, *Geschichte des Qorans*, II, p. 13.

[27] *Materials for the History of the Text of the Qur'ān*, pp. 20–113.

[28] Cf. *Die Richtungen der islamischen Koranauslegung* (1920), pp. 26 f.

[29] Cf. Goldziher, op. cit., p. 27. On the following page the author gives two anecdotes clearly showing how strongly the difficulty was felt and how great the relief when the syntactical operation was proposed.

[30] Cf. Goldziher, op. cit., p. 37.

[31] Cf. op. cit., p. 40.

[32] Cf. Goldziher, op. cit., p. 44 f.

[33] That the *tafsīr* that goes under his name is spurious may be taken for granted.

[34] An impression of Muslim scholarship in the field of Qur'ānic exegesis may be gained from Margoliouth, *Chrestomathia Baidawiana* (London, 1894), which gives a translation of Baiḍāwī's commentary on Sūrah 3 with extensive notes.

[35] Kenneth Cragg, *Counsels in Contemporary Islam* (Edinburgh, 1965), p. 177. For a survey of more recent Qur'ānic exegesis cf. Baljon, *Modern Muslim Koran Interpretation* (Leiden, 1961).

[36] Cf. Andreae, 'Traditionens religiösa betydelse i Islam', *Religionshistoriska studier tillägnade Edvard Lehmann* (Lund, 1927), pp. 195–223.

[37] H. A. R. Gibb, *Mohammedanism. An Historical Survey* (Oxford, 1950), p. 97.

[38] Cf. for this idea Friedlaender, *The Heterodoxies of the Shiites*, Index s.v. *ġaibah*.

[39] Cf. Widengren, *Muḥammad*, pp. 86 f., 88, 91 f., 94 f.

[40] For Shaykh Muhammad Ashraf's position cf. Guillaume, *Islam*, 2nd ed. (repr. 1964), pp. 163 ff.

[41] G. Parrinder, *Religion in an African City* (Oxford University Press, 1955), p. 65.

[42] Ibid., p. 66.

[43] Cf. Trimingham, *A History of Islam in West Africa* (Oxford University Press, 1963), pp. 81, 98 n. 1, 159, 177, 187.

[44] Matthews and Akrawi, *Education in Arab Countries of the Near East* (Washington, 1950), p. 45.

[45] Ibid.

[46] Ibid., p. 50.

[47] Rosenthal, *Islam in the Modern National State* (Cambridge, 1965), p. 363.

[48] Ibid., p. 364.

[49] *Muslim Devotions* (London, 1961).

[50] Cf. the edition of Massignon, Paris 1913, p. 109, list of Qur'ānic quotations.

[51] Cf. Massignon, *Essai sur les origines au lexique technique de la mystique musulmane* (Paris, 1922), p. 84: 'c'est du Qur'ān, constamment récité, médité, pratiqué, que procède le mysticisme islamique'.

[52] Massignon exaggerated his position by neglecting to a great extent above all the Christian influences, so well demonstrated by Andrae and Wensinck.

[53] Sūrah 18:23.

[54] *The Kashf al-Maḥjūb*, new ed. by R. A. Nicholson (London, 1936), pp. 396 f.

[55] Padwick, p. 13.

[56] Ibid., p. 14.

Index

'Abdullāh ibn 'Abbās, 223
Abraham, Testament of, 12
Abu Bakr, 15, 220
Abydos, rites at, 31
Africa, Islamic mission in, 231 f.
Akiba, 59 f., 104–5
Albert the Great, 122
Alexander the Roman, 37, 39
Alexandrian Church Fathers, 120
Allegorical method of interpretation, 119–21
Allen, Th. G., 33
al-Ṭabarī, 224
Amand de Mendieta, Fr Emmanuel, 188–9
Amerbach, Bonifacius, 127
Anabaptists, 149
Anglican approach to Orthodox Church, 200
Anglicans and Methodists, conversations between, 147–52; Report 1963, 147
Apastāk ut Zand, see Avesta *and* Zand
Apollos of Alexandria, 70
Apostolic tradition in Catholic Church, 95 f.; *see also under* Tradition
Aquinas, Thomas, St, 121, 122, 205; teaching on sacraments, 124
Arabic sacred literature and study of Hebrew literature, 55; *see also* Qur'an
Arberry, A. J., 212, 222
Aristotle, 205
Art, religious, 7, 12, 30 f.; Islamic, 8; Jewish, 8
Artaxšēr I, founder of Sasanian dynasty, 38, 48, 50
Auerbach, Erich, 117 f., 121
Augsburg, Confession of, 174, 199
Augustine, St, 120, 124, 172
Avesta, 36 ff.; Pahlavi written translation, 41–3, 50 f.; text of Zerva-

nite type, 44 f.; tradition in oral transmission, 46, 48 f., 52; as written literature, 48–9, 50–1; canon of, 48–9, 50–1; dating of, 51

Babylonian Tablets of Destiny, 215; *Enuma Elish*, 2, 14
Bahman Yašt, apocalyptic literature, 41, 43 ff., 51
Bahram I, II and III, 50
Baiḍāwī, 225
Bailey, H. W., 36 f., 46, 49
Bakhuizen van den Brink, J. N., 155
Baptism, 87 n., 143–4, 202
Baptists: supremacy of Scripture, 138, 143
Barlaam the Calabrian, apophatic theology of, 204
Barth, Karl, 136, 188
Basil, Bishop of Ancyra, 197
Basil of Caesarea, St, 172, 189, 203
Bell, G. K. A., 200
Berdyaev, Nicolas, 206
Bevan, Edwyn, 192
Bible, 2, 16 n., 142 f.; linguistic study of, 122; and Luther, 130 ff.; spiritual meaning, 130; witness of God's revelation, 141; in Roman Catholic Church, 172; in Orthodox Church, 190 f., 194; Greek text in Orthodox Church, 191
Bleeker, C. J., 9
Blondel, Maurice, 175
Boethius, 205
Bonaventura, 121
British church life, 136–41; conversations between denominations, 146–52
Bruni, Leonardo, 127
Buck, A. de, 31 f.

237